Lecture Notes in Artificial Intelligence   10444

Subseries of Lecture Notes in Computer Science

More information about this series at http://www.springer.com/series/1244

Vladimír Mařík · Wolfgang Wahlster
Thomas Strasser · Petr Kadera (Eds.)

Industrial Applications of Holonic and Multi-Agent Systems

8th International Conference, HoloMAS 2017
Lyon, France, August 28–30, 2017
Proceedings

 Springer

Editors

Vladimír Mařík
Czech Technical University
Prague
Czech Republic

Thomas Strasser
Austrian Institute of Technology
Vienna
Austria

Wolfgang Wahlster
German Research Center for AI
Saarbrücken
Germany

Petr Kadera
Czech Technical University
Prague
Czech Republic

ISSN 0302-9743   ISSN 1611-3349   (electronic)
Lecture Notes in Artificial Intelligence
ISBN 978-3-319-64634-3   ISBN 978-3-319-64635-0   (eBook)
DOI 10.1007/978-3-319-64635-0

Library of Congress Control Number: 2017947733

LNCS Sublibrary: SL7 – Artificial Intelligence

Printed on acid-free paper

This Springer imprint is published by Springer Nature
The registered company is Springer International Publishing AG
The registered company address is: Gewerbestrasse 11, 6330 Cham, Switzerland

Preface

It is real pleasure to declare that the research activities around holonic and multi-agent systems for industrial applications have continued and even increased their importance during the past 15 years. The number of both the scientific topics and the achievements in the subject field is growing steadily, especially because of their direct relevance to the German Industry 4.0 initiative and similar initiatives worldwide. The influence of the multi-agent and holonic system philosophy on the Industry 4.0 visions is more than clear.

HoloMAS has been the pioneering event in this field, but we can see that there are multiple conferences like the IEEE SMC annual conference, ETFA, INDIN, or INCOM that aim their attention at advanced industrial solutions based on intelligent agents. However, the HoloMAS conference keeps its orientation, character, and flavor. It remains strongly industry oriented.

This year's conference was the 11th in the sequence of HoloMAS events. The first three (HoloMAS 2000 in Greenwich, HoloMAS 2001 in Munich, and HoloMAS 2002 in Aix-en-Provence) were organized as workshops under the umbrella of DEXA. Starting in 2003, HoloMAS achieved the status of an independent conference organized bi-yearly on even years, still under the DEXA patronage (HoloMAS 2003 in Prague, HoloMAS 2005 in Copenhagen, HoloMAS 2007 in Regensburg, HoloMAS 2009 in Linz, HoloMAS 2011 in Toulouse, HoloMAS 2013 in Prague, HoloMAS 2015 in Valencia). The HoloMAS line of scientific events created a community of researchers who are active in the subject field. They have started to cooperate on large EU projects, e.g., on the IP project ARUM in 2012 or DIGICOR in 2016, and they have jointly submitted several new project proposals since the last HoloMAS event.

The research of holonic and agent-based systems attracts the very strong interest of industry and receives increasing support from both the public sector and private institutions. We can see increased interest from the IEEE System, Man, and Cybernetics Society, namely, from its Technical Committees on Distributed Intelligent Systems and on Cybernetics for Intelligent Industrial Systems. Another IEEE body – Industrial Electronics Society – supports the related R&D field through its Technical Committee on Industrial Agents (http://tcia.ieee-ies.org/). Its mission is to provide a base for researchers and application practitioners for sharing their experiences with application of holonic and agent technologies in the industrial sector, especially in assembly and process control, planning and scheduling, and supply chain management. There are a number of impacted journals that provide space for articles dealing with industrial agents like *IEEE Transactions on SMC: Systems*, IEEE *Transactions on Industrial Informatics*, *Journal of Production Research*, *Journal of Intelligent Manufacturing* or *JAAMAS*.

It is our pleasure to inform you that for HoloMAS 2017 there were 27 papers submitted, from which the Program Committee selected 19 papers to be included in this volume. The papers are organized into five sections. Issues of scheduling are the focus of the first section (three papers). The next one is aimed at knowledge engineering approaches exploring holonic and multi-agent principles (four papers). There is also one specific section aimed at results from simulation, modeling, and reconfiguration (four papers). The fourth section is dedicated to the very hot field of energy systems and smart grids leveraging the MAS approach (four papers). This application area seems to be growing in importance in the past few years, because some of the results could be easily applied to industrial practice. The last section is dedicated to applications in various fields, e.g., smart cities, sensor networks, environmental protection, and gas turbines.

In general, we are very pleased that the papers accepted for publication follow the main innovation trends in the field of holonic and multi-agent systems and display the current state of the art keeping the industrial orientation of the research in mind. Thus, HoloMAS 2017 reflected the progress in the field, but retained its original character and focus.

The MAS technology represents an excellent and promising theoretical background for developing an Industry 4.0 solution. The MAS theory can be used with advantage to support research activities and to bring new features to these solution explorations, e.g., AI principles, machine learning, data mining, and data analytics in general. But the implementations explore – as a rule – the SOA (service-oriented architecture) approaches on an ever broader scale. These are critically simplifying real-life solutions.

This volume of the HoloMAS 2017 proceedings presents the current trends in intelligent manufacturing. It confirms that additional techniques, like ontology knowledge structures, machine learning, etc. represent very important and promising topics for further research. These are expected to enrich the current solutions and to help bring the Industry 4.0 visions to industrial practice.

The HoloMAS 2017 conference represented another successful scientific event in the HoloMAS history and created a highly motivating environment, challenging future research and fostering the integration of efforts in the subject field. This conference offered – as usual - information about the state of the art in the MAS industrial application field with a focus on Industry 4.0 needs to specialists in neighboring research fields covered by the DEXA multi-conference event.

We are very grateful to the DEXA Association for providing us with this excellent opportunity to organize the HoloMAS 2017 conference as part of the DEXA event. We would like to express many thanks to Gabriela Wagner and Lucie Budinová for all their organizational efforts, which were of key importance for the success of our conference.

June 2017

Vladimír Mařík
Wolfgang Wahlster
Thomas Strasser
Petr Kadera

HoloMAS 2017

7th International Conference on
Industrial Applications of Holonic and Multi-Agent Systems
Lyon, France, August 28–30, 2017

Conference Co-chairs

Wolfgang Wahlster   German Research Center for Artificial Intelligence
                           (DFKI), Germany
Vladimír Mařík   Czech Technical University in Prague, Czech Republic
Thomas Strasser   Austrian Institute of Technology, Austria

Program Committee

Reiner Anderl   Technical University of Darmstadt, Germany
Jose Barata   Universidade Nova de Lisboa, Portugal
Theodeor Borangiu   University of Bucharest, Romania
Robert W. Brennan   University of Calgary, Canada
Luis Camarinha-Matos   Universidade Nova de Lisboa, Portugal
Patrikakis Charalampos   Piraeus University of Applied Sciences, Greece
Armando W. Colombo   University of Applied Sciences Emden-Leer, Germany
Ulrich Epple   RWTH Aachen, Germany
Amro M. Farid   Dartmouth University, USA
Adriana Giret   Universidad Politechnica de Valencia, Spain
Kenwood Hall   Rockwell Automation, USA
Zdeněk Hanzálek   Czech Technical University in Prague, Czech Republic
Jürgen Jasperneite   Fraunhofer IOSB-INA, Germany
Václav Jirkovský   Czech Technical University in Prague, Czech Republic
Petr Kadera   Czech Technical University in Prague, Czech Republic
Toshiya Kaihara   Kobe University, Japan
Martin Klíma   CertiCon, a.s., Czech Republic
Matthias Klusch   German Research Center for Artificial Intelligence
                           (DFKI), Germany
Kari Koskinen   Aalto University, Finland
Jose L.M. Lastra   Tampere University of Technology, Finland
Paulo Leitao   Polytechnic Institute of Braganca, Portugal
Wilfired Lepuschitz   PRIA, Austria
Francisco Maturana   Rockwell Automation, USA
Duncan McFarlane   Cambridge University, UK
Munir Merdan   PRIA, Austria
Thanh Nguyen Ngoc   Polytechnic University of Wroclaw, Poland

Petr Novák	Vienna University of Technology, Austria
Marek Obítko	Rockwell Automation, Czech Republic
Boris Otto	Technical University Dortmund, Germany
Stuart Rubin	SPAWAR Systems Center, San Diego, USA
Nestor Rychtyckyj	Ford Motor Company, USA
Arndt Schirrmann	Airbus Group, Germany
Tim Schwartz	German Research Center for Artificial Intelligence (DFKI), Germany
Ilkka Seilonen	Aalto University, Finland
Petr Skobelev	Smart Solutions, Russia
Alexander Smirnov	SPIIRAS, Russia
Václav Snášel	Technical University, Ostrava, Czech Republic
Pavel Tichý	Rockwell Automation, Czech Republic
Damien Trentesaux	University of Valenciennes, France
Pavel Václavek	Brno University of Technology, Czech Republic
Jiří Vokřínek	Czech Technical University in Prague, Czech Republic
Valeriy Vyatkin	Aalto University, Finland and Luleå Techniska Universitet, Sweden
Michael Weinhold	Siemens AG, Germany
Haibin Zhu	Nipissing University, Canada
Alois Zoitl	Fortiss, Germany

Organizing Committee

Lucie Budinová	Czech Technical University in Prague, Czech Republic
Gabriela Wagner	DEXA Society, Austria

Contents

Scheduling

Method of Adaptive Cargo Flow Scheduling for ISS RS Based on Multi-agent Technology

P.O. Skobelev[1,2(✉)], O.I. Lakhin[2,3], and I.V. Mayorov[2,3]

[1] Samara National Research University,
Moskovskoye shosse, 34, Samara 443086, Russian Federation
petr.skobelev@gmail.com
[2] Samara State Technical University,
Molodogvardeyskaya str., 244, Samara 443100, Russian Federation
lakhin@smartsolutions-123.ru
[3] Smart Solutions, Ltd., Business center "Vertical", office 1201,
Moskovskoye shosse 17, Samara 443013, Russian Federation

Abstract. Problem statement: The problem of real-time cargo flow scheduling for the Russian Segment of the International Space Station (ISS RS) is considered. Strategic and tactical scheduling of flight plans, delivery, return, disposal and allocation of RS ISS cargo flow, including more than 3500 entities, is a very complex and time-consuming task. To solve this problem one has to consider numerous factors, constraints and preferences, such as changing demand in fuel, water and supplies, ballistics and solar activity, peculiarities of spaceship types and docking modules. Changes in dates of launch, landing, docking and undocking, number of crew members and other parameters influence the flight program and cargo flow. These changes require dynamic re-scheduling in the chain of changes of interconnected parameters that should be specified, recalculated and coordinated. The problem is represented as a dynamical balance of interests between demands and resources. Methods: A method of adaptive ISS RS cargo flow scheduling in real-time is suggested, considering cargo priorities. The method is based on multi-agent technology for solving conflicts through negotiations of agents. This method is capable of flexible and efficient adaptation of ISS RS cargo flow schedule depending on events in real-time. Results: The developed method is used in the interactive multi-agent system for scheduling of flight program, cargo flow and resources of ISS RS. Practical relevance: The developed system has been implemented in industrial operation and is used for cargo flow scheduling of ISS RS resources. The system provides the following advantages: ISS cargo flow scheduling similar to the schedules created by the experienced operators; flexible and quick reaction to the events that cause cargo flow re-scheduling; reduction of manual labor and increased decision-making efficiency by 2–3 times; real-time monitoring and control of the schedule implementation.

Keywords: Decision-making support · Adaptive planning · Multi-agent technology · Cargo flow scheduling · Events

© Springer International Publishing AG 2017
V. Mařík et al. (Eds.): HoloMAS 2017, LNAI 10444, pp. 3–10, 2017.
DOI: 10.1007/978-3-319-64635-0_1

1 Introduction

Providing life support and scientific research at the Russian Segment of the International Space Station (ISS RS) requires continuous planning of cargo delivery, return or disposal, including scientific equipment for space experiments, spare units, repair materials, and instruments as well as fuel, air, water and food for astronauts, and results of space experiments. Strategic and tactical scheduling of flight plans as well as delivery, return, disposal and allocation of ISS RS cargo flow, including more than 3500 entities, is a very complex and time-consuming task. When solving this task one has to consider numerous factors, constraints and preferences, such as changing demand in fuel, water and supplies, ballistics and solar activity, peculiarities of spaceship types and docking modules, etc. At that, any event can influence the flight program and cargo flow schedule. For example, changes in dates of launch and landing, docking and undocking, crew members, etc., require dynamic re-scheduling in the chain of changes of interconnected parameters that should be specified, recalculated and coordinated in a proper way.

In order to solve complex and dynamic tasks of this class, the multi-agent approach [1, 2] is being widely used. It is one of the most perspective directions in the field of artificial intelligence, according to which solution of a complex task can be searched in a distributed way with the use of principles of self-organization and evolution of living creatures [3–5]. In the suggested approach the concept of Demand and Resource networks (DRN) is used, where plan is built as a flexible network of links between demand and resource agents [6, 7].

The paper studies the method of adaptive planning of ISS RS cargo flow, which elaborates previously proposed method of conjugate interactions in DRN due to use of cargo priorities. The paper also demonstrates advantages of the developed solution for adaptive processing of events, which does not require either stop or restart of the system, as well as its future development.

2 The Problem of Cargo Flow Scheduling of ISS RS

To formulate mathematical problem statement of planning transportation vehicle resources, it is assumed that each of the demands (orders) for resources and each resource can have their own criteria of decision-making (e.g. time limits, prime cost, risk, etc.), and their significance can change in the course of task execution.

To unify the criteria, preferences and constraints for demands and resources, a concept "satisfaction" of corresponding agents is introduced.

The structure of ISS RS cargo flow schedules can be described through a set of resource and demand plans for cargo delivery, return or disposal, where bottom level resources are presented as certain places in the transportation vehicle. The larger plans are containers for equipment and tanks for fuel, water and gas, etc.

Each plan of level h (transportation vehicle flight, cargo containers, fuel tanks, etc.) has the corresponding aims of resources and orders, the state of which is described through satisfaction functions $u_j^{res\,h}$ depending on criteria i from the set of $\{x_i^h\}$ with weight $\alpha_{ij}^{res\,h}$, which show, how much criteria deviate from expected values $x_{ij}^{id\,h}$ for the resource j according to plan h. Satisfaction functions are defined as piecewise linear ones depending on arguments. Values of satisfaction functions lie in the segment from 0 to 1. Criteria are brought additively to one satisfaction function. In this model resource target satisfaction function (res) at the plan h depends on deviation of criteria x_i^h, on values of criteria at the preceding level h−1, and values of resource and task satisfaction at the selected level of the plan. Similarly, satisfaction function of orders (tasks) $u_n^{task\,h}$ with weight $\beta_{mn}^{task\,h}$ at the level h of the plan; as criteria, a set $\{y_n^h\}$ is considered. At the level of such plans priorities $\{w_j^{res\,h}\}$ and $\{w_n^{task\,h}\}$ are introduced for resources and tasks, correspondingly. Then the task of cargo delivery plan optimization comes to maximization of resource and demand satisfaction for plans of the level h−1... H:

$$u^h = u^{res\,h} + u^{task\,h}$$
$$= \sum_j w_j^{res\,h} u_j^{res\,h}$$
$$+ \sum_n w_n^{task\,h} u_n^{task\,h}$$
$$= \sum_j w_j^{resh} \sum_i \alpha_{ij}^{res\,h} f_{ij}^{res\,h}(x_i^h - x_{ij}^{id}, x_i^{h-1}, f_{ij}^{res\,h-1}) \qquad (1)$$
$$+ \sum_n w_n^{task\,h} \sum_m \beta_{mn}^{task\,h} f_{mn}^{task\,h}(y_m^h - y_{mn}^{id}, y_n^{h-1}, f_{mn}^{task\,h-1})$$
$$x^{res\,h*} = \max_{x_i^h}(u^{res\,h})$$
$$y^{task\,h*} = \max_{y_m^h}(y^{task\,h}),$$

where $x^{res\,h*}$ and $y^{res\,h*}$ are optimal values of criteria of resource and task variables for plans of level h. For plan of bottom level 1 functions of satisfaction components f_{ij} with $h = 1$ depend only on deviations of arguments,

$$x_i \in D^I, \; y_m \in D^M \; \forall i, j, \quad I = Dim(D^I), \; M = Dim(D^M)$$

Variables x and y lie in the area of criteria of resources D^I and demands D^M, I and M are dimensions of the corresponding spaces.

Therefore, the planning task is formulated in the system as the task of satisfaction maximization of all the participants. Recursiveness of the task (1) of plan levels and non-linearity of dependence on decisions at the preceding level allow for iterative decision with the help of "attached" network multi-agent schedulers, that is proved by results of experimental implementation in various applications.

In the result, the solution ("good schedule") should be found as a balance of interests of orders and resources. It can be achieved by discovering and solving conflicts through negotiations and coordinated decision-making by those participants, the state of which can be influenced by a new event.

3   Approach to Problem Solution

In the suggested approach solution of any complex task of allocation, planning and optimization of resources is considered as a search for balance of interests of all participants. The balance is achieved by successive approach: from the most rough, simple, but quick solution to more complex and better ones. This is important for quick and flexible adaptation of plans depending on events in real time.

For this purpose a set of basic software agents is proposed, which try to achieve the assigned targets (ideal values of indicators) and continue improving them even after achieving maximum.

For example, during planning, cargo "wants" to be delivered in time and with minimal expenses. Transportation vehicle "wants" to be used most efficiently, that is not to be under- or over-loaded. Cargo gets activated and quickly finds a free space in the vehicle. Further, the vehicle itself can be activated, which will evaluate its state and try to improve it by attracting the cargoes it needs.

Benefits in efficiency when using multi-agent technology are achieved due to the switch to situational decision-making in real time, when user (and the system itself in the future) will be able to manage criteria significance.

The developed approach is based on the "holon" concept, proposed for designing multi-agent systems in the paper [8]. According to it, multiplicity and cohesion of multi-level plans are assumed. Besides, special classes of agents were first introduced, namely orders (cargoes), products (here, flights), and resources (transportation vehicles) as well as master-agent for coordination of all decisions.

This approach is applied for solving the task of multicriterial planning or allocation of orders to resources. Priorities of cargoes, volumes, types, risks, etc. are traditionally considered as criteria for the task. Implementation of multi-agent approach for solving the task of adaptive cargo flow scheduling is based on the previously developed concept of demand and resource networks and the method of conjugate interactions to manage resources at the virtual market in real time [5, 9].

Requirement of "real time" is directly connected with ensuring efficient resource use, because delays in decision-making of resource allocation can lead to loss of ISS RS support quality or complete failure in delivering cargo in time. In these conditions, when neither the number of orders nor the number of resources is known in advance, traditional methods of allocation, planning and optimization of resources appear to be practically useless.

We suggest using a method which develops the previously elaborated method of conjugate interactions through the use of priorities. It gives the opportunity to solve tasks of managing heterogeneous ISS RS resource allocation in real time.

4   Modification of the Method of Conjugate Interactions

The suggested approach considers peculiarities of cargo flow scheduling at ISS RS and cargo priorities of various purposes. The modified method consists of two stages: primary initialization of cargo allocation on flights and proactive improvement of states of orders and cargoes.

It is assumed that demands in cargo flow are given initially, and there is the initial flight program. All cargoes have their weights, types, virtual costs, and time span of delivery assigned.

When a new demand for cargo occurs, the following actions take place:

1. Creation of a new cargo agent is initiated.
2. New cargo agent interviews flight agents of transportation vehicles included in the ISS RS flight plan, about principle possibility of delivery planning within the flight, and receives answers.
3. New cargo agent analyzes and ranges possible variants depending on their profitability. Evaluation is based on how much the variant corresponds with the requirements of a new cargo, which are ranged according to priority.
4. If there is enough space for cargo placement at the selected flight of transportation vehicle (cargo fits by weight and size), delivery of this cargo will be included in the cargo flow schedule.
5. Negotiations about conflict analysis and search of its resolution begin by replacing conflicting cargoes on flights as well as those who are involved in the conflict further. Protocols of conflict resolution are used which are connected with shifts within the resource, displacement to another resource and change between resources.
6. Order of agent activation depends on priorities of cargo groups and situation in the DRN.
7. Each agent at the stage of proactive plan improvement tries to improve its position to increase satisfaction function.
8. Work of the method is over when none of the agents can improve the situation, planning time is up, or decision is slightly improved within the given boundaries.

In the result, the DRN represents an example of self-organizing system, forming and changing schedules of resources as well as adapting its behavior under events occurring in real time.

5 Efficiency Evaluation of the Method of ISS RS Cargo Flow Adaptive Scheduling

To evaluate the efficiency of the developed method of ISS RS cargo flow adaptive scheduling, an experimental study has been carried out, analyzing dependence of time of event processing and new cargo plan formation on the load of transportation vehicle by cargoes.

The stated problem was solved with the use of one of solution methods, namely branch and bound method and modified method of conjugate interactions.

In the set of conducted experiments, from 100 to 1000 cargoes were assigned. Results of experiments at the same determined set of input data (Fig. 1) showed:

- The modified method of conjugate interactions finds possible solutions in less time than the exact branch and bound method;
- Values of target functions evaluated by the modified method of conjugate interactions deviate from the global extremum is approximately 5%.

According to the results of the study, one can conclude that the modified method of conjugate interactions appears to be more efficient for practical solving of the considered problem.

In the second set of experiments (1000 cargoes) conflict-free planning stage and pro-active planning stage of the modified method of conjugate interactions were compared. Adaptive planning algorithm demonstrated an almost 15% benefit over the non-adaptive one, which uses conflict-free cargo flow scheduling as they occur.

In the third set of experiments productivity of the system was evaluated. Experimental studies in load testing were carried out, which showed that time for processing of events coming into the system is acceptable when 150 users simultaneously work with it. Moreover, the system has no degradation when the number of users increases regularly.

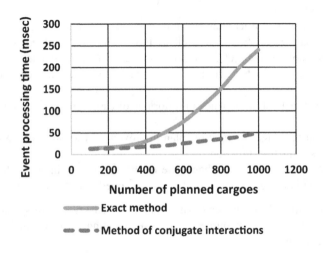

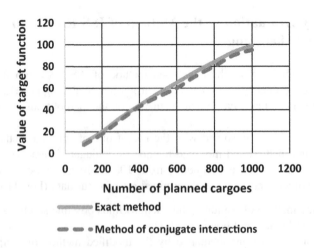

Fig. 1. Results of experimental studies of a new plan formation rate depending on event

Experiments showed that use of the method for adaptive cargo flow planning of ISS RS based on multi-agent technology, which is grounded on principles of self-organization, and evolution, demonstrated its advantage. Besides, it proved its working capacity and efficiency for solving the task of ISS RS cargo flow scheduling as well as responsiveness and flexibility in rescheduling of ISS RS cargo flow in real time.

6 Conclusions

The paper considered problem statement and method of cargo flow adaptive scheduling, which is applied in designing an intelligent system for management of ISS RS cargo flow based on multi-agent technology.

In this implementation of the system for cargo flow planning, multi-agent technology provides the following benefits:

- scheduling of ISS RS cargo flow similar by its parameters to those created by experienced dispatchers;
- possibility of coordination of plans by all participants of the planning process;
- reduction of manual labor in cargo flow scheduling as well as complexity and labor intensity of calculations;
- increase in decision-making efficiency by 2–3 times;
- possibility of monitoring and control of plan execution in real time;
- decrease in dependence on human factor, including errors.

"The developed system has been implemented for Rocket and Space Corporation "Energia" and now is used for ISS RS cargo flow scheduling in every day operations".

Acknowledgments. This work is also a part of a large R&D project. The aim of this project is to develop a set of scientific and technical solutions and to create an intellectual decision support system (IDSS) for managing labor, financial and time resources in complex rocket and satellites projects. IDSS was used on the final stage of the project for developing the solution on the client side.

This paper was prepared with the financial support of the Ministry of Education and Science of the Russian Federation - contract №14.578.21.0137, project unique ID is RFMEFI57815X013.

References

1. Wooldridge, M.: An Introduction to Multi-agent Systems, p. 340. Wiley, Chichester (2002)
2. Voß, S.: Meta-heuristics: the state of the art. In: Nareyek, A. (ed.) LSPS 2000. LNCS, vol. 2148, pp. 1–23. Springer, Heidelberg (2001). doi:10.1007/3-540-45612-0_1
3. Xhafa, F., Abraham, A.: Metaheuristics for Scheduling in Industrial and Manufacturing Applications. Springer, Heidelberg (2008). 342 p.
4. Kennedy, J., Eberhart, R.: Particle swarm optimization. In: Proceedings of IEEE International Conference on Neural Networks, vol. 4, pp. 1942–1948 (1995). doi:10.1109/ICNN.1995. 488968
5. Rzevski, G., Skobelev, P.: Managing Complexity. WIT Press, Southampton (2014). 202 p.

6. Vittikh, V., Skobelev, P.: Metod sopryazhennyh vzaimodejstvij dlya upravleniya raspredeleniem resursov v real'nom masshtabe vremeni (Open multi-agent systems for decision-making support). Avtometriya J. Sib. Branch Russ. Acad. Sci. **6**, 45–61 (2002). (in Russian)
7. Skobelev, P., Vittikh, V.: Mul'tiagentnye modeli vzaimodejstviya dlya postroeniya setej potrebnostej i vozmozhnostej v otkrytyh sistemah (Models of self-organization for designing demand-resource networks). Autom. Control J. Russ. Acad. Sci. **1**, 177–185 (2003) (in Russian)
8. Vittikh, V.A., Larukhin, V.B., Tsarev, A.V.: Actors, holonic enterprises, ontologies and multi-agent technology. In: Mařík, V., Lastra, J.L.M., Skobelev, P. (eds.) HoloMAS 2013. LNCS, vol. 8062, pp. 13–24. Springer, Heidelberg (2013). doi:10.1007/978-3-642-40090-2_2
9. Skobelev, P.: Multi-agent systems for real time adaptive resource management. In: Leitão, P., Karnouskos, S (eds.) Industrial Agents: Emerging Applications of Software Agents in Industry, pp. 207–230. Elsevier (2015)

Total Setup Time Minimisation in Production Scheduling with Alternatives

Zdeněk Hanzálek[1,2]([✉]), Roman Čapek[1], and Přemysl Šůcha[1,2]

[1] FEE, Czech Technical University in Prague,
Karlovo náměstí. 13, 121 35 Prague 2, Czech Republic
zdenek.hanzalek@cvut.cz
[2] CIIRC, Czech Technical University in Prague,
Jugoslávských partyzánů 1580/3, 160 00 Prague 6, Czech Republic

Abstract. The research presented in this paper is focused on the scheduling problem with alternative process plans where the goal is to minimise the sum of all the performed setup times in the schedule. The setup times play an important rôle in scheduling problems, yet they are, in most cases, considered only as an additional constraint, not as a part of the objective function. We propose a model, based on the resource constrained project scheduling problem with alternative process plans, release times and deadlines, that includes the setup times in the scheduling criterion. Both the exact mathematical model and the new heuristic algorithm are proposed to solve the problem. The effectiveness of the proposed two-phase heuristic algorithm, designed with the intention to solve the large instances of the problem, is evaluated on a wide set of instances.

1 Introduction

This article is dedicated to the *resource constrained project scheduling problem* with *alternative process plans* while the *total setup time* is minimised. Up to our knowledge, there is no existing solution approach for such a problem and therefore, a new model and a new heuristic algorithm is proposed for the considered problem with the intention to solve large instances with up to 1000 activities.

Sequence dependent setup times (also called *changeovers*) are crucial for the problems where the resources are very expensive in terms of wasting their time by unnecessary setups. Setup times represent the time necessary to reconfigure the resource or to change its functionality. During this time period, no work on the resources can be performed, which can cause the entire process flow to be inefficient. The problem in minimisation of the total setup time is a part of many manufacturing processes (we "sell the machinery time") as well as it is often a crucial constraint in the optimisation of algorithms for the field-programmable gate arrays (FPGAs) where the reconfiguration of the available resources is very time consuming. In other words, the minimisation of the time and the costs related to setting up the resources is a natural demand that can be applied in

© Springer International Publishing AG 2017
V. Mařík et al. (Eds.): HoloMAS 2017, LNAI 10444, pp. 11–23, 2017.
DOI: 10.1007/978-3-319-64635-0_2

many different optimisation problems. Yet the setup times are almost always considered only as a problem constraint, not as a part of the criterion. One of the main goals of this research is to fill the gap in this area, i.e. to propose a generic approach to deal with the minimisation of the total setup time.

In this article, we consider shared resources and precedence constraints among activities. The classification of the resource constraint project scheduling problem (RCPSP) is used for the problem representation. Furthermore, alternative process plans are considered in the scheduling model to cover the flexibility of the studied processes. The alternative process plans allow one to define more possible ways how to finish the process, differing in the required resources, time constraints or even in the number of activities and precedence relations among them. As a result, not all of the given activities will be present in the final schedule. The considered problem can be classified as the resource constrained project scheduling problem with alternative process plans (RCPSP-APP) where the goal is to minimise the total setup time (TST), equal to the sum of the overall performed setup time (TST) in the schedule.

2   Literature Review

The resource constrained project scheduling problem (RCPSP), which is used in this article, is a well-known problem with many applications. According to [18], RCPSP can be defined as a set of activities with specific requirements that have to be processed on a particular work centre with limited capacity. [5,7] proposed a formal notation and categorisation for the RCPSP problems as well as for their extensions. Other reviews of the models and the solution methods can be found e.g. in [6,8,9,13,15,16,20,21,25]. The multi-mode resource constrained project scheduling problem (MRCPSP), which is an extension of RCPSP with more execution modes for each activity, has been studied in [12,25, 26,28,29]. Apart from the non-renewable resources, each MRCPSP problem can be represented as the RCPSP-APP problem: each activity with multiple modes is to be transformed into the appropriate number of single-mode activities while only one is always selected in the schedule.

Therefore, the formalism of the alternative process plans is a generalisation of the multi-mode behaviour of activities in the MRCPS problem. It allows us to model how to complete projects more than one way, while not only the resource demands, but also the number of activities, the precedence relations, etc. can differ among the alternative process plans. [2,3] defined a structure called *Nested temporal network with alternatives* (NTNA) to model alternative process plans. [4] formulated a constraint-based representation of the alternative activities. [11] dealt with the RCPSP extended by the alternative process plans and the sequence dependent setup times. The authors presented a mixed integer linear programming (MILP) model for the exact solution of small instances and a heuristic called *iterative resource scheduling with alternatives* (IRSA) for larger ones. [19] proposed three algorithms for the jobshop problem with processing alternatives. [22,23] focused on RCPSP with alternatives that is close to the jobshop problem and proposed agent based metaheuristic algorithms to minimise the makespan. [27] presented an integration model of process planning and scheduling problems which are carried out simultaneously. The authors developed a genetic algorithm to minimise the schedule length.

Allahverdi et al. [1] dealt with the setup times in general and published a survey in which many different problems related to the setup times are summarised. The authors also reported on solution approaches and proposed a notation for all of these problems. [31] published a study for a metal casting company concerning the minimisation of the total setup costs in which the authors demonstrate the importance of setup times by calculating the savings to the company. [14] dealt with the general shop problem with the sequence dependent setup times. The authors proposed a two phase Pareto heuristic to minimise the makespan and the total setup costs. In the first phase, the makespan is minimised and, in the second phase, the total setup costs are minimised, while the makespan is not allowed to get worse. [30] focused on a single machine earliness tardiness problem with sequence dependent setup times. The objective function is to minimise the total setup time, earliness and tardiness. [24] proposed a hybrid simulated annealing algorithm for the single machine problem with sequence dependent setup times. The objective function is given by the sum of the setup costs, delay costs and holding costs.

3 Paper Contribution and Outline

The main contribution of this paper is the formulation of novel problem, incorporating the alternative process plans and a criterion based on the performed setup times into the area of the resource constrained project scheduling problems. The strength of the proposed model, formulated using the mixed integer linear programming, is in the combination of the well known RCPSP formalism with the additional flexibility gained by the alternative process plans and the total setup time minimisation. Such a problem has not been studied before in this range. There were only a few attempts to deal with the scheduling problems where the criterion reflects the setup times. The closest problem that can be found in the literature, when compared to the approach studied in this article, was published by [14] who focused on the job shop problem with the alternative machines while the makespan and the total setup time is minimised. Compared to the problem studied in [14], the model proposed in this paper is developed for more general problems, namely for non-unary resources, deadlines of activities and more complex precedence rules including alternative process plans.

The second contribution lies in the newly developed algorithm able to solve the instances of the RCPSP-APP problem with up to 1000 activities. The effectiveness of the algorithm is evaluated using the datasets published in [10] while the proposed algorithm outperforms the results presented in [14]. Moreover, the algorithm presented in this paper is able to solve instances with 1000 activities within dozens of seconds.

The rest of the paper is organised as follows: Sect. 4 provides a definition of the considered problem for which the mathematical model is presented in Sect. 5.

A new heuristic algorithm is proposed in Sect. 6. Section 7 presents the results of the performance evaluation of the developed algorithm and Sect. 8 concludes the work.

4   Problem Statement

The problem considered in this paper is defined by a set of activities, a set of resources, a set of constraints and an optimality criterion. Let $\mathcal{A} = \{1 \ldots n\}$ be the set of n activities representing the project to be scheduled. Furthermore, let $\mathcal{A}_\mathcal{E} = \mathcal{A} \cup \{0, n+1\}$ be the extended set of activities, where dummy activities 0 and $n+1$ with zero processing time restrict the whole project. Activity 0 represents the start and activity $n+1$ the end of the project. There are m resource types $\mathcal{R} = \{R_1 \ldots R_m\}$ where each resource type $R_q \in \mathcal{R}$ has a discrete capacity $\theta_q \geq 1$, i.e. there are θ_q resource units available for resource type R_q. Each activity $i \in \mathcal{A}_\mathcal{E}$ has the following parameters: processing time $p_i \geq 0$, release time $r_i \geq 0$, deadline $\tilde{d}_i \geq 0$ and the resource demand $R_i^k > 0$ for one resource type $R_k \in \mathcal{R}$. In this article, only mono-resource activities are considered, meaning that each activity demands for only one resource type. Additional constraints of the problem are defined by the alternative process plans, the non-negative start to start time-lags and the sequence dependent setup times.

The alternative process plans are defined using the nested temporal network with alternatives (NTNA) presented by [3]. NTNA is a directed acyclic graph $G = (V, E)$ where each node $i \in V$ corresponds to activity $i \in \mathcal{A}_\mathcal{E}$ and each edge $e = (i, j) \in E$ represents one temporal constraint in the form of a non-negative start to start time-lag $s_i + l_{ij} \leq s_j$ (where $l_{ij} \in \mathbb{R}_0^+$), i.e. a minimal amount of time between the start times of activities i and j. Furthermore, each node i of the graph has an input label $in_i \in \{0, 1\}$ and an output label $out_i \in \{0, 1\}$, denoting the type of input and output branching, which can be either parallel or alternative. Based on the NTNA instance, some of the activities, called the *selected* activities, will be present in the schedule and the rest, called the *rejected* activities, will not be. When there is a parallel branching at the input/output of the selected activity i ($in_i = 0 / out_i = 0$), all its direct predecessors/successors have to be selected. If activity i is rejected, all its direct predecessors/successors have to be rejected as well. On the contrary, when there is an alternative branching at the input/output of the selected activity i ($in_i = 1 / out_i = 1$), exactly one of its direct predecessors/successors has to be selected. If activity i is rejected, all its direct predecessors/successors have to be rejected.

Both parallel and alternative branchings can be further nested one in another. An example of the NTNA instance is shown in Fig. 1 where the parallel branchings are denoted as *PAR* and the alternative branchings are denoted as *ALT*. Several time-lags are used to demonstrate how the temporal constraints are defined, see e.g. time-lag $l_{17} = 8$ that forces activity 7 to start at least 8 time units after the start time of activity 1. All the parameters related to the activities are also included; *res* determines the resource type required by each activity. The setup times are depicted for each resource separately.

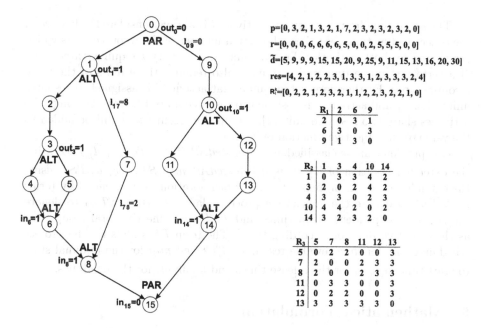

Fig. 1. Nested temporal network with alternatives - example

The sequence dependent setup times $st_{ij} \geq 0$ are given for all pairs of the activities assigned to the same resource type, i.e. for all $(i,j) \in \mathcal{A}^2$: $(\exists k : \mathrm{R}_i^k > 0 \wedge \mathrm{R}_j^k > 0)$. The term setup time (in our case sequence dependent setup time) st_{ij} denotes the minimal time between the completion time of activity i and the start time of activity j, if activities i and j are scheduled subsequently on the same resource type and they share at least one resource unit. The setup time can be different for each pair of the activities and therefore the actual values are determined based on the sequence of the activities. For more details, the reader is referred to [6].

The goal of the scheduling process is to select one process plan and to schedule the corresponding activities to the available resources with respect to both the temporal and the resource constraints. A process plan is a subset of all activities such that the constraints for the selection defined for the corresponding NTNA instance are satisfied. The objective function is the minimisation of the total setup time (TST), given by the sum of all setup times performed in the schedule. To represent a schedule, the following variables are used: $s_i \in \mathbb{R}_0^+$, $v_i \in \{0,1\}$ and $z_{ivk} \in \{0,1\}$. Variable s_i denotes the start time of activity $i \in \mathcal{A}_\mathcal{E}$, v_i determines whether activity i is selected ($v_i = 1$) or rejected ($v_i = 0$). Finally, if $z_{ivk} = 1$ then activity i is scheduled on resource unit v of resource type k; $z_{ivk} = 0$ otherwise. For the purpose of the objective function evaluation, variable $f_{ij} \in \{0,1\}$ is defined as follows: If activities i and j are scheduled subsequently on the same resource type and they share at least one unit of its resource capacity, then $f_{ij} = 1$; $f_{ij} = 0$ otherwise. The objective function is then formulated as $TST = \sum_{\forall i \in \mathcal{A}} \sum_{\forall j \in \mathcal{A}} f_{ij} \cdot st_{ij}$.

The setup time from activity i to activity j is always considered only once in the objective function, regardless the actual number of the resource units which are shared by both activities. Lets assume that activity i requires three units of a certain resource type and activity j also requires three units of the same resource types. Furthermore, lets assume that activity i is assigned to resource units $\{1, 2, 4\}$ and activity j is assigned to resource units $\{2, 3, 4\}$. Although the activities share two resource units, the setup time from i to j will be added to the value of the objective function only once.

Our problem can be classified as $PS|nestedAlt, l_{ij}^{min}, ST_{SD}, r_j, \tilde{d}_j|TST$ using the extended notation of [7] or as $m1|nestedAlt, min, ST_{SD}, r_j, \tilde{d}_j|TST$ using the extended notation proposed by [17]. Both notations are extended by terms $nestedAlt$ to denote the alternative process plans (see [11]), ST_{SD} to denote the sequence dependent setup times and TST to define the total setup time as the objective function according to [1]. The term PS stands for the project scheduling, $m1$ for m renewable resources, l_{ij}^{min} and min for the minimal start to start time-lags, r_j for the release times and finally $\tilde{d}_j$ for the deadlines.

5 Mathematical Formulation

The mathematical formulation using the mixed integer linear programming (MILP) for the problem defined in the previous section is formulated below. For a higher efficiency of the model, variable z_{ivk} is substituted by variable z_{iu}, i.e. only one index u is used to reference the assigned resource units of a certain resource type. The mutual conversion between (v, k) and u is given as follows:

$$u = \sum_{q=1}^{k-1} \theta_q + v \text{ and } k = arg\min_{k} \left\{ \sum_{q=1}^{k} \theta_q \geq u \right\}; v = u - \sum_{q=1}^{k-1} \theta_q.$$

In addition to variables s_i, v_i, f_{ij} and z_{ivk} (z_{iu}) defined in the previous section, auxiliary binary variables g_{ijk}, x_{ijk} and y_{ijk} are used. Variable g_{ijk} determines whether activities i and j are selected and assigned to the same resource unit k such that i is a direct predecessor of j on such resource unit. Similarly, variable x_{ijk} determines whether activities i and j are selected and assigned to the same resource unit k such that i is an arbitrary (direct or propagated) predecessor of j on such resource unit. Finally, variable y_{ijk} determines whether both activities i and j are assigned to resource unit k.

$$\min \sum_{\forall i \in \mathcal{A}} \sum_{\forall j \in \mathcal{A}} f_{ij} \cdot st_{ij}$$

subject to:

$$v_i = \sum_{\forall j:(i,j) \in E} v_j \qquad \forall i \in \mathcal{A_E} : out_i = 1 \qquad (1)$$

$$v_i = \sum_{\forall j:(j,i) \in E} v_j \qquad \forall i \in \mathcal{A_E} : in_i = 1 \qquad (2)$$

$$v_i = v_j \qquad\qquad \forall (i, j) \in E : out_i = 0 \wedge in_j = 0 \qquad (3)$$

$$\sum_{i \in \mathcal{A}_\mathcal{E}} v_i \geq 1 \qquad\qquad\qquad\qquad\qquad (4)$$

$$s_i \geq r_i - (1 - v_i) \cdot UB \qquad\qquad \forall i \in \mathcal{A}_\mathcal{E} \qquad (5)$$

$$s_i + p_i \leq \tilde{d}_i + (1 - v_i) \cdot UB \qquad\qquad \forall i \in \mathcal{A}_\mathcal{E} \qquad (6)$$

$$s_i + l_{ij} \leq s_j + UB \cdot (2 - v_i - v_j) \qquad\qquad \forall (i, j) \in E \qquad (7)$$

$$s_j + p_j + st_{ji} \leq s_i + UB \cdot (x_{iju} + 1 - y_{iju}) + UB \cdot (2 - v_i - v_j)$$
$$\forall (i, j) \in \mathcal{A}^2 : i \neq j; \forall u \in \{1 \ldots K\} \qquad (8)$$

$$s_i + p_i + st_{ij} \leq s_j + UB \cdot (2 - x_{iju} - y_{iju}) + UB \cdot (2 - v_i - v_j)$$
$$\forall (i, j) \in \mathcal{A}^2 : i \neq j; \forall u \in \{1 \ldots K\} \qquad (9)$$

$$\sum_{u=C+1}^{C+\theta_q} z_{iu} = R_i^q \cdot v_i \qquad \forall i \in \mathcal{A}; \forall q \in \{1 \ldots m\}; C = \sum_{j=1}^{q-1} \theta_j \qquad (10)$$

$$z_{0u} = 1 \qquad\qquad \forall u \in \{1 \ldots K\} \qquad (11)$$

$$z_{n+1\,u} = 1 \qquad\qquad \forall u \in \{1 \ldots K\} \qquad (12)$$

$$y_{iju} \geq z_{iu} + z_{ju} - 1 \forall (i, j) \in \mathcal{A}_\mathcal{E}^2 : i \neq j; \forall u \in \{1 \ldots K\} \qquad (13)$$

$$y_{iju} \leq z_{iu} \qquad \forall (i, j) \in \mathcal{A}_\mathcal{E}^2 : i \neq j; \forall u \in \{1 \ldots K\} \qquad (14)$$

$$x_{iju} \leq y_{iju} \qquad \forall (i, j) \in \mathcal{A}_\mathcal{E}^2 : i \neq j; \forall u \in \{1 \ldots K\} \qquad (15)$$

$$\sum_{j=1}^{n+1} g_{iju} = z_{iu} \qquad\qquad \forall i \in \mathcal{A}; \forall u \in \{1 \ldots K\} \qquad (16)$$

$$\sum_{i=0}^{n} g_{iju} = z_{ju} \qquad\qquad \forall j \in \mathcal{A}; \forall u \in \{1 \ldots K\} \qquad (17)$$

$$g_{iju} \leq x_{iju} \qquad\qquad \forall (i, j) \in \mathcal{A}_\mathcal{E}^2; \forall u \in \{1 \ldots K\} \qquad (18)$$

$$f_{ij} \cdot UB \geq \sum_{\forall u \in \{1 \ldots K\}} g_{iju} \qquad\qquad \forall (i, j) \in \mathcal{A}_\mathcal{E}^2 \qquad (19)$$

where:

$$s_i \in \mathbb{R}_0^+; \; v_i, f_{ij}, z_{iu}, g_{iju}, x_{iju}, y_{iju} \in \{0, 1\}; \qquad (20)$$

$$K = \sum_{q=1}^{m} \theta_q; UB > \sum_{\forall i \in \mathcal{A}_\mathcal{E}} \max \left(p_i + \max_{\forall j \in \mathcal{A}_\mathcal{E}} st_{ij}, \max_{\forall j \in \mathcal{A}_\mathcal{E}} l_{ij} \right)$$

There are three types of constraints in the model - constraints for the selection of activities, temporal constraints and resource constraints. The goal is to minimise the sum of all the performed setup times in the schedule, i.e. the total setup time.

First, the constraints for the selection of the activities are stated. Equation (1) and (2) define the rules for the selection of activities in alternative branchings,

Eq. (3) defines the rule for the selection of the activities in parallel branchings and Eq. (4) forces the schedule to have at least one selected activity (empty schedule has no relevant significance).

Second, the temporal constraints are given in three formulas. The start time of each activity is constrained by the release time and the deadline - (5) and (6). Both constraints are applied for the selected activities only. The non-negative start to start time-lags are defined in Formula (7).

The rest of the formulas then serve to define the resource constraints, including the determination of the performed setup times in the schedule. Formulas (8) and (9) prevent more activities (from overlapping) on one resource unit in one moment. Equation (10) ensures that the number of the assigned resource units is equal to the resource demand for each activity. Equations (11) and (12) are used to assign dummy activities 0 and $n + 1$ to each resource unit of each resource type, which then ease the definition of the constraints related to the setup times. Formulas (13) and (14) constrain the value of variable y_{ijk} - if both activities are scheduled on the same resource unit, then y_{ijk} is equal to 1; 0 otherwise. Formula (15) determines the value of variable x_{ijk} - if both activities i and j are assigned to the same resource unit k, they must be scheduled sequentially. Equation (16) forces each activity to have only one direct successor on each assigned resource unit. Similarly, Eq. (17) forces each activity to have only one direct predecessor on each resource unit. Formula (18) prevents the cycles in values of variable g_{ijk} for each resource unit. Finally, Formula (19) determines whether a particular setup time has to be taken into consideration in the objective function, i.e. whether activities i and j are scheduled subsequently on the same resource unit.

6   Heuristic Algorithm

This section is dedicated to the description of the heuristic algorithm designed to solve the large instances of the problem defined in Sect. 4. The goal is to find a schedule determined by the selection of activities (variable v_i), their start times (variable s_i) and their assignment to resources (variable z_{ivk}) such that all the constraints are satisfied and the total setup time (TST) value is minimised.

The basic scheme of the proposed heuristic algorithm, called $STOAL$ (Setup Time Optimization ALgorithm), consists of two phases - the initial phase to find any feasible solution and the local search for the improvement of the objective value. The initial phase is inspired by the IRSA algorithm published in [11] and the local search, based on a time separation technique, is inspired by the work of [14]. If a feasible solution is not found (due to the presence of deadlines) in the initial phase, the local search is not started at all and the algorithm is terminated. Detailed description of the STOAL algorithm is available from the authors upon request.

7   Performance Evaluation

Two sources of instances have been used for the performance evaluation of the algorithm proposed in Sect. 6, designed to solve the problems with alternative process plans. First, the STOAL algorithm is evaluated on randomly generated instances and compared with the IRSA algorithm proposed by [11]. Second, the standard benchmarks of [10] are used and the results of the STOAL algorithm are compared with the results reported in [14]. Furthermore, various settings of the STOAL algorithm are discussed and tested on large instances of the problem (up to 1000 activities). The STOAL algorithm was implemented in the C# language and the experiments were performed on a PC with an Intel Core 2 Quad CPU at 2.83 GHz with 8 GB of RAM.

7.1   Comparison with IRSA Algorithm on Random Instances

Random instances of the problem defined in Sect. 4 are generated to compare the STOAL algorithm with the existing IRSA algorithm, designed for the minimisation of the schedule length for the RCPSP with alternative process plans and positive and negative time-lags. As reported in [11], the IRSA algorithm was originally implemented in the Matlab environment, but for the purpose of this article, we have re-implemented the algorithm in the C# language to get a fair comparison. Since IRSA does not consider resources with non-unary capacities, all the instances contain only unary resources and all activities have resource demand equal to 1. There are three different sets of generated instances: *loose*, *medium* and *tight* which differ in the specification of release times and deadlines. Each set further contains 100 instances for each of 20, 50, 100 and 200 activities per instance.

The instances were generated with the following settings: the parameters for each activity i were randomly selected from the intervals $p_i \in \langle 2, 10 \rangle$, $r_i \in \langle 0, k_1 \cdot n \rangle$, $\tilde{d}_i \in \langle k_1 \cdot \frac{n}{2}, k_2 \cdot n \rangle$ where n is the number of activities in a particular instance and k_1 and k_2 are constants depending on the type of the instance (*loose/medium/tight*); namely $k_1 = 5$ and $k_2 = 15$ for the *loose* instances, $k_1 = 7$ and $k_2 = 13$ for the *medium* instances and $k_1 = 10$ and $k_2 = 10$ for the *tight* instances. For each instance, the release times and deadlines are sorted in non-decreasing order and assigned to the activities based on the precedence relations from activity 0 towards activity $n + 1$. Each activity has the resource demand equal to one, i.e. $R_i^q = 1$, for one resource type q. The number of resource types m is randomly chosen from interval $\langle 1, 2 \rangle$ for 20 and 50 activities per instance and from interval $\langle 1, 5 \rangle$ for 100 and 200 activities per instance. The setup times st_{ij} are generated in the interval $\langle 5, 10 \rangle$ and the non-negative start to start time-lags l_{ij} in the interval $\langle 0, 20 \rangle$. The structural properties of the generated NTNA instances are as follows: If node i starts the parallel branching, the number of successive nodes lies in interval $\langle 5, 10 \rangle$. Similarly, if node i starts the alternative branching, the number of direct successors lies in interval $\langle 2, 4 \rangle$.

Table 1 shows the comparison of the results obtained by the IRSA algorithm and by the STOAL algorithm. Column *feas* determines the percentage ratio of feasible solutions found by each algorithm. Column *TST* contains an arithmetic average value of the objective function for instances that were successfully solved by both algorithms. Column *time* determines the average computational time (in milliseconds) to solve a single instance regardless of whether a solution was found or not. Finally, column TST^{impr} states the improvement of the STOAL algorithm over the IRSA algorithm in terms of the TST value.

Table 1. Comparison with IRSA algorithm using new random instances

		IRSA			STOAL			
n	$Type$	$Feas$ [%]	TST	$Time$ [ms]	$Feas$ [%]	TST	$Time$ [ms]	TST^{impr} [%]
20	Loose	100	102	5	100	76	3	25.50
50	Loose	100	254	36	100	215	12	15.35
100	Loose	100	494	112	100	427	77	13.56
200	Loose	94	942	322	100	824	141	12.53
20	Medium	62	77	4	69	76	2	1.01
50	Medium	58	226	29	60	221	14	2.10
100	Medium	69	386	98	64	371	57	3.92
200	Medium	72	707	293	68	662	112	6.37
20	Tight	44	65	4	41	63	2	1.03
50	Tight	31	183	25	32	183	15	0.00
100	Tight	26	302	86	33	295	48	2.30
200	Tight	37	597	266	42	592	119	0.92

The number of feasible solutions found is almost the same for both tested algorithms, but the STOAL algorithm outperforms the IRSA algorithm in both the TST value and the solution time. The fact that the success rate in finding feasible solutions is equal proves that the STOAL algorithm is very effective for the considered temporal constraints, since the IRSA algorithm was developed with the main aim to find any feasible solution. The most significant difference in terms of the objective value can be observed for the *loose* instances where the flexibility of the activities is higher and, therefore, the optimisation can be performed in a wider scope.

7.2 Comparison with Algorithm of Focacci [14]

For a further evaluation of the STOAL algorithm, the instances of the general job shop problem proposed by [10] are used. As a reference, the results for such instances reported in [14] are considered. The problem studied in [10] is a subproblem of the problem defined in Sect. 4 since there are no release times or deadlines, no alternative process plans and the resources are considered to be unary. The objective function reported in [14] is twofold, first the makespan in minimised and then the total setup time is being minimised without a deterioration of the makespan value.

Focacci Table 2 shows the comparison of the STOAL algorithm with the one published by [14]. Compared with the algorithm described by [14], the STOAL algorithm improved the value of the total setup time by more than 16% in average. The price for the better value of the TST is the higher value of the makespan, by almost 19% in average. Such a trade-off between the makespan and the total setup time shows the good efficiency of the STOAL algorithm proposed in terms of the total setup time criterion.

The big trade-off between TST and makespan is probably incurred by the alternative process plans. The two criteria should be more linked in the classical problems without alternatives. The makespan criterion probably makes more sense, since it includes the setup time as well. On the other hand the sole TST criterion may be useful when the setup is costly (e.g. including the waste of the material).

Table 2. Comparison with [14] using instances of [10]

Set	Focacci		STOAL			
	TST	C_{max}	TST	C_{max}	TST^{impr} [%]	C_{max}^{det} [%]
t2-ps12	1 530	1 445	1 010	1 920	33.99	32.87
t2-ps13	1 430	1 658	1 330	1 872	7.00	18.93
t2-pss12	1 220	1 362	950	1 599	22.13	17.4
t2-pss13	1 140	1 522	1 140	1 610	0	5.78
Average	1 330	1 497	1 110	1 825	16.54	18.74

8   Conclusion

This paper fills the gap in the literature, where only very few pieces of work have been dedicated to scheduling problems with setup times as a part of the criterion. The setup times are usually considered only as a constraint. The proposed innovative model combines the RCPSP problem with the alternative process plans and the criterion to minimise the total setup time in the schedule. Furthermore, the model includes the release time and deadline for each activity and the non-negative start to start time-lags for precedence constrained activities. For such a model, of the studied problem, the mathematical formulation, using the mixed integer linear programming (MILP), is proposed.

The two-phase heuristic algorithm is then developed to solve the large instances of the considered problem. The goal of the algorithm first phase is to find any feasible solution and the second phase, based on the time separation of the schedule, is dedicated to improve the existing schedule in terms of the total setup time. The STOAL algorithm is compared with two reference algorithms. The experiments show a very good performance of the STOAL algorithm in both the quality of the solutions and the running time.

In the future research, we want to concentrate on situations where tasks are owned by agents representing, e.g. departments of a company. In this case, the resources are shared by the agents, and the problem becomes a multiobjective optimization problem. This extension requires a realistic definition of a fair use of resources with respect to the objective of the individual agents.

Acknowledgments. This work was supported by the Grant Agency of the Czech Republic under the Project FOREST GACR P103-16-23509S and by the Project AI&Reasoning CZ.02.1.01/0.0/0.0/15_003/0000466 and the European Regional Development Fund.

References

1. Allahverdi, A., Ng, C., Cheng, T., Kovalyov, M.Y.: A survey of scheduling problems with setup times or costs. Eur. J. Oper. Res. **187**(3), 985–1032 (2008)
2. Barták, R., Čepek, O.: Temporal networks with alternatives: complexity and model. In: Proceedings of the Twentieth International Florida Artificial Intelligence Research Society Conference (FLAIRS), Florida, USA, pp. 641–646. AAAI Press (2007)
3. Barták, R., Čepek, O.: Nested temporal networks with alternatives: recognition and tractability. In: Proceedings of the 2008 ACM Symposium on Applied Computing (SAC), Ceara, Brazil, pp. 156–157. ACM (2008)
4. Beck, J.C., Fox, M.S.: Constraint-directed techniques for scheduling alternative activities. Artif. Intell. **121**(1), 211–250 (2000)
5. Blazewicz, J., Ecker, K.H., Pesch, E., Schmidt, G., Weglarz, J.: Scheduling Computer and Manufacturing Processes. Springer, New York (1996). doi:10.1007/978-3-662-04363-9
6. Brucker, P.: Scheduling Algorithms. Springer, New York (2007). doi:10.1007/978-3-540-69516-5
7. Brucker, P., Drexl, A., Mohring, R., Neumann, K., Pesch, E.: Resource-constrained project scheduling: notation, classification, models, and methods. Eur. J. Oper. Res. **112**(1), 3–41 (1999)
8. Brucker, P., Knust, S.: Complexity results for single-machine problems with positive finish-start time-lags. Computing **63**(4), 219–316 (1998)
9. Brucker, P., Kunst, S.: Complex Scheduling. Springer, New York (2006). doi:10.1007/3-540-29546-1
10. Brucker, P., Thiele, O.: A branch & bound method for the general-shop problem with sequence dependent setup-times. Oper. Res. Spectr. **18**(3), 145–161 (1996)
11. Čapek, R., Šůcha, P., Hanzálek, Z.: Production scheduling with alternative process plans. Eur. J. Oper. Res. **217**(2), 300–311 (2012)
12. De Reyck, B., Herroelen, W.: The multi-mode resource-constrained project scheduling problem with generalized precedence relations. Eur. J. Oper. Res. **119**(2), 538–556 (1999)
13. Demeulemeester, E., Herroelen, W.: A branch-and-bound procedure for the multiple resource-constrained project scheduling problem. Manage. Sci. **38**(12), 1803–1818 (1992)
14. Focacci, F., Laborie, P., Nuijten, W.: Solving scheduling problems with setup times and alternative resources. In: Artificial Intelligence Planning Systems 2000 Proceedings (AIPS), pp. 1–10. AIPS (2000)
15. Hartmann, S., Briskorn, D.: A survey of variants and extensions of the resource-constrained project scheduling problem. Eur. J. Oper. Res. **207**(1), 1–14 (2010)

16. Herroelen, W., De Reyck, B., Demeulemeester, E.: Resource-constrained project scheduling: a survey of recent developments. Comput. Oper. Res. **25**(4), 279–302 (1998)

17. Herroelen, W., De Reyck, B., Demeulemeester, E.: A classification scheme for project scheduling. In: Weglarz, J. (ed.) Handbook of Recent Advances in Project Scheduling, pp. 1–26. Kluwer Academic Publishers, Dordrecht (1999)

18. Kadrou, Y., Najid, N.M.: A new heuristic to solve RCPSP with multiple execution modes and multi-skilled labor. In: Proceedings of the IMACS Multiconference on Computational Engineering in Systems Applications (CESA), pp. 1–8. IEEE (2006)

19. Kis, T.: Job-shop scheduling with processing alternatives. Eur. J. Oper. Res. **151**(2), 307–322 (2003)

20. Kolisch, R., Hartmann, S.: Experimental investigation of heuristics for resource-constrained project scheduling: an update. Eur. J. Oper. Res. **174**(1), 23–37 (2006)

21. Kolisch, R., Padman, R.: An integrated survey of deterministic project scheduling. Omega Int. J. Manag. Sci. **29**(3), 249–272 (2001)

22. Leung, C.W., Wong, T.N., Maka, K.L., Fung, R.Y.K.: Integrated process planning and scheduling by an agent-based ant colony optimization. Comput. Ind. Eng. **59**(1), 166–180 (2010)

23. Li, X., Zhang, C., Gao, L., Li, W., Shao, X.: An agent-based approach for integrated process planning and scheduling. Expert Syst. Appl. **37**(2), 1256–1264 (2010)

24. Mirabi, M.: A hybrid simulated annealing for the single-machine capacitated lot-sizing and scheduling problem with sequence-dependent setup times and costs and dynamic release of jobs. Int. J. Adv. Manuf. Technol. **54**(9–12), 795–808 (2010)

25. Neumann, K., Schwindt, C., Zimmermann, J.: Project Scheduling with Time Windows and Scarce Resources. Springer, Heidelberg (2003). doi:10.1007/978-3-540-24800-2

26. Salewski, F., Schirmer, A., Drexl, A.: Project scheduling under resource and mode identity constraints: model, complexity, methods and application. Eur. J. Oper. Res. **102**(1), 88–110 (1997)

27. Shao, X., Li, X., Gao, L., Zhang, C.: Integration of process planning and scheduling - a modified genetic algorithm-based approach. Comput. Oper. Res. **36**(6), 2082–2096 (2009)

28. Van Peteghem, V., Vanhoucke, M.: An experimental investigation of metaheuristics for the multi-mode resource-constrained project scheduling problem on new dataset instances. Technical report, Faculty of Economics and Business Administration (Ghent University) (2011)

29. Van Peteghem, V., Vanhoucke, M.: Using resource scarceness characteristics to solve the multi-mode resource-constrained project scheduling problem. J. Heuristics **17**(6), 705–728 (2011)

30. Wang, L., Wang, M.: A hybrid algorithm for earliness-tardiness scheduling problem with sequence dependent setup time. In: Proceedings of the 36th Conference on Decision and Control, pp. 1219–1223. IEEE (1997)

31. Yuan, X.M., Khoo, H.H., Spedding, T.A., Bainbridge, I., Taplin, D.M.R.: Minimizing total setup cost for a metal casting company. Winter Simul. Conf. **2**, 1189–1194 (2004)

Agent-Based Shop Floor Scheduling

Martin Klima[✉], Jan Gregor, Ondrej Harcuba, and Vladimir Marik

CertiCon a.s., Prague, Czech Republic
{martin.klima,jan.gregor,ondrej.harcuba,
vladimir.marik}@certicon.cz

Abstract. Shop floor scheduling problem is known for a long time and is considered an academic exercise for solving by constraint solvers or for linear solvers. In a small production scale it can be solved easily. For a large scale production, the problem becomes too large and we need major heuristics to solve it. We introduce a way to decompose the major problem into smaller sub-problems and to quickly find a satisfying solution using human thinking inspired heuristics. The results combines scalable agent based solution and multiple constraint solver instances running in parallel.

Keywords: Shop floor scheduling · Agents · Distributed computing · Constraint solver

1 Introduction

Shop-floor scheduling of operations is known for a long time as classical NP-hard problem [2, 5, 6]. Constraint programming is a classical way of solving the problem [3]. For small scale production, where only a few operations should be scheduled and where there is only a few production operators/workers involved, the problem is easy to solve in a reasonable time. As the production grows, the time to find a solution is growing to an extreme. In this article we introduce a method to deal with large scale production and we demonstrate it on a use-case of Airbus A350 fuselage assembly. In the introduced solution we first decompose the global problem of scheduling of all operations that are to be done in the shop into multiple localized smaller problems. The problem is to some degree similar to [7]. There are other attempts to involve agent distributed logic into a optimization problem [8]. The localization of a problem is made on a time-space principle and is highly inspired by the work organization on the production line. Each small problem is solved separately by an autonomous unit. Agent technology is an ideal match for solution of multiple problems in parallel. Agent can autonomously validate input data, solve the given problem using various strategies, analyse quality of solution, and negotiate with other agents to consider eventual changes in the solution. All these operations may run in most cases in parallel on one or multiple machines.

© Springer International Publishing AG 2017
V. Mařík et al. (Eds.): HoloMAS 2017, LNAI 10444, pp. 24–36, 2017.
DOI: 10.1007/978-3-319-64635-0_3

2 Airbus Use Case

The agent-based shop floor scheduling is inspired by the work organization at the Airbus assembly line. An instance of an agent is in this case reflecting some of the physical objects in the factory. To understand the concepts, we first have to describe the processes in the production line, decision making criteria, responsibilities and information flows.

There are multiple assembly lines in Airbus factory, each is specialized to a dedicated product. The products are for example fuselages for A350 airplane, wings for A350, fuselages for A380, etc. All these production lines are running in parallel, each working on several products (e.g. fuselages) in different stages of production. The production is "tacted". Every tact, typically lasting for two days, a new fuselage is started to be assembled while one is finished.

One production line is only a small part of a larger system – numerous lines form a production hall, factory, factory cluster, etc. A holonic principle is apparent in such a complex system. For example factories (Hamburg, Toulouse, Getafe, Filton) need to coordinate their production in a similar manner as their individual production lines, see Fig. 1.

Logistics from external suppliers and in-factory logistics is organized on just in time principle minimising the need for storages and warehouses.

In our scheduling solutions, we are focussing primarily on one assembly line, but the solution can be generalized on multiple lines, or in more aggregated sense to several cooperating factories.

Figure 1 demonstrates the organization of production on three levels: the factory, the assembly line and the station level, it demonstrates the holonic principle of production.

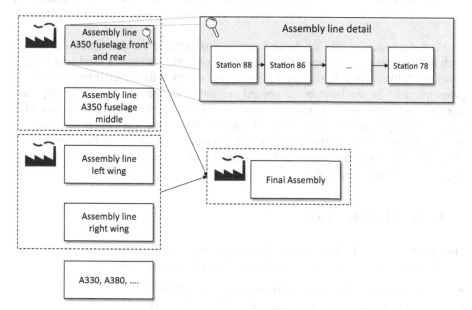

Fig. 1. Factories, assembly lines, stations in Airbus use-case

On the factory level each factory is producing specific parts of the airplane and serves as a source of products to another factory (in this case the Final Assembly). Internally, each factory is composed of one or more assembly lines, each assembly line is composed of multiple stations. In Fig. 1 a detail of an assembly line for A350 middle and rear fuselage parts is displayed in the upper right corner. This particular assembly line is composed of 6 assembly stations. The fuselages flow between the individual stations similarly to the flow of products between factories. Stations are numbered in a decreasing order by numbers meaning the planned number of days until take-off.

Each station is equipped with its specific tooling corresponding to the planned set of operation. Each station has a number of workers assigned with a distribution of qualifications that corresponds to the planned operations. Each worker has at least one qualification.

Individual operations are described in a technological documentation. Multiple different job dependences exist as expressed in Table 1.

Table 1. Most frequent job dependence type examples

#	Dependence type	Description
1	J2 starts after J1 ends	Job J2 must not start before J1 has finished. This is the most frequent type of dependence used
2	J2 starts after J1 starts	Job J2 must not start before J1 has started
3	J2 starts within T time units after J1 ends	Job J2 must start in a given time frame after job J1 has finished. This is a typical dependence for gluing operations when the glue has been applied and two components must be attached
4	J2 starts after T time units after J1 starts	Job J2 must not start in time window from J2 end to J2 end + T. This is a typical situation for gluing or welding. After welding, the components must cool down in T time

More dependences may be defined considering both start and end times of jobs. Such job dependences are constrains that must be obeyed to achieve a valid scheduling solution. Multiple other dependences do exist, for example the material required for a given job must be available in the needed amount when the jobs start, similarly the workers, tools, and location constrains must be fulfilled. In the Airbus scenario, multiple jobs are grouped to so called Work Orders (WO). One work order is typically assigned to just one worker representing a set of operation he/she should do during one shift. A worker may have multiple WO assigned for one shift and multiple workers may cooperate on a single WO.

3   Basic Scheduler Tasks

The operative scheduler has multiple tasks to accomplish. These tasks are similar to a well-known shop-floor scheduling problem. The tasks are the following:

- Assign particular jobs, resp. WOs to individual workers.
- Assign proper starting and ending times to the jobs (WOs).

- Assign tools to jobs (WOs).
- Assign work place to jobs (WOs).

The assignment must be valid, e.g. compliant with all given constraints:

- Flow of jobs must follow constrains of the technological process given by job dependences, see Table 1.
- Conflicts in resource usage must be eliminated. There are sharable resources that are assigned to individual jobs and that may be utilized by just one job at a time. These resources are workers and tools. Both workers and tools are released after the job is finished.
- Workers must be assigned to individual jobs considering their skills. Every job requires typically just one skill, but in general multiple skills may be required. Only those workers, who have the required combination of skill, may be assigned to a particular job. Skills are recorded in a Skill Matrix table, see Table 2.

Table 2. Skill matrix

Worker		Skills					
ID	Name	Mechanical assembly	Electrical assembly	Hytraulics	Inspection MI1	Inspection EI1	Inspectioin HI1
2456	John brown	X					
7345	Marian green	X	X				
9427	Peter red			X	X		
5813	Simon blue				X	X	X

- Worker's availability is limited to one shift per day. Vacations, holidays, end eventual sicknesses are recorded as non-availabilities and are given as an input to the scheduler. Ad-hoc non-availabilities of workers are considered as disruptive events and are a reason for operative re-scheduling. In specific cases an overtime can be applied, in such a case the workers may stay at work beyond the regular shift end.
- Tool availability is known similarly to the worker's availability. Major tools have planned maintenance intervals, minor tools like screw drivers are not considered in the scheduling at all. Planning of maintenance operations is not a subject of shop floor scheduling.
- Material availability. Material is a consumable resource and therefore cannot be reused after the job is done. In the scheduling the material is considered as a binary condition available/non-available. When non-available, jobs requiring a particular material are blocked, resp. postponed until the material is available.
- Shifts and work hand-over. The scheduler should minimize the risk of work interruption due to end of shift. Work hand-over is a non-recommended practise. If possible, a particular job should be finished in the same shift it begun. Close to the end of shift (minutes to the end) no new jobs should be started (unless an overtime is considered).

3.1   Advanced Scheduler Tasks

The above mentioned shop-floor scheduling is well described in literature and is considered as technically solved. In the Airbus case, there are nevertheless some special requirements and internal processes that need a special attention. First of all, the number of jobs, WOs, workers, other resources and consequently the size of Skill Matrix is very large. Classical scheduling techniques like constraint programming do fail here due to the non-polynomial nature of the problem.

The Airbus case brings some specific aspects of scheduling that influence the global solution and make it possible to use some decomposition of the problem, parallel computing and take advantage of the agent approach.

The advanced tasks are related to balancing work between stations and factories (the holonic principle). The advanced tasks are:

- Moving a job (multiple jobs) from one station to another. Depending on chosen production strategy, moving jobs from one station to another may be allowed. If this is the case, the stations and their schedule are no longer independent, they influence each other in multiple aspects – the space occupancy, tool sharing, and depending on the chosen strategy, on the human resources sharing. The everyday practice confirms that moving jobs (in this context such a practise is called Traveling Work Strategy - TWS) is very beneficial. A consequence of TWS is that cycle time changes may be introduced, shortage of resources may propagate across the stations or exactly the opposite – extra resources may become available. Enabling TWS is a subject of managerial decision. Typically TWS is enabled after a short ramp-up phase. During the ramp-up phase a strategy called Stop&Fix is typically used – no traveling work is enabled, all jobs planned to be performed at a given station have to be finished there. The Stop&Fix strategy results in major cycle time prolongation, nevertheless it is beneficial for initial education period at the beginning of production.

- Changing the cycle time. A cycle time may be adjusted most typically due to job working time extension, e.g. if a given job was not finished in the planned time. A cycle time may be changed to a later one or, under some specific conditions to an earlier one. When the TWS is enabled, jobs may be postponed for a later station in the production line making it possible to shorten the production tact. Figure 2 shows a schematic situation of three stations in a production line, each currently performing several jobs. End of the last job denotes the possible earliest cycle time for a given station (t_1 for Station 86, t_2 for Station 90, and t_3 for Station 88). The originally planned cycle time is marked as t_p. It is obvious, that Station 88 is blocking other stations in proceeding with the cycle, the time t_3 is therefore the valid end of cycle. If we accept the t_3 as end of cycle, Station 90 and Station 86 may benefit from this situation by either proceeding with new jobs, or by gaining disturbance event robustness (an eventual disturbance event is likely to be resolved in the extra time at the end of the cycle). In the same way, the Station 90 and Station 86 may waste resources by leaving them unutilized at the cycle end. The scheduler should propose optimal utilization of resources whenever possible, for example offering unutilized people from stations 90 and 86 to the problematic station 88.

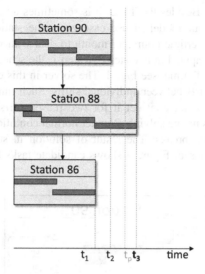

Fig. 2. Station duration and cycle times

A combination of moving job and adjusting cycle time is a typical real-live situation. In our example in Fig. 3, the scheduler may propose to move the last task in Station 88 to the next cycle and let it finish at Station 86. This will result to shortening the cycle to time t_2 or to the planned time t_p, depending on the chosen strategy.

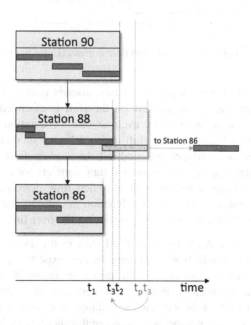

Fig. 3. Traveling work enabled

- Introducing overtime. Besides the TWS, it is sometimes advantageous to use over time. The praxes in our modelled use case gives the station manager a certain amount of available overtime hours per month to deal with work delays. The over time, if allowed, is computed in two steps: In step 1, the schedule for each station is solved in a "condensed" time, see Fig. 4. The solver in this case does not consider any extra time that exists between individual shifts. Such time does exist in reality but the scheduler does not consider it for two reasons: 1/shortening the solving domain greatly speeds up the solving, 2/under normal conditions no work should be placed into these work breaks. The result of solution in step 1 is analysed and overtime may be proposed. Figure 4 shows candidate tasks for overtime in red.

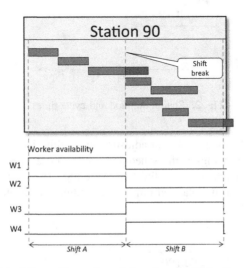

Fig. 4. Scheduling with condensed time domain (Color figure online)

In step 2, when overtime is proposed, the time domain is extended by time breaks between shifts and availability of workers on the shift is extended, see Fig. 5. The availability of workers may be extended even beyond the duration of the break. For example, let's consider a break between shifts being 1 h plus yet one hour for working shifts overlapping. In the overlapping period, all the workers from previous and the current shift are available at the shop floor and they compete for resources like space and tools. When proposing schedule with extended time domain, human resource utilization will be included into the criterial function in order to minimize the number of workers who have to stay at the shop floor during the over time.

- Introducing extra shift. An extra shift (third shift in the day) may be introduced when the optimized production is running bellow expected performance. Introducing a shift is nevertheless beyond the operative nature of the scheduler, it is going into the area of capacity planning. The scheduler is evaluating several KPIs of the production wherefrom the expected expedition of a product (MSN) is the key one. When the deadline is not met beyond given threshold, the scheduler indicates a need to introduce a new shift. Since the new shift needs a well prepared set of data like human resources and material delivery times, the scene can be recalculated when this data is given.

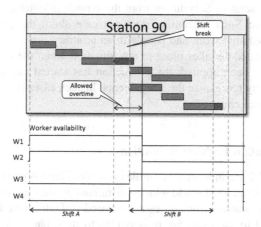

Fig. 5. Scheduling with expanded time domain – overtime

3.2 Scheduling Algorithm in General

Our solution is based on a holonic principle stemming from the fact, that every unit (station, production line, factory) is a self-sufficient unit that under ideal conditions should be able to produce products as planned without any external help. It should not propagate its internal problems to the outer world. Propagating problems to other entities, such as neighbouring stations is costly and not welcomed. Anyway, when necessary, problems may be propagated and should be resolved as close to their source as possible (next station in the line at best). The scheduling is therefore aligned along the following principles.

1. Compute local optima for every station.
2. Use local resources only.
3. Propagate problems when no other solution found.
4. Negotiate with other stations when absolutely necessary.

The formed principles are very native to human thinking, forming a simple to understand heuristic. They result in problem resolution that minimizes the need to reorganize production (remember there are many people involved, who must be instructed to change their assignments). Scheduling may not find a global optima, rather it will find a feasible sub-optimal schedule.

Every station is represented by an independent software unit – an agent. Each such an agent has its own internal scheduling engine that optimizes its own schedule. The agent continuously evaluates the quality of the schedule and if necessary, it starts to negotiate problems with other agents. The need to negotiate may be twofold: either the agent itself is getting into troubles (not able to keep up with deadlines), or the agent is doing exactly the opposite – has unused (human) resources that can be given at disposal to other stations. Both the cases may result in re-adjusting the schedules of other stations.

An important principle is a difference between re-adjusting a schedule and scheduling from the scratch. Scheduling from the scratch is suitable for those stations that did not start yet. Such scheduling does not care about the current (corrupted) schedule and may reassign work and people in an arbitrary way.

Re-adjusting a schedule takes place in any situation when the current (corrupted) schedule has already been applied, the production has started and it would be very cumbersome to greatly reorganize the assignments. In such cases the scheduler follows a strategy of "Minimal change".

3.3   Station to Station Problem Resolution

Stations in our model are independent entities that have their own set of resources to perform their tasks. In an ideal world with no disturbances, they are fully self-sufficient and there is not cross station problem resolution needed. Unfortunately, such situation does not correspond to the everyday reality. Due to disturbances in the production, many jobs are delayed, halted due to non-conformity and many jobs are newly added as a result of a non-conformity resolution activities of the engineering department. The Stations are therefore no longer independent and they do influence each other. An example of mutual influence is traveling work (when TWS is enabled) and change of cycle time. Let's have a look how the changes propagate and how they can be resolved.

The stations can be displayed in a matrix where on the horizontal axes there is the time and on the vertical axes there is the position of the station and the product (fuselage) being produced in the station, see Fig. 6. The individual cells represent

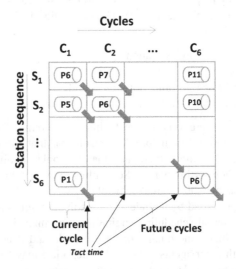

Fig. 6. Cycles and stations (Color figure online)

stations at one cycle, denoted by letters C_1 to C_6. Marked Current cycle displays the situation as it is now, C_2 to C_6 are future cycles. The matrix could continue as long as the production is planned to run. The six cycles are the minimal scheduling horizon that lets all products produced in the Current cycle to finish. At any next cycle a new product is started at station S_1 while one is finished and transported away from station S_6. The traversing of a particular product in the matrix is marked by orange arrows. These arrows also denote the possible traveling work trajectory, for example any work that could not be done on product P6 in cycle C_1 will be rescheduled for the next cycle C_2 in the subsequent station S_2. If this fails due to insufficient resources, the work will be placed to C_3 at S_3, and so on.

The above matrix also nicely shows the mutual influence of stations in different situations. Some of the situations has been described when the traveling work and cycle time was introduced. We will inspect the influence deeper and show some examples.

Figure 7 shows a situation when product P_6 located at Station S_4 has caused cycle prolongation request. Such a prolongation will affect all products in the given Cycle, in this case C_{13}, as marked by orange arrows. P_7 and P_5 (and all other products in C_{13}) are to end earlier than P_6, therefore in the extra time Δt there is nothing to do and the workers would stay idle. This can render resource utilization suboptimal solution, nevertheless, there is a chance to accept more traveling work by all station in C_{13}. Green arrows show this kind of propagation potentially shortening the duration of Cycle C_{14}.

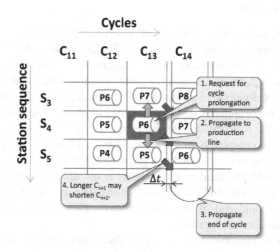

Fig. 7. Problem propagation Example 1 (Color figure online)

In the next example a situation in Cycle C_{13} is shown when an event occurred on product P_6 resulting in lack of resources needed to handle already accepted traveling work from Cycle C_{12}. Since cycle C_{13} is still in the future, it is possible to recalculate the schedule and to offer a new solution. Already accepted jobs sourcing from P_6 S_3C_{12} are returned back to cell S_3C_{12} and the process of scheduling is repeated from C_{12}.

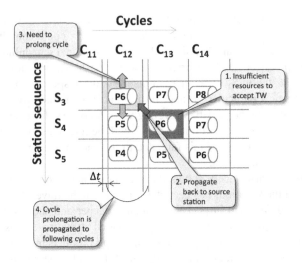

Fig. 8. Problem propagation Example 2

Since it is no more possible to let the job travel to C_{13}, a cycle time extension is needed (or overtime may be used). See Fig. 8 for details.

3.4 Finding a Solution

We have shown the major principles of agent based scheduling using a combination of constraint programming and agent negotiation. So far we have for the sake of simplicity considered only one solution for every agent. Let's imagine a situation when every agent has enough time to search the whole solution space and to find a locally optimal solution. Locally optimal means the best solution a particular agent can find for itself. We can use for example a lead time criterial function – the sooner to do all the jobs, the better. In the real situation nevertheless, even the local solution space is too big to be investigated completely in a reasonable time. Therefore we need to consider all good enough solutions we can find in a given time frame. As a result of this we are dealing with a twofold problem: either an agent is not able to find any solution in a given time, or the agent can find too many solutions. The first situation is simpler – no solution found is a valid end of computation and a clear message to the user. The second situation need more attention.

Let's consider a situation when an agent finds 100 different solutions that are equally good, e.g. their criterial function gives the same value. The agent could take them all and start branching the solution by negotiating all of the solutions with the neighbouring agents who may also find big number of their local solutions and thus branch the solution even more. We will see that many of the branches will at one point reach a dead end – no valid solution found by one of the agents, but the rest may succeed and finally we may end up by an avalanche of solutions. Too many solutions are for the management of the production line as useless as none.

The way to solve the problem of too many solutions is definition of groups of equivalent solutions. We define several categories of equally good solutions that will be represented by just one, typically randomly chosen. Defining a group of equivalent solutions is a subject for the management – we introduce this way new type of heuristics. An example of such a groups is: all solutions where the timespan is equal (criterial function) and where the assignment of human resources to individual jobs is the same. In other words the same people are doing the same work, possibly in different times are considered to be the same. Every agent is given a constant amount of time in which it will find a number of solutions and group them according the classes of equivalence. In praxes it results in a handful of different solutions that are further branched. The management of the factory is interested in about 5 (max 10) significantly different solutions to choose from.

4 Implementation and Practical Results

The scheduler was tested on real production data from Airbus Hamburg factory producing A350 fuselages. The implementation of the scheduler is based on Jade agent platform, Fig. 9 shows the internal structure of agents. SchedulerMainAgent is responsible for communicating with external data sources. SolvingAgent creates structure of StationAgents corresponding to production line, e.g. every instance of StationAgent corresponds to a product-cycle. Each StationAgent holds its own instance of a Choco constraint solver [9]. Individual StationAgents run in parallel (on different machines) and communication their solutions found to the SolutionAgent, that is combining their solutions into a global one. SolutionAgent evaluates the quality of the global solutions and groups it into classes of equivalence as described in Sect. 3.4. It is also responsible for stopping further computations, pausing and resuming StationAgents. The solution agent may create new station setup (tasks to be solved, their dependency, resources, resource availability, time offset) for every StationAgent and command it to re-schedule with new conditions. In case multiple different strategies should be computed in the same time, multiple instances of all StationAgents can be created and one instance of SolutionAgent per strategy.

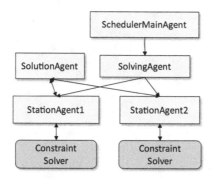

Fig. 9. Agents and communication

In praxes the first valid solution is found within several seconds on a 4 core Intel i7 machine. The solution outperforms the existing scheduler, which is part of Airbus Visual Line 2 solution for up to 30% in the work efficiency KPI. The lead time of a product based on a real data testing has been improved by 28% using the traveling work strategy. Utilization of workers has risen from 62% to 88%.

References

1. Java Agent DEvelopmpent Framework. http://jade.tilab.com/
2. Manne, A.S.: On the job shop scheduling problem. Oper. Res. **8**(2), 219–223 (1960)
3. Zeballos, L.J., Quiroga, O.D., Henning, G.P.: A constraint programming model for the scheduling of flexible manufacturing systems with machine and tool limitations. Eng. Appl. Artif. Intell. **23**(2), 229–248 (2010)
4. McKay, K.N., Safayeni, F.R., Buzacott, J.A.: Job shop scheduling theory: What is relevant? Interfaces **18**(4), 84–90 (1998)
5. McFarlane, D., Sarma, S., Chirn, J.L., Wong, C.Y., Ashton, K.: The intelligent product in manufacturing control and management. In: 15th Triennial World Congress, Barcelona, Spain, July 2002
6. Morariu, C., Morariu, O., Borangiu, T.: Advanced shop-floor scheduling with genetic algorithm for combined horizon optimization in holonic manufacturing systems. In: Mařík, V., Lastra, J.L.M., Skobelev, P. (eds.) HoloMAS 2013. LNCS, vol. 8062, pp. 25–36. Springer, Heidelberg (2013). doi:10.1007/978-3-642-40090-2_3
7. Wang, C., Ghenniwa, H., Shen, W.: Real time distributed shop floor scheduling using an agent-based service-oriented architecture. Int. J. Prod. Res. **46**(9), 2433–2452 (2008)
8. Baker, A.D.: A survey of factory control algorithms which can be implemented in a multi-agent heterarchy: dispatching, scheduling, and pull. J. Manuf. Syst. **17**(4), 297–320 (1998)
9. Choco Constraint Solver Web Site (2017). http://www.choco-solver.org/

Knowledge Engineering

Enabling Semantics within Industry 4.0

Václav Jirkovský[1]([⊠]) and Marek Obitko[2]

[1] Czech Institute of Robotics, Informatics, and Cybernetics,
Czech Technical University in Prague, Zikova 4, 166 36 Prague, Czech Republic
`vaclav.jirkovsky@cvut.cz`
[2] Rockwell Automation R&D Center,
Argentinska 1610/4, 170 00 Prague, Czech Republic
`mobitko@ra.rockwell.com`

Abstract. Manufacturing faces increasing requirements from customers which causes the need of exploiting emerging technologies and trends for preserving competitive advantages. The apriori announced fourth industrial revolution (also known as Industry 4.0) is represented mainly by an employment of Internet technologies into industry. The essential requirement is the proper understanding of given CPS (one of the key component of Industry 4.0) data models together with a utilization of knowledge coming from various systems across a factory as well as an external data sources. The suitable solution for data integration problem is an employment of Semantic Web Technologies and the model description in ontologies. However, one of the obstacles to the wider use of the Semantic Web technologies including the use in the industrial automation domain is mainly insufficient performance of available triplestores. Thus, on so called Semantic Big Data Historian use case we are proposing the usage of state of the art distributed data storage. We discuss the approach to data storing and describe our proposed hybrid data model which is suitable for representing time series (sensor measurements) with added semantics. Our results demonstrate a possible way to allow higher performance distributed analysis of data from industrial domain.

Keywords: Industry 4.0 · Ontology · Triplestore · Big data · Distributed data processing · Historian

1 Introduction

Manufacturing companies have been facing increasing requirements from their customers, and therefore they should begin with exploiting emerging technologies and trends for preserving their competitive advantages. The manufacturing domain went through many milestones, and the most significant were the three preceding industrial revolutions—the introduction of mechanical production facilities (the first revolution); the electrification and the first assembly line (the second revolution); the first computer in industrial domain together with automation (the third revolution).

© Springer International Publishing AG 2017
V. Mařík et al. (Eds.): HoloMAS 2017, LNAI 10444, pp. 39–52, 2017.
DOI: 10.1007/978-3-319-64635-0_4

Nowadays, we are witnessing the expansion of new technologies which are going to form the new industrial revolution. The fourth industrial revolution differs from the previous revolutions because it was announced apriori [9]. The fourth era of manufacturing (also known as Industry 4.0) is represented mainly by the employment of (advanced) Internet technologies into industry. We may observe various marketing announcement of released Industry 4.0 solutions however real realizations are still in the future [9]. Nevertheless, many of corresponding technologies are already available, but they are applied in different areas, e.g. the consumer industry.

A good way of describing Industry 4.0 may be by the means of its main components—Cyber-Physical System (CPS), Internet of Things (IoT), Smart Factory, and Internet of Sevices (IoS). Cyber-Physical Systems (the cornerstone for achieving the new industrial paradigm) are integrated structures involving communications, computation, control, and sensing. The aiming of CPSs is a tight integration among controlled physical processes and controlling digital computing systems [6]. CPSs are building blocks of advanced systems which form Industry 4.0 as described in [19]—Smart Grids, Smart Cities, Smart Factories, Smart Buildings, and Smart Homes.

Next, the integration of the Internet of Things and the Internet of Services within manufacturing process has initiated the fourth industrial revolution according to [12]. The IoT represents cooperation of "smart components" (primarily CPSs), e.g., RFID, sensors, actuators, mobile phones. The objective of the IoT is to ensure achievement of common goals by means of previously mentioned cooperation. The common goals are also achieved with the help of IoS. The IoS enables service vendors to offer their services via the Internet within the scope of a factory. The next step is the transfer of the IoS concept from a single factory to entire factory networks (Connected Enterprises [4]) so that factories can offer special production technologies instead of just a production types.

Furthermore, the last key term used to describe Industry 4.0 is so called Smart Factory. Based on the given CPS and IoT definitions, the Smart Factory is a factory where CPS communicate over the IoT and assist people and machines in the execution of their tasks [14].

In the context of smart factories as well as connected enterprises, an implementation and an operation of CPSs together with a management of the corresponding automation infrastructure is one of the requirements for enabling Industry 4.0. The management of CPSs concerning IoT leads to the problem of the collaborative automation paradigm [7]. The promising solutions are based on the use of Multi-Agent Systems (MAS) and Service-Oriented Architectures (SOA) [18].

The essential requirement is the proper understanding of given CPS data models together with a utilization of knowledge coming from various systems across a factory as well as an external data sources. This problem may be expressed as integration problem and the suitable solution is the employment of Semantic Web technologies and model description in ontologies. The Semantic Web technologies include RDF (Resource Description Framework) for describing data in the form of triples subject-predicate-object and OWL (Web Ontology Language) for describing ontologies, i.e., describing the model of the data. An application of Semantic Web technologies should facilitate the semantic heterogeneity reduction [16]. Furthermore, the exploiting of ontologies is also necessary due to a virtualization of the different phases of the manufacturing process. The virtual factory (virtual twin) is ideal for factory and production planning, virtual commissioning, production monitoring as well as training.

The use of ontologies for expressing required knowledge and data brings many competitive advantages [16]. On the other hand, this approach has several drawbacks. The biggest obstacle to the expansion of the use of the Semantic Web technologies in the industrial automation domain is a mainly insufficient performance of available triplestores[1]. The poor performance of triplestores is very evident for example in the case of handling sensor measurements (i.e., time series). Thus, we are introducing our proposed data model which is suitable for storing RDF triples representing time series (sensor measurements) in this paper. It is needed to have an efficient infrastructure for RDF triples processing as well.

The paper is organized as follows: first, we provide a general overview of triplestores and their features regarding their utilization in industrial domain. Next, we present possible data models for RDF triples storage. Then, the triple data storage corresponding to the proposed data model is illustrated on the Semantic Big Data Historian system. Finally, the approach is demonstrated on data from the hydro-electric power station.

2   Enabling Semantics within Industry 4.0

For automated integration of disparate data sources it is needed to bring semantic description of the data. Semantics adds meaning to data so that it is known what the data mean, what we they represent, what are the constraints, what can be the consequences etc. For computing, the semantics is described in the form of ontologies. An ontology defines "explicit specification of conceptualization"— it describes the conceptual view of the modelled real world (e.g., sensors) and specifies it explicitly. In other words, ontology defines data model so that data can be understood and integrated.

The way of representing data and ontologies described in this paper is based on Semantic Web technologies. These technologies were designed to enable integration of data from heterogenous and changing World Wide Web. For describing data, the RDF (Resource Description Framework) uses the form of triples *subject-predicate-object*, such as *my temperature sensor-measures-temperature*. The triples then form a graph of data that can be integrated via common relationships so that previously unconnected data can be related together. For the storage of such data, so called triple stores are used. The data can be queried,

---

[1] A triplestore is a database for the storage and retrieval of triples through semantic queries.

usually using the SPARQL language which provides means for expressing triples patterns to be matched in the data.

On top of RDF, the Web Ontology Language (OWL) is built to provide primitives for modelling ontologies. The OWL provides primitives for description of classes, properties that can have object or data values, individuals and constraints. These modelling primitives are then used to describe the model of the data and the constrains then define the semantics, i.e., how data can or cannot be related, what consequences can be derived etc. The ontology in OWL language is expressed using RDF and thus can be stored in triplestores together with data.

As already mentioned above, our aim is to use triplestores to store, query and retrieve the data, such as time series of measured sensor data. For processing of huge amounts of data, including their analysis, a scalable approach is needed. Let us discuss the solutions for our use case, so called Semantic Big Data Historian (SBDH).

2.1   Related Work

There are many various already existing triplestores which offer mainly "database" for RDF triples (based on different technologies) and subsequently different support of data querying, inferring, etc.

The important triplestores characteristics include triplestore performace (required time for query processing) and the capability to store as many triples as possible. Widespread and well-known RDF triplestores [5,13,17,23] are based on a centralized approach. These solutions have become unsatisfactory in current trend of increasing data production due to their limited scalability.

In addition to those centralized approach solutions there are several promising distributed solutions. Apache Accumulo [2] is an open-source, distributed, column-oriented store. It offers automatic load balancing and partitioning, data compression, and security labels. Next, HadoopRDF [10] combines Hadoop and Sesame[2] triplestore. Sesame is installed on each node of Hadoop cluster. Data querying is done by SPARQL language—queries are decomposed and spread across the Hadoop cluster. Retrieved data are subsequently joined using MapReduce algorithm.

The available triplestores optimize the triple storage for general data models. On the other hand, when we consider deployment within industrial automation domain we know that the prevalent amount of data are sensor measurements. Thus, we are introducing the possible solutions of how to optimize RDF triple storage model for the time series data in the following paragraphs.

2.2   Data Models for Triple Store

We identified three different approaches for storing RDF data in a distributed way according to the method of data model handling:

---

[2] http://www.openrdf.org.

- **Single file model:** preserves the triple construct of classical RDF.
- **Vertical partitioning model:** splits RDF triples according to their properties.
- **Entity class-based model:** utilizes high-level entity class graph to create RDF partitions [21]. First, similar entities (subjects) are grouped (according to similarity measure) into an entity class. Corresponding entity class graph is then partitioned. This model is not discussed in detail in the following sections because it is not used in our Semantic Big Data Historian.

Single File Model. The single file model preserves the RDF triples in the form (subject, predicate, object). In other words, data are stored within a database system in one file/table. The database system is then responsible for splitting the file into blocks, replicating the blocks, etc.

The system based on this approach and HDFS (Hadoop Distributed File System) is for example PigSPARQL [21]. Furthermore, SHARD [20] uses a variation of the single file model where triples with the same subject are merged into a one line of a file/table.

```
:CO2ds048 rdf:type :CO2ObsValue :hasQuantityValue 355.0
       :hasQuantityUnitOfMeasurement  :parts-per-million
```

Vertical Partitioning Model. The previously described single file model is easy to implement but has some disadvantages. The main obstacle is the I/O cost during query processing. A more suitable model is represented by vertical partitioning model. In this model, triples are partitioned with the respect to their property and stored in files named according the corresponding property name. The vertical partitioning model is employed for example in [15]. In the case of SBDH, the file `hasQuantityUnitOfMeasurement` contains the following data:

```
:CO2ds048 :parts-per-million
:THSds075 :percentage
:THSds075 :degreeCelsius
:PRSds032 :hectopascal
```

This model overcomes deficiencies of the single file model but data are not homogenously distributed in files in some cases (e.g., the type file is usually very big file). In the case of SBDH, the biggest file would be `hasQuantityValue` as this relation is the most used one.

Further file splitting can be performed for ensuring homogeneous data distribution among files. HadoopRDF creates partitions according to data property and object as well. For example, the triple (`:THSds075` `:hasQuantityUnitOfMeasurement` `:percentage`) would be stored in a file named `hasQuantityUnitOfMeasurement#percentage`.

Hybrid SBDH Model. Our current realization of the SBDH storage architecture is based on combining single file model and vertical partitioning-like model. This hybrid model replaced previously used single file model which had insufficient performance due to the high I/O costs during query processing. The single file model is unsuitable for time-series data storage. Especially for queries with range filter expressions and order constraints the acceptance was not acceptable.

The vertical partitioning is used for all sensors measurements where the partitions are created with the respect to subject and property accompanied by timestamp. For example, the file `CO2ds048#hasQuantityValue` contains the following data:

```
2012-04-29T00:00:10  355.0
2012-04-29T00:00:40  355.1
2012-04-29T00:01:10  355.0
```

Other triples are stored according to the single file model. The different data handling of sensors measurements reflects the fact that an amount of measurements is significantly bigger than the rest of data.

3   Architecture

The system utilizing processing of RDF triples for subsequent advanced data analysis is described in this section. The realization of the data storage layer is presented after the description of the whole system architecture.

3.1   Semantic Big Data Historian

We introduce the architecture of Semantic Big Data Historian (SBDH) in the following paragraphs. Generally, a historian software is used in the industrial automation to gather data and then to provide an access to the data and possibly also analytics of them. The historian software is usually optimized to allow fast and compressed storage of data, but not much attention is paid to analytics or to heterogeneous data integration. We propose this solution to overcome common deficiencies of available solutions in case of handling (i.e., storing, processing and querying) of RDF triples. The architecture of the implemented SBDH is illustrated in the Fig. 1.

The historian architecture is divided into four main layers—data acquisition layer, transformation layer, data storage layer, and analytic layer.

- *Data acquisition layer*—collects data from (smart) sensors, other systems related to a given application (for example from MES/ERP systems—information about shifts, supply chain, ...), and relevant external data sources (e.g., weather forecast, traffic information). Various data sources are gathered and connected mainly via OPC UA [11]. The platform heterogeneity (various developers and manufacturers) has to be resolved by this layer.

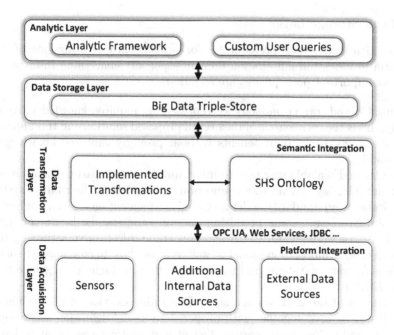

Fig. 1. Architecture overview of Semantic Big Data Historian

- *Transformation Layer*—transforms data to the unified semantic form according to SHS ontology. This layer is responsible for data pre-processing (corrections of damaged data, etc.) if needed. Created triples are subsequently stored in the corresponding storage system. The semantic heterogeneity is solved by this layer.
- *Data storage layer*—we have evaluated several triple stores during SBDH development. The most promising solutions were 4Store[3], CumulusRDF[4], and Hadoop[5] together with Jena Elephas[6]. Every mentioned solution has a certain limitation (performance issues, limitations caused by design) and thus we implemented the Data storage layer by means of Apache Spark[7] and Apache Cassandra[8]. The data storage layer is described in the Sect. 3.2 in detail.
- *Analytic layer*—this layer provides access to directly connected storage layer for custom analytic programs or custom user queries.

[3] http://4store.org.
[4] https://code.google.com/p/cumulusrdf/.
[5] http://hadoop.apache.org.
[6] https://jena.apache.org.
[7] http://spark.apache.org.
[8] http://cassandra.apache.org.

3.2 Data Storage Layer

We have identified several prerequisites for enabling proper utilization of RDF data form in industrial automation domain especially concerning Industry 4.0. The most important prerequisites are as follows:

- A suitable and correct ontology for representing required knowledge. Apparently, this is the cornerstone of the overall proposed solution and this approach has more drawbacks than benefits without properly captured knowledge in the ontology.
- Modular and scalable way how to interconnect system parts. There are several suitable ways for an interconnection of all parts of distributed system. A suitable way/standard/model is strongly dependent on a given application domain. Nowadays, some promising and versatile standards are coming to the fore—for example, OPC UA [8]. This standard offers versatile approach how to design information model as well as a way how to communicate across various operating systems and from a shop floor to highest enterprise levels (e.g. ERP[9]).
- Realization of the data storage layer. The right selection of the technology which will be used together with proper data model definition according to a given application should ensure efficient and faultless system operation. In this section, we discuss and present the possible solution in detail.
- Analytical and querying tools. An appropriately operating system is valueless without any reasonable tool which is able to access information stored in the system. It means the way how to query data by a user or another system via a proper API as well as the basic/advanced tools for conducting analytical tasks.

In this section, we focus on the realization of the data storage layer of the SBDH. It is the essential component (together with a corresponding ontology) of the system which is intended for handling and storing RDF data. The realization of the data storage layer influence an efficiency of data management and processing itself as well as a scalability of possible applications.

We have tested many different systems for the storage layer implementation during years of the SBDH development. Solutions based on available triplestores have several drawbacks but the main insufficiency is their performance. Thus, we decided to build up our prototype upon some Big Data framework.

The First Version of SBDH Storage Layer. The first version of SBDH prototype has the storage layer based on Apache Hadoop together with Jena Elephas. This solution has many advantages, for example, it offers very robust environment for massive distributed parallel data processing; very efficient cluster management with the help of YARN[10]—providing the computational resources

---

[9] ERP—Enterprise resource planning system.
[10] YARN—Yet Another Resource Negotiator.

(e.g., CPUs, memory, etc.) needed for application executions; and there are available many additional tools for extending data processing and conducting various analytical tasks—Hive[11], HBase[12], Mahout[13], KNIME[14] connected by means of Hive connector, etc.

The Hadoop Distributed File System (HDFS) is designed to work with sequence files [1]. The SequenceFile is a flat file consisting of binary key/value pairs and is used in MapReduce [3] as input/output formats. This input/output format has many benefits—more compact than text files, offers support for data compression (particular records or whole blocks of records), are designed for parallel processing, etc. Unfortunately, SequenceFiles have one main disadvantage—they are append only [22]. The "append only" mode helps maintain easy data consistency. On the other hand, it is not sufficient for our realization of the SBDH storage layer. We have encountered fundamental problems during integrating (storing and processing) various data compared to simple storing of sensor data. Thus, the architecture of the SBDH storage layer has been changed and re-implemented with the help of Apache Spark together with Apache Cassandra.

Data Storage Layer Based on Apache Spark and Apache Cassandra. More suitable solution for the data storage layer for SBDH seems to be combination of Apache Spark together with Apache Cassandra.

Apache Spark is a fast and general-purpose computing system which provides high-level APIs in Java, Scala, Python, and R. It also provides a set of additional tools including SparkSQL for SQL and Structured data processing, MLib for machine learning, GraphX for graph processing, and Spark Streaming. Spark may be deployed in three different modes depending on the used cluster manager—Standalone, Apache Mesos, and Hadoop YARN. The standalone deployment mode uses a simple cluster manager included with Spark which is sufficient for clusters that are not big. On the other hand, Mesos and YARN cluster managers should be utilized for huge clusters for improving the cluster performance.

Apache Cassandra is a NoSQL database project which originated at Facebook and is maintained by Apache Software Foundation. It is built on Amazon DynamoDB[15] and Google Big Table[16]. Cassandra was designed as distributed database for managing large amounts of structured data across many commodity servers and for offering high availability. In comparison to the common NoSQL databases, the Cassandra uses a hybrid model between key-value and column oriented database—based on defining super-columns and column-families. The topology of a Cassandra cluster is "masterless ring" due to overcome a legacy master-slave architectures. The advantages of the Cassandra database could be

---

[11] https://hive.apache.org.
[12] https://hbase.apache.org.
[13] http://mahout.apache.org.
[14] https://www.knime.org.
[15] https://aws.amazon.com/dynamodb/.
[16] https://cloud.google.com/bigtable/.

summarized as follows—continuous availability, linear scale performance, operational simplicity and easy data distribution across multiple data centers.

In the proposed data storage layer, Spark and Cassandra clusters are deployed to the same set of machines. Cassandra serves as data storage and Spark worker nodes are co-located with Cassandra and perform the data processing tasks. When a job is created, the Spark workers load data into memory and perform the required data processing. Very important fact of such a processing is that there is no overhead with superfluous network traffic. Finally, the results are written back to the Cassandra tables or propagated to another systems. The architecture of the SBDH data storage layer is illustrated in the Fig. 2.

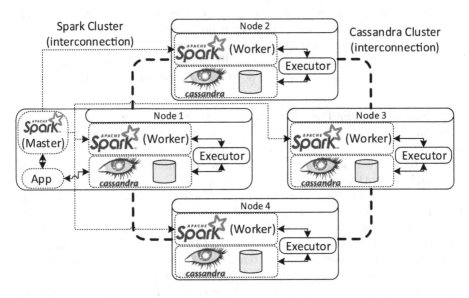

Fig. 2. Example of data storage layer architecture combining Apache Spark and Apache Cassandra

Data are stored in Cassandra tables by means of the Hybrid SBDH Model. The Hybrid SBDH Model is adapted according to given data nature, i.e., data corresponding to general entities are vertically partitioned by a predicate (e.g., the table named hasQuantityUnitOfMeasurement contains corresponding subjects and objects—:CO2ds048 :parts-per-million, etc.) and time-related data are stored according to the hybrid SBDH model (e.g., the table with composite name (subject#object) CO2ds048#hasQuantityValue contains objects representing measurements together with their timestamp—2012-04-29T00:00:10 355.0, etc.). The emerging problem is how to automatically recognize the right model for given entities in this approach. We handle this problem as follows—if the concept is connected with some object with the type timestamp then we store the data in hybrid SBDH model.

4   Use Case and Results

Let us describe briefly one of the applications of the ontology model utilization for representation and handling data from a hydroelectric power plant. This scenario is used for verifying the concept of CPSs integration by means of SHS ontology and the SBDH and verifying the possibility of handling a huge amount of RDF triples by a suitable triplestore. In our application, we process data measured by 38 sensors in the power plant including for example measurement of fall of water, frequency, power factor, and real power. All data from power plant sensors are read with 5 s sampling rate. These data sources are connected via implemented adapters to comply with the SHS ontology.

The significant problem is the performance issue in the context of CPS data processing—especially in the case when data are stored as RDF triples. Our sensors produce 656,640 samples per day. If we transform these data into triples, then the volume of data is equal to 5,253,120 triples per day and it corresponds to 1,917 mil. triples per year (Fig. 3).

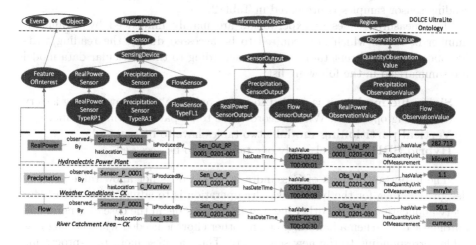

Fig. 3. Example of hydroelectric data model described in SHS ontology

We conducted several tests for demonstrating the suitability of the proposed hybrid SBDH model. The hardware for these tests was the computer with two hard disks (SSD + magnetic HDD), 32 gigabytes of memory and CPU was Intel Core i7-7700T.

The cluster of Spark and Cassandra nodes was deployed using Docker containers. First, we conducted tests with two Spark workers and two Cassandra nodes. The importance of two separated hard disk resides in ensuring independent data storage for each cluster node. Shared data storage affects the speed of reading/writing operations. The objective of this test was the performance comparison of single file model, vertical partitioning model, and hybrid SBDH model. The test was focused on writing and reading sensor measurement sequence.

Table 1. Comparison of different data models - writing data

	Single file	Vertical partitioning	Hybrid SBDH
Write 1000 sensor samples	36.522 s	29.612 s	13.027 s
Write 10000 sensor samples	94.428 s	70.298 s	34.412 s
Write 100000 sensor samples	299.647 s	296.767 s	149.293 s

Table 2. Comparison of different data models - reading data

	Single file	Vertical partitioning	Hybrid SBDH
Read 3000 sensor samples	60.022 s	20.012 s	9.716 s
Read 10000 sensor samples	113.428 s	22.298 s	10.231 s

The performance comparison of the different data models during writing sensor samples is presented in Table 1. Next, the performance comparison during reading sensor samples is presented in Table 2.

The measured times of experiments are mainly influenced by a different number of tables which are required to be accessed during the reading/writing operations. Different tables accesses according to the particular data model are summarized in the following list:

- **Single file model**—it is needed to access only one table but filtering is very demanding operation. Whole records have to be parsed during filtering.
- **Vertical partitioning model**—two tables have to be accessed.
- **Hybrid SBDH model**—only one table has to be accessed.

The important feature of Cassandra is that it does not allow table joins by design. The idea for the best Cassandra operation is to adjust table schema for every application. On the other hand, it is not possible in the case of general and automatic data schema handling, i.e., no other effort is needed while adding new table corresponding to the new sensor, etc. Thus, a subsequent post-processing is needed within the higher level of the system (using Apache Spark in our case), and it is also very time demanding operation. Therefore, the outcomes of vertical partitioning model experiments show that this solution is not as usable as other ones.

Furthermore, it is important to be aware that the single file and vertical partitioning models store data from more sensors into one table. Therefore, next experiments were conducted to find out how the number of sensors stored in a table affects reading performance.

The experiment demonstrating dependency between the number of sensors and the reading time is described in Table 3. It is apparent that the reading time is not increasing together with the sensor number in linear way according to our experiments.

Table 3. Vertical partitioning various number of sensors stored in one table—reading of 10,000 sensor samples

# of sensors	Vertical partitioning
1 sensor	22.298 s
2 sensors	24.321 s
3 sensors	28.982 s
4 sensors	30.842 s

5   Summary and Conclusions

The needs to improve the performance of triplestores are pervading many domains including the industrial automation domain. The task of ensuring efficient RDF data processing is essential for the way towards the usage of the Semantic Web technologies for data linking and analysis within Industry 4.0. The semantic description of data from industrial automation domain using ontologies brings many advantages—easy understanding of a given data model, easy data integration, and better consistency maintenance.

In this paper, we have introduced hybrid SBDH data model which is focused mainly on storage of sensor data. Next, we introduced Semantic Big Data Historian architecture—the system which utilizes semantic data description. Then we discussed the realization of SBDH storage layer to overcome performance issues. Finally we demonstrated the advantages of semantic data description on the hybrid SBDH layer.

The performance of hybrid SBDH model was the best compared to the single file and vertical partitioning model concerning the case of time series processing. The conclusion is that the proposed approach should enable and facilitate expanded use of Semantic Web technologies within Industry 4.0, at least for the use case described in this paper. Our future work includes using the SBDH with improved performance for advanced data analysis.

Acknowledgment. This research has been supported by Rockwell Automation Laboratory for Distributed Intelligent Control (RA-DIC) and by institutional resources for research by the Czech Technical University in Prague, Czech Republic.

References

1. SequenceFile (2009). https://wiki.apache.org/hadoop/SequenceFile
2. Accumulo (2011). https://accumulo.apache.org
3. MapReduce (2011). https://wiki.apache.org/hadoop/MapReduce
4. The Connected Enterprise (2017). http://www.rockwellautomation.com/global/capabilities/connected-enterprise
5. Aasman, J.: Allegro Graph: RDF Triple Database. Oakland Franz Incorporated, Cidade (2006)

6. Cao, X., Liu, L., Shen, W., Laha, A., Tang, J., Cheng, Y.: Real-time misbehavior detection and mitigation in cyber-physical systems over WLANs. IEEE Trans. Ind. Inf. **13**(1), 186–197 (2017)

7. Colombo, A.W., Bangemann, T., Karnouskos, S.: A system of systems view on collaborative industrial automation. In: 2013 IEEE International Conference on Industrial Technology (ICIT), pp. 1968–1975. IEEE (2013)

8. Commission, I.E., et al.: IEC 62541: OPC Unified Architecture (all parts), February 2010

9. Drath, R., Horch, A.: Industrie 4.0: hit or hype?[industry forum]. IEEE Ind. Electron. Mag. **8**(2), 56–58 (2014)

10. Du, J.-H., Wang, H.-F., Ni, Y., Yu, Y.: HadoopRDF: a scalable semantic data analytical engine. In: Huang, D.-S., Ma, J., Jo, K.-H., Gromiha, M.M. (eds.) ICIC 2012. LNCS, vol. 7390, pp. 633–641. Springer, Heidelberg (2012). doi:10.1007/978-3-642-31576-3_80

11. Girbea, A., Suciu, C., Nechifor, S., Sisak, F.: Design and implementation of a service-oriented architecture for the optimization of industrial applications. IEEE Trans. Ind. Inf. **10**(1), 185–196 (2014)

12. Group, I.W., et al.: Recommendations for implementing the strategic initiative industrie 4.0. Final report, April 2013

13. Harris, S., Gibbins, N.: 3store: Efficient Bulk RDF Storage (2003)

14. Hermann, M., Pentek, T., Otto, B.: Design principles for industrie 4.0 scenarios. In: 2016 49th Hawaii International Conference on System Sciences (HICSS), pp. 3928–3937. IEEE (2016)

15. Husain, M., McGlothlin, J., Masud, M.M., Khan, L., Thuraisingham, B.M.: Heuristics-based query processing for large RDF graphs using cloud computing. IEEE Trans. Knowl. Data Eng. **23**(9), 1312–1327 (2011)

16. Jirkovsky, V., Obitko, M., Marik, V.: Understanding data heterogeneity in the context of cyber-physical systems integration. IEEE Trans. Ind. Inf. **13**(2), 660–667 (2017)

17. Kolas, D., Emmons, I., Dean, M.: Efficient linked-list RDF indexing in parliament. SSWS **9**, 17–32 (2009)

18. Leitão, P., Colombo, A.W., Karnouskos, S.: Industrial automation based on cyber-physical systems technologies: prototype implementations and challenges. Comput. Ind. **81**, 11–25 (2016)

19. Obitko, M., Jirkovský, V.: Big data semantics in industry 4.0. In: Mařík, V., Schirrmann, A., Trentesaux, D., Vrba, P. (eds.) HoloMAS 2015. LNCS, vol. 9266, pp. 217–229. Springer, Cham (2015). doi:10.1007/978-3-319-22867-9_19

20. Rohloff, K., Schantz, R.E.: High-performance, massively scalable distributed systems using the mapreduce software framework: the shard triple-store. In: Programming Support Innovations for Emerging Distributed Applications, p. 4. ACM (2010)

21. Schätzle, A., Przyjaciel-Zablocki, M., Lausen, G.: PigSPARQL: mapping SPARQL to pig Latin. In: Proceedings of the International Workshop on Semantic Web Information Management, p. 4. ACM (2011)

22. Vohra, D.: Practical Hadoop Ecosystem: A Definitive Guide to Hadoop-Related Frameworks and Tools. Apress (2016)

23. Wilkinson, K., Sayers, C., Kuno, H., Reynolds, D.: Efficient RDF storage and retrieval in Jena2. In: Proceedings of the First International Conference on Semantic Web and Databases, pp. 120–139 (2003). CEUR-WS.org

Semi-automatic Ontology Matching Approach for Integration of Various Data Models in Automotive

Václav Jirkovský[1(✉)], Petr Kadera[1], and Nestor Rychtyckyj[2]

[1] Czech Institute of Robotics, Informatics, and Cybernetics, Czech Technical
University in Prague, Zikova 4, 166 36 Prague, Czech Republic
{vaclav.jirkovsky,petr.kadera}@ciirc.cvut.cz
[2] Ford Motor Company, Dearborn, MI, USA
nrychtyc@ford.com

Abstract. All manufacturing companies need to be able to closely monitor the processes, labor, tooling, parts and throughput on the assembly plant floor. This might be a challenging task because of a large number of plant floor applications that operate using different hardware and software tools. In many cases, there are a large number of devices that need to be monitored and from which critical data must be extracted and analyzed. This situation calls for the use of an architecture that can support data from heterogeneous sources and support the analysis of data and communication with these devices. Ontologies can be developed to facilitate a proper understanding of the problem domain, and subsequently, knowledge from external sources can be shared through linked open data or directly integrated (mapped) using an ontology matching approach. In this paper, we demonstrate how ontological data description may facilitate interoperability between a company data model and new data sources as well as an update of stored data via ontology matching. The MAPSOM system (system for semi-automatic ontology matching) is introduced and described in this paper, and subsequently, an example of new data model integration is demonstrated using the MAPSOM system.

Keywords: Heterogeneity · Ontology · Ontology matching · Self-organizing map · Active learning

1 Introduction

All manufacturing companies need to be able to closely monitor the processes, labor, tooling, parts and throughput on the assembly plant floor. This is often complicated because of a large number of plant floor applications that operate using different hardware and software tools. In many cases, there are a large number of devices that need to be monitored and from which critical data must be extracted and analyzed. This situation calls for the use of an architecture

© Springer International Publishing AG 2017
V. Mařík et al. (Eds.): HoloMAS 2017, LNAI 10444, pp. 53–65, 2017.
DOI: 10.1007/978-3-319-64635-0_5

that can support data from heterogeneous sources and support the analysis of data and communication with these devices. Another factor to consider are the significant differences between the hardware/software at different manufacturing facilities even though they may be building the same product. This can be due to a variety of reasons including the availability of tooling at different locations around the world, local differences and the need to support different versions of hardware and software at many plants. In many cases, the data also needs to be localized to support a plant and textual data may require translation using either machine or human translation. Other issues that need to be addressed include different units of measurement between locations (imperial vs. metric) and even different formats for dates between plants around the world. All of these factors contribute to the difficulty of the problem in developing a solution for integrating manufacturing data on the plant floor.

There are a number of different solutions that can be currently applied to this data heterogeneity problem. A data warehouse can be built to include the various data sources that are present, but this will require the development of a data model that will represent all of the different data sources. This is a difficult process because the different variations and inconsistencies between disparate data sources need to be correctly represented in the common data model. In many cases, the same data element has different names and formats in separate databases which then need to be merged into a single data model. The data model needs to be maintained and modified as new data sources are incorporated into the production system. Commercial vendor solutions can also be applied but often require the use of proprietary data representation models that cannot be easily integrated with external systems.

An ideal solution would allow for the usage of a simplified data representation model that can support various data sources and uses an open standard that can exchange information easily between systems. This solution should also allow for easy maintainability as there will be frequent additions and modifications to the data model. It would also consolidate manufacturing data using a global open standard and would be able to represent and communicate with these different data sources. It is also important that the proposed solution supports knowledge expressiveness and reasoning as well as the ability to keep track of the source of each data item. These requirements led us to select the use of semantic technologies to develop a common architecture for the manufacturing data model.

Semantic technologies are built around common XML-based representation standards such as RDF/OWL and provide a framework for building applications that support heterogeneous data sources. Ontologies can be developed to facilitate a proper understanding of the problem domain, and subsequently, knowledge from external sources can be shared through linked open data or directly integrated (mapped) using an ontology matching approach. Within the framework of this work we utilized our previous experiences with the development of manufacturing ontologies and will be building upon those ontologies in this work [15,16]. Other advantages for semantic technologies include flexibility, standardization, expressiveness, provenance and a reasoning/inferencing capability. There are many vendors who have built tools to support these semantic web standards which can support manufacturing data integration and analysis.

The goal of this paper is to demonstrate how ontological data description may facilitate interoperability between a company data model and new data sources as well as an update of stored data via ontology matching. Furthermore, a user involvement in the ontology matching process is a very important feature within the automotive industry. Knowledge management and a matching of new data models are very important not only within automotive but also in every distributed environment including agent-based and SOA-based industrial systems.

This paper is organized as follows: first we provide a general overview of the heterogeneity problem. Then, we introduce the ontology matching problem including similarity measures aggregation and user involvement possibilities in the ontology matching problem. Next, we demonstrate an integration of the Ford supply chain ontology and MS Excel spreadsheet representing a list of spare parts together with many important details on MAPSOM system which utilize a self-organizing map, visualization methods, and active learning for ontology matching.

2 Heterogeneity

An essential prerequisite for an accurate integration is to reduce heterogeneity between data models—the shared ontology and a data source for integration in our case. Many different types of heterogeneity have been defined and discussed e.g. in [1,4,5]. The most obvious types of heterogeneity are as follows [6]:

- **Syntactic heterogeneity** represents the situation when two data sources are expressed in different representational language. In the case of ontologies, this situation happens when ontologies are modeled in different representation formalisms, e.g., OWL[1] and KIF[2].
- **Terminological heterogeneity** stands for different names of the same entity in different data models. An example may be a usage of different natural language—Wing vs. Křídlo (Czech term); or usage of synonyms—Wing vs. Fender.
- **Semantic heterogeneity** (a.k.a. logical mismatch) represents differences in modeling the same domain of interest. This logical mismatch arises due to a utilization of different axioms for defining the same elements from data sources. Two different mismatches may be distinguished: 1. the conceptualization mismatch—differences between modeled concepts; 2. the explicitation mismatch—differences how the concepts are expressed as discussed in [19]. Moreover, [2] identifies and describes three essential reasons for conceptual differences:

---

[1] Web Ontology Language - https://www.w3.org/OWL.
[2] Knowledge Interchange Format - http://www-ksl.stanford.edu/knowledge-sharing/kif.

- Difference in coverage—two data models describe different (possibly over-lapping) parts of the world at the same level of detail and from the same perspective.
  - Difference in granularity—two data models describe the same part of the world from the same perspective but with different levels of detail.
  - Difference in scope—two data models describe the same part of the world with the same level of detail but from a different perspective.
- **Semiotic heterogeneity** stands for a different interpretation of entities by various people. In other words, entities from two different data models with the same semantic interpretation may be interpreted by an interpreter (human, expert system, etc.) with regard to the context. The semiotic het-erogeneity is difficult to detect and solve by computer and often by a human as well.

In general, more than one type of heterogeneity occurs at once. It is caused for example because of various ad-hoc tailored system integration, etc.

3   Ontology Matching

In this section, we introduce the ontology matching problem [6]. The term ontol-ogy is defined as an explicit specification of a conceptualization [7] sometimes extended with the requirement for a shared conceptualization. In other words, an ontology represents a conceptualization of some particular domain which is shared among users (if everybody has his unique ontology they cannot commu-nicate to each other) and is expressed by using a particular explicit means.

The goal of ontology matching is to find correspondent entities expressed in different ontologies. The simplest possible relation between elements is a one-to-one relation, e.g., Person maps to Human. Furthermore, there are more complex types of a semantic relationship, e.g., Student maps to Undergrad-Student and Postgrad-Student as well.

Ontology matching systems are widely used especially in the Semantic Web domain where the systems are responsible for the integration of a lot of large ontologies. Thus, the techniques for finding relations have to be fully auto-matic. However, even though many researchers have been trying to develop fully automatic and faultless matching systems, there are many cases where faultless matching could be achieved only by means of a skilled user supervision.

The goal of this paper is to introduce a hybrid matching system prototype which is responsible for matching elements from an MS Excel[3] file (XLS) to an ontology. We assume an XLS is a general spreadsheet file, i.e., we are not limited for example to Parcelized Ontology Model [9]—the approach how to store an ontology in an XLS. This approach has several differences comparing to a matching of two ontologies. The first difference is the way of elements extraction for matching. Naturally, ontology elements to be matched are clearly given (strings representing concepts, object properties, etc.). On the other hand,

---

[3] Microsoft Excel https://products.office.com/en-us/excel.

we must consider what should be the element for matching within an XLS. Should it be a content of cells, column names, sheet names, or the name of the XLS file? The second difference is the process of the subsequent XLS and ontology mapping. In this case, it is more difficult to decide what is a concept, an instance (an individual), a property (data or object) in the source XLS and more in merged ontology as an outcome of ontology mapping. For example, an XLS could be in many cases decomposed as a table name—a concept name; table columns—concept properties; table rows—individuals belonging to the concept.

A problem of the ontology matching (i.e., find out related entities) may be expressed as a problem of finding the most similar entities. There are many various already implemented similarity measures for computing a similarity of entities. In the following paragraphs, essential types of similarity measures are shortly introduced.

3.1   Basic Similarity Measures

String-Based Techniques. These methods are based on comparing strings as the name indicates. They compare a name, labels or comments of entities (e.g., a concept represented specific cultivar of apple could be characterized by following strings: name—anton; label—Antonovka apple?; comment (1)—A popular small green culinary apple variety from Russia; comment (2)—It has ability to tolerate extreme cold). A prefix or suffix similarity measure tests if one string is a prefix or suffix of another. Next, very widely used similarity measure is n-gram. This method computes the number of common n-grams (sequences of n characters) between two strings.

Language-Based Techniques. This group of similarity measures rely on using Natural Language Processing (NLP) methods. NLP is used for facilitating an extraction of meaningful terms. NLP methods can by divided into intrinsic methods (i.e., linguistic normalization) and extrinsic. Extrinsic methods utilize external resources, e.g., WordNet [14]. WordNet is an electronic lexical database for English, based on the notion of synsets or sets of synonyms. Furthermore, WordNet provides hypernyms and meronyms as well.

Structure-Based Techniques. These techniques aim to compare a structure of entities that can be found in ontologies. Structure-based techniques can be divided into comparison of an internal structure of an entity or the comparison of the entity together with surrounding entities. An example of a structure based similarity measure is the structural topological dissimilarity on a given hierarchy [18]. Extensional Techniques. This approach is applicable when concept individuals are available. The idea is based on the fact that if two concepts have the same individuals then they should represent identical concept.

Semantic-Based Techniques. Semantic-based methods belongs to the deductive methods. These methods alone do not perform well when they are utilized for an inductive task like the ontology matching. Thus, semantic based techniques are suitable for verification or amplification of pre-alignments (i.e., entities which are presupposed to be equivalent). Examples of semantic-based techniques are propositional satisfiability, modal satisfiability techniques, or description logic based techniques.

3.2 Similarity Aggregation

The basic similarity measures are suitable for different dissimilarity kinds. Therefore, the basic measures may be utilized as building blocks of some complex solution. There are several techniques how to use these blocks together for ontology matching. The most widely used method is to aggregate them.

There are several proposed and implemented methods for the similarity measures aggregation. We will provide short overview of these methods in the following paragraphs.

Weighted Product and Weighted Sum. Triangular norms are well-known as conjunction operators in the uncertain calculi and weighted product (belonging to the triangular norms) may be used for ontology matching. The weighted product between two objects x, x' from set of objects O is as follows:

$$sim(x, x') = \prod_{i=1}^{n} sim_i(x, x')^{w_i},$$

where $sim_i(x, x')$ is the ith similarity measure of objects x, x'. Analogously, the weighted sum can be considered for example as a generalization of the Manhattan distance with weighted dimensions.

Multidimensional Distances. This aggregation is suitable for independent basic similarity measures. An example of multidimensional distances is Minkowski distance:

$$sim(x, x') = \sqrt[p]{\sum_{i=1}^{n} sim_i(x, x')^p},$$

where $sim_i(x, x')$ is the ith similarity measure of objects x, x'.

Machine Learning Approaches. There are several proposed approaches for utilizing machine learning methods for the ontology matching problem. A similarity measures aggregation may be converted into a supervised machine learning problem with the help of training data containing a set of similarity measure values corresponding to every matching pair together with a value representing positive or negative mapping as described in [8]. Thus, general machine learning methods can be utilized for ontology matching problems, e.g., support vector machines (SVM), decision trees and neural networks.

3.3 Semi-automatic Ontology Matching

A fully automatic ontology matching systems are not suitable for all application domains. A system with the highest possible precision and recall is needed for communication among experts and systems from different domains, e.g. in manufacturing or in medicine. One of the possible examples for such a problem is described in [11]. Semi-automatic or manual ontology matching solutions overcome previously mentioned deficiencies. However, these solutions are usually more time consuming.

In other words, semi-automatic solutions are based on a user involvement in ontology matching process. There are three areas in which users can be involved in a matching solution: (i) by providing initial alignments (and parameters) to the matchers, (ii) by dynamically combining matchers, and (iii) by providing feedback to the matchers in order for them to adapt their results [6].

Furthermore, historical records of the prior matching may be used for improving a precision and a recall of an ontology matching. Existing matches positive/negative and a user action history can enhance a matching process to be more interactive and personalized [3].

4 Validation Study

In this section, we introduce our solution of the hybrid ontology matching problem. This solution is based on semi-automatic ontology matching system named MAPSOM and its corresponding extension for processing MS Excel files. Next, the approach is demonstrated on the integration of the Ford supply chain ontology and MS Excel file containing spare part information.

4.1 MAPSOM

We have extended our previously proposed and developed semi-automatic ontology matching system MAPSOM [10] to be able to compute possible matching pairs between the Ford supply chain ontology and MS Excel file containing spare parts items. This system combines a machine learning approach for a similarity measures aggregation and a user involvement into the ontology matching problem.

The similarity measure aggregation is based on a self-organizing map also known as Kohonen self-organizing maps (SOM/KSOM) [13]. In general, self-organizing maps are a type of neural networks with unsupervised training algorithm. The basic functionality of a SOM is an ability to assign similar input vectors to the same neuron of a SOM output layer.

The user involvement is represented by verification of computed matching values—by means of SOM visualization (see Fig. 4); and next by the active learning process—used for tuning of classified data.

The overall matching process consists of following steps:

1. Compute desired similarity measures for element pairs
2. Train SOM
3. Compute clusters by means of a hierarchical clustering
4. Compute initial classification (positive or negative) of all neurons as well as of clusters.
5. A user may verify classified neurons and clusters in this step.
6. Conduct active learning process—the most probably badly classified neurons of each cluster are put forward a user.

After these steps, a user has a set of corresponding entities from the both data models (ontology and XLS file) and is ready for subsequent mapping.

4.2 Data Models Matching

Data Models for Subsequent Matching. The Ford supply chain ontology captures the risk management in the Ford global supply chain. Every car model depends on many different suppliers, and important capability is to be able to determine which vehicles at which plants would be impacted by a potential shortage, e.g., a limited supplier plant operation, a disaster (e.g. tsunami), etc. The Ford ontology captures all needed knowledge about vehicles, manufactures, and processes, and therefore the ontology can infer required information. Furthermore, the ontology would be able also to identify if Ford is dependent on one supplier plant for multiple vehicles.

The second source of items for matching is an Excel file (XLS) containing Ford spare part records. The XLS file has about 62 various columns identifying particular parts. A predominant number of columns contain specific numerical codes or strings composed of abbreviated labels. Obviously, a manual integration of such a data would be very time consuming and because of big volume of records probably impossible. Furthermore, a data preprocessing is needed for enabling an automatic model matching. The data preprocessing is described in the following paragraphs. An example of spare part records is illustrated in the Fig. 1.

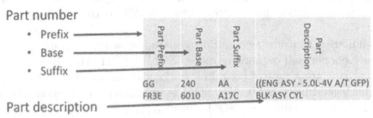

Fig. 1. A segment of Ford spare parts MS Excel file

Data Preprocessing. The essential step preceding matching of models is data preprocessing. Data for matching could be enriched with additional and valuable information during this step.

Part numbers conceal a lot of important information which may make the matching more precise. Thus, we need to parse and decode these items. Part numbers are divided into three categories—regular parts (e.g., a cylindrical block); hardware and utility parts (e.g., machine screws); special service tools. Furthermore, two different part coding notations may be distinguished—before and after 1998.

In this paragraph, we provide a detail description of regular parts. Regular parts consist of tree part—prefix, base, and suffix. The prefix is represented by a four-digit alphanumeric character and denotes year, model, and engineering office of a given part. The base part has four or five digits and indicates a part. For example, base part number series 2000–2874 represent brakes. The suffix indicates change level, i.e., A: original design; B: changed once, etc. An example of spare part number decoding is illustrated in Fig. 2.

Fig. 2. An example of a spare part decoding

Next, every spare part has a description. This description is formed from abbreviations and therefore it could be hardly utilized for data models matching. We used Ford Speak for decoding a part description. The Ford Speak is database of acronyms, definitions, and terms originally designed for facilitating data exchange between manufacturers. Items from the Ford Speak may have more than one value, and we cannot decide which is the correct one. This fact decreases accuracy and increases complexity of a matching but a utilization of a part description is probably impossible without this preprocessing step. The decoding of a spare part description is illustrated in Fig. 3.

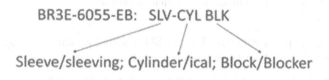

Fig. 3. An example of the part description decoding

Models Matching. After preprocessing, the data models matching by means of MAPSOM system may be conducted. Steps of the matching task and their order are stated in the Sect. 4.1. A SOM had a hexagonal topology and 25 neurons in both dimensions in our experiments. A training algorithm had following parameters [12]—a neighborhood function: Gaussian (parameter: 0.5); a neighborhood size: 5; an adaptation of learning rate: linear; an initial value of learning rate: 0.4. First, we trained self-organizing map. Training data were pairs composed of ontology elements from Ford supply chain ontology and preprocessed elements from MS Excel spare part list. A number of iteration was set to 1000 but after 300 iterations there were no evident changes of the output layer neuron weights. Thus, we could stop the learning algorithm after 300 iterations. The trained SOM within MAPSOM system is illustrated in Fig. 4. Next, we have to conduct initial classification of neurons. We used a Boolean conjunctive classifier [8] for an initial neuron classification as well as for a subsequent cluster classification.

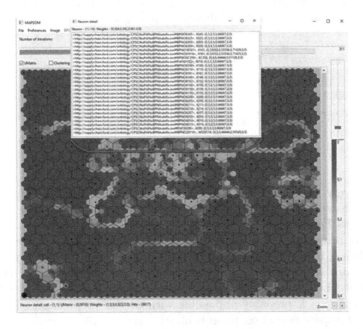

Fig. 4. The trained SOM visualization by means of U-Matrix together with demonstration of data pairs represented by a particular neuron

Subsequently, pairs with the help of SOM visualization could be analyzed. We have several ways how to process it:

– **Clusters and their classification**—a cluster classification is computed according to its center of gravity. Clearly, the cluster classification is dependent on a count of clusters (centroids are translating). Therefore, MAPSOM system offers an option for varying different numbers of clusters according to a given data.

- **U-Matrix visualization**—important neurons as well as neuron clusters may be recognized by means of U-Matrix (unified distance matrix) visualization [17]. U-Matrix displays distances between neurons (blue color - a short distance; red color - a long distance), and thus we can recognize an important neuron in the middle of trained SOM in Fig. 4. In general, neurons with decidedly positive and negative classification have a longer distance to remaining neurons in many cases. It enables a recognition of positive matching even without initial classification.
- **Hit histogram**—this additional information denotes how many pairs are represented by a particular neuron. Hit histogram may be combined with U-Matrix visualization as well as with visualization of clusters.

The last step of models matching is an active learning process. A utilization of this process has several benefits. First, the found positive matching pairs may be improved during this step (the least probable matchings are presented for verification and user can change a classification of a corresponding neuron or a cluster). In other words, a user should be capable of verifying correctness of discovered neuron classifications. We used active learning mainly for verification of a given matching in our case.

5 Discussion

The knowledge management task is a difficult task even in the case of one data model. Furthermore, an integration of various data models together with a maintenance of their consistency is very complex task which is essential in many applications and domains including agent-based and SOA-based industrial systems. Semantic Web technologies may offer solution for these tasks. There are many already proposed and implemented systems for ontology matching which could be used for integration of various data sources.

In many cases, manual matching could be very time consuming or even impossible due to huge number of matching entities. Thus, many researchers and developers try to develop fully-automatic matching systems. These systems are capable to process very big number of entities. On the other hand, the precision of the matching has to be taken into account in many domains, i.e., healthcare, industrial domain, etc. A user involvement in semi-automatic matching system is the best solution how to process huge data amount and ensure a satisfactory precision of matching.

A user should be involved not only within the matching process itself. A user may provide additional valuable information for the matching—mainly in the preprocessing phase. In this paper, we have shown that the preprocessing phase could be essential for enabling matching in many applications. Here, available information in XLS file are not sufficient for any reasonable matching. Thus, a user is able to extend knowledge about matching items by decoding part numbers and abbreviated part description. Apparently, a user is not involved for example in converting all part numbers manually but in providing a definition for the system how to convert part numbers and corresponding descriptions. A blind automatic matching approach cannot achieve such outcomes.

A user-friendly visualization of matching data during the matching process is essential for proper understanding of data as well as a matching process itself. A suitable visualization method is strongly dependent on methods and technologies which are used for the matching. However, visualization methods have to reflect several assumptions because of ensuring usable and efficient user interaction, i.e., offer a capability to manipulate with a whole set of similar entities (for example change a classification of the proposed matching), provide a mechanism which recommends suitable data for user verification, etc.

6   Conclusions and Future Work

In this paper, we introduced the approach how to utilize ontology matching for semi-automatic various data model integration and how important is the user involvement in this process together with the preprocessing phase. The approach is demonstrated on the matching task where spare parts are matched to the Ford supply chain ontology.

In this article, we focused on spare part matching to the ontology elements. In future work, we will be aimed at a utilization of preprocessed (extended) XLS data for a derivation of new concepts, properties, and relationships and how to conduct the most precise mapping between the original ontology and the new derived ontology segments. This extension of the ontology should offer a better interoperability as well as efficiency for supply chain management. We would like to automate the process of ontology management (e.g., adding new concept into an existing ontology) by means of a utilization of ontology learning methods and cover a creation of following ontology parts step by step—terms, concepts, concepts hierarchy, relations, relations hierarchy, axioms. We especially will emphasize a user involvement in previously mentioned research directions for achieving the best outcomes required within the automation domain.

Acknowledgment. This work is supported through the Ford Motor Company University Research Proposal (URP) program and by institutional resources for research by the Czech Technical University in Prague, Czech Republic.

References

1. Batini, C., Lenzerini, M., Navathe, S.B.: A comparative analysis of methodologies for database schema integration. ACM Comput. Surv. (CSUR) **18**(4), 323–364 (1986)
2. Benerecetti, M., Bouquet, P., Ghidini, C.: On the dimensions of context dependence: partiality, approximation, and perspective. In: Akman, V., Bouquet, P., Thomason, R., Young, R. (eds.) CONTEXT 2001. LNCS, vol. 2116, pp. 59–72. Springer, Heidelberg (2001). doi:10.1007/3-540-44607-9_5

3. Bernstein, P.A., Melnik, S., Churchill, J.E.: Incremental schema matching. In: Proceedings of the 32nd International Conference on Very Large Data Bases, pp. 1167–1170. VLDB Endowment (2006)

4. Bouquet, P., Ehrig, M., Euzenat, J., Franconi, E., Hitzler, P., Krotzsch, M., Serafini, L., Stamu, G., Sure, Y., Tessaris, S.: Specification of a Common Framework for Characterizing Alignment (2005)

5. Euzenat, J.: Towards a principled approach to semantic interoperability. In: Proceedings of IJCAI 2001 Workshop on Ontology and Information Sharing, pp. 19–25 (2001). (No commercial editor)

6. Euzenat, J., Shvaiko, P., et al.: Ontology Matching, vol. 18. Springer, Heidelberg (2007)

7. Gruber, T.R., et al.: A translation approach to portable ontology specifications. Knowl. Acquis. $5(2)$, 199–220 (1993)

8. Ichise, R.: Machine learning approach for ontology mapping using multiple concept similarity measures. In: Seventh IEEE/ACIS International Conference on Computer and Information Science, ICIS 2008, pp. 340–346. IEEE (2008)

9. Standardized product ontology register and transfer by spreadsheets – Part 1: Logical structure for data parcels. International standard, International Electrotechnical Commission, Geneva, CH (2014)

10. Jirkovský, V., Ichise, R.: MAPSOM: user involvement in ontology matching. In: Kim, W., Ding, Y., Kim, H.-G. (eds.) JIST 2013. LNCS, vol. 8388, pp. 348–363. Springer, Cham (2014). doi:10.1007/978-3-319-06826-8_26

11. Jirkovský, V., Obitko, M.: Ontology mapping approach for fault classification in multi-agent systems. IFAC Proc. Vol. $46(9)$, 951–956 (2013)

12. Kohonen, T.: Essentials of the self-organizing map. Neural Netw. 37, 52–65 (2013)

13. Kohonen, T.: The self-organizing map. Neurocomputing $21(1)$, 1–6 (1998)

14. Miller, G.A.: WordNet: a lexical database for English. Commun. ACM $38(11)$, 39–41 (1995)

15. Ostrowski, D., Rychtyckyj, N., MacNeille, P., Kim, M.: Integration of big data using semantic web technologies. In: 2016 IEEE Tenth International Conference on Semantic Computing (ICSC), pp. 382–385. IEEE (2016)

16. Rychtyckyj, N., Raman, V., Sankaranarayanan, B., Kumar, P.S., Khemani, D.: Ontology re-engineering: a case study from the automotive industry. In: Proceedings of the Thirtieth AAAI Conference on Artificial Intelligence, pp. 3974–3981. AAAI Press (2016)

17. Ultsch, A.: Self-organizing neural networks for visualisation and classification. In: Opitz, O., Lausen, B., Klar, R. (eds.) Information and Classification, pp. 307–313. Springer, Heidelberg (1993). doi:10.1007/978-3-642-50974-2_31

18. Valtchev, P., Euzenat, J.: Dissimilarity measure for collections of objects and values. In: Liu, X., Cohen, P., Berthold, M. (eds.) IDA 1997. LNCS, vol. 1280, pp. 259–272. Springer, Heidelberg (1997). doi:10.1007/BFb0052846

19. Visser, P.R., Jones, D.M., Bench-Capon, T.J., Shave, M.J.: Assessing heterogeneity by classifying ontology mismatches. In: Proceedings of the FOIS, vol. 98 (1998)

Ontology-Based Cooperation
in Cyber-Physical Social Systems

Alexander Smirnov[1,2], Tatiana Levashova[1,2(✉)],
and Alexey Kashevnik[1,2]

[1] St. Petersburg Institute for Informatics and Automation of the Russian
Academy of Sciences, 39, 14th line, St. Petersburg 199178, Russia
{smir,tatiana.levashova,alexey}@iias.spb.su
[2] ITMO University, 49, Kronverkskiy pr., St. Petersburg 197101, Russia

Abstract. The paper describes the research on cooperation of cyber-human resources in a cyber-physical social system. An ontology for a cyber-physical social system is proposed and specialized for the robotics assembly domain. A task from this domain is used to demonstrate scenarios of robot-robot cooperation and robot-human cooperation. Communications that support the cooperation processes are performed through online communities by messaging. Examples of messages and their format are given when the scenarios have been described.

Keywords: Cyber-physical social systems · Ontology · Robot cooperation · Robot-human cooperation · Online community

1 Introduction

Cyber-Physical Social Systems (CPSSs) are a new generation of networked systems, wherein human resources are an integral part. In these systems, humans are not only service consumers, but "collaborators" as well. Collaboration of humans and cyber resources provide great benefits. For instance, cyber resources can learn from humans in the process of their collaboration and then, if it is possible, to substitute the humans. Humans and cyber resources can jointly do a job that cyber resources themselves are not able to do. Distribution of a task assuming combination of routing work and intelligence between cyber resources and humans may facilitate task execution or even lead to new task solutions. Many other examples of beneficial cyber- and human collaboration can be found. The CPSSs unite cyber- and social worlds naturally and in this way provide a great opportunity to take advantages from collaboration.

A building block for collaboration is cooperation [1]. Cooperative working is tightly coupled with information exchange. Appropriate communication mechanisms are useful for partners to maintain a set of shared beliefs and to coordinate their actions towards the shared goal [2]. If communication between cyber resources, which are kinds of machines, can be formalized, effectively producing types of inter-human communication (shared visual information, gests, speech) on cyber resources is not currently feasible [3].

© Springer International Publishing AG 2017
V. Mařík et al. (Eds.): HoloMAS 2017, LNAI 10444, pp. 66–79, 2017.
DOI: 10.1007/978-3-319-64635-0_6

Cooperation of humans and cyber entities is the focus of the present research. In this direction, a core ontology of a CPSS is proposed. The ontology defines the basic concepts that are needed to organize cooperation of cyber- and social worlds. The core ontology is specialized for the robotics and automation domain. A product assembly task from this domain is used to demonstrate scenarios of robot-robot cooperation and robot-human cooperation. Robots and humans use the specialized (domain) ontology for the communication. The research proposes the cooperative partners to communicate through online communities by messaging. The advantages of this are (1) an explicit form of knowledge being communicated; (2) the common way of communication; (3) no need to recognize different communication modalities.

The rest of the paper is structured as follows. Section 2 provides an overview of the related research. Ontology of a cyber-physical social system is proposed in Sect. 3. In Sect. 4 two cooperation scenarios in the robotics assembly domain are discussed. Some concluding remarks and the research limitations are summarized in the Conclusion.

2 Related Research

Cooperation in cyber-physical social systems is tightly related to the research on collaborative networks and cooperation & collaboration in cyber-human environments supported by communication mechanisms. Some of such studies are considered below.

Collaborative network is a network consisting of a variety of autonomous entities (e.g., organizations, robots, people, etc.) that are geographically distributed and heterogeneous in terms of their operating environment, culture, social capital and goals, but that collaborate to better achieve common or compatible goals, and whose interactions are supported by computer network [1]. Different forms of collaborative networks are distinguished. Virtual organizations, virtual communities, dynamic supply chains, etc. are among them. CPSSs have not been explicitly listed as one of the forms. Nevertheless, when it comes to collaboration supported by computer mediated communication, these systems manifest themselves as a kind of collaborative network.

In collaborative networks, ontologies are given the role of a knowledge source that facilitates the mutual understanding among the network members [4]. For instance, in the CoBASA architecture, cooperation of manufacturing agents is regulated by contracts [5]. The ontology validates the definitions and concepts of these contracts. The socio-technical aspect of collaboration in a community is the basis for the ontology proposed in the framework of virtual enterprises [6]. A collaboration ontology purposed to describe the social collaboration processes from an external point of view is suggested to capture and share knowledge about collaboration [7]. This ontology builds a common vocabulary for the key concepts of collaboration and the relations and dependencies between them. ColOnto (Collaborative networks Ontology) [8] is the result of elaboration of the approach to modelling collaborative networked organizations by four dimensions (structural, componential, functional, and behavioral) [4]. The main concepts organizing the general level of the mentioned ontologies are actor, objective (goal), policy, task, service, process, resource; actor can be company, organization, or person. Some of these concepts have formed the basis for the core ontology proposed in this paper.

The base for cooperation and collaboration in cyber-human environments is communication acts. In this direction, a number of approaches treat different communication modalities (explicit like verbal, deictic or based on gaze, gestures, facial expressions, or implicit like postures) [2, 9–11]. Some approaches contend with problems of speech communication in natural language. An ontological semantic technology [12] is widely used in these approaches. The technology relies upon repositories of world and linguistic knowledge. The repositories consist of the ontology, containing language independent concepts and relationships between them; one lexicon per supported language; and the Proper Name Dictionary (PND), which contains names of people, countries, organizations, etc. [13]. This technology is used, for instance, for robotic reasoning [14], for communication between a firefighting-robot and a human [15], and for human-robot collaboration in CHARMS – an environment of hybrid human-robot-agent-collaboration [16].

Just like the collaborative networks, the cyber-human environments use ontologies to provide the partners with the domain semantics that is in the centre of communication acts. Besides the semantics, ontologies in the collaborative networks and cyber-human environments serve as knowledge repositories. These repositories can provide with different kinds of knowledge, e.g. a task structure, a classification of gests, a description of partner skills and competencies, etc.

An analysis of ontologies used in different approaches has shown that most approaches tend to develop own ontologies. Some of these approaches take a general ontology as the basis for domain-specific ontologies. For instance, DOLCE[1] ontology is used in the manufacturing control area for communication between autonomous and cooperative holons (physical resources and logic entities) [17]. UFO (Unified Foundational Ontology)[2] is proposed to be used for business modeling [18] and to integrate several collaborative software applications aiming at effectively collaboration support within organizations [19]. UFO and SUMO (Suggested Upper Merged Ontology)[3] were investigated as the upper-level ontologies to build the foundation of an IEEE standard ontology for robotics and automation [20]. The standard is indented to provide a unified way of representing knowledge and to provide a common set of terms and definitions, allowing for unambiguous knowledge transfer among any group of humans, robots, and other artificial systems. Today, the core ontology for robotics and automation (CORA) is grounded in SUMO. The CORA ontology has been extended in the collaborative CORA by introducing concepts related to human-robot collaboration [21].

OpenCyC[4] and UFO ontologies seem to be the most popular to model enterprises and particularly CPSSs (e.g., [11, 22]). The popularity of OpenCyC is due to the presence of common sense knowledge. Such knowledge can be naturally used to organize communication between cyber components (e.g., robots) and humans. UFO ontology was constructed with the primary goal of developing foundations for conceptual modelling. The engaging quality of this ontology is a detailed account of

---

[1] http://www.loa.istc.cnr.it/old/DOLCE.html.

[2] https://oxygen.informatik.tu-cottbus.de/drupal7/ufo/?q=node/1.

[3] http://www.adampease.org/OP/.

[4] http://www.opencyc.org.

universals such as unary or binary relations [23]. A core ontology suitable to model CPSSs is expected as a result of the NIST project "Reference Architecture for Cyber-Physical Systems" [24]. The project addresses the development of a cyber-physical system framework with common vocabulary, analysis methodology, reference architecture concepts and use cases to serve as the basis for shared development, information exchange, and new formal methods applicable across domains. This project is in progress so far.

The ontology proposed in the paper is a core ontology of CPSS. It offers concepts and relationships to model structural, componential, and partly functional dimensions of a CPSS. A specialization of this ontology in domains serves as a means to organize cooperation of partners from cyber and social worlds in these domains. The ontology provides the partners with the domain semantics for the communication. In the paper, communication through online communities by messaging is suggested. The main advantage of this approach is explicit form of knowledge being communicated, which facilitates communication between the two worlds.

So far, the proposed ontology has not been grounded in any general ontology. The authors are in favourof UFO as a candidate to provide the ontology with the upper level.

3   Ontology of Cyber-Physical Social System

The ontology of CPSS (Fig. 1) comprises the main concepts and relationships that have been identified as relevant to model such systems. This ontology is inspired by the ontology for resource self-organization in cyber-physical-social systems [25]. The structure dimension of a CPSS provides the main concepts around which the ontology is built.

A CPSS consists of cyber space, physical space, and mental space [26]. These spaces are represented by sets of *resources*. The physical space consists of various *physical devices*. These devices are supplied with computing components. Such components allow the devices to perform computations, process data, information and knowledge, communicate, and as a consequence be interoperable. The physical devices united on the communication basis organize the *cyber space*. This space in the ontology is represented by *cyber resources*. Inherence of computing components in cyber resources is modelled by the equivalence axiom: *(is-a Physical device) and (embeds some Computation)* ≡ *Cyber resource*. The mental space is represented by *humans* with their knowledge, mental capabilities, and sociocultural elements.

In terms of collaborative networks, actors are participants of cooperative & communicative activities [4]. In this research, the CPSS' resources form the category of *Actors*. The actors *perform Roles*. A role defines *services* that an actor provides in a given context. In the figure, this idea is modelled as the actors perform *roles* and roles, in turn, provide *services*. The ontology represents concept role at the very abstract level. A corresponding specialization of this concept is required to denote specific roles that resources perform in the CPSS, the communication network, or the application domain. The resources may change their roles in the process of scenarios executions. Services provided by one role are *consumed* by other ones.

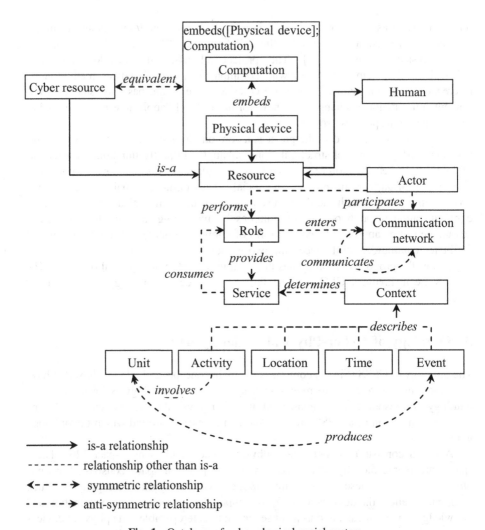

Fig. 1. Ontology of cyber-physical social system

Sorts of the services depend on the domain in which the CPSS is used. They may be computational functions, actions, communication services, etc. Services can be a simple service that a certain resource provides or a complex service requiring cooperation or collaboration of several resources. The paper does not treat the complex notion of services in corpore. Perspectives to this notion vary. The reference ontology [23] for services provides means to elaborate this notion minutely. The perspective on services accepted in this paper is that the services carry out processes.

Services expected in the current situation are determined by *context*. Information systems use various inferences, procedures, rules, etc. to analyze context and determine what services are expected. A widely adopted in ubiquitous and pervasive environments definition of *context* is any information that can be used to characterize the situation of an entity [27]. Such context is characterized by categories of individuality, activity, location, time, and relations [28]. On the other hand, *context* is a situation, which could be seen as a course of events; this situation evolves organizing new relationships between the entities involved in it [29]. Uniting the two perspectives, the ontology proposes to characterize context by categories of *unit*, *activity*, *location*, *time*, and *event*. The *unit* category describes the entity itself. The name *unit* is introduced instead of *individual* in order not to be confused with individuals in Web Ontology Language OWL[5]. *Location* and *time* provide the spatio-temporal coordinates of the entity. *Activity* is a process of performance of the task the entity is involved in. *Event* is occurrence happening at a determinable time and place; event can be produced by either some entity or some factors. Events are instantaneous whereas activities last in time [30]. The relations category is omitted since it is not a contextual category. It is a standard category used to characterize ontology concepts and comprises all the relationships specified in the ontology.

Interoperability of the CPSS' resources is supported by communication mechanisms. *Communication network* is an association of resources interconnected to information exchange. The resources joint this network with communication *roles* defined for this network.

The presented ontology is considered as a core ontology [31]. In domains of ontology usage, the ontology concepts are supposed to be extended and specialized.

4 Cooperation

The ontology (Fig. 1) is specialized to organize cooperation in the robotics and automation domain. This domain implies communicating knowledge between robots and humans and therefore is a good application domain for a CPSS. A product assembly task is used to demonstrate cooperation activities. The focus of this section is robot-robot cooperation and robot-human cooperation.

The CPSS ontology specialized to the domain in question is presented in Fig. 2. *Robots* are a kind of cyber resources in this domain. The assembly scenario supposes that either one robot participates in the *assembly* process or several robots cooperate to perform the *assembly task*. In the former case, *assembly task* is accomplished by one instance of the concept *Robot*, in the latter case, by a set of instances. The assembly task is defined as a task to assemble a *product* from *components*.

In the paper, robots and humans are proposed to use the technology of online communities to communicate, i.e. in the ontology, *online community* is a kind of *community network*. *Online community* is a virtual community whose members interact with each other via the Internet. As opposed to social networks, an online community unites its members (cyber- and social resources here) based on a common interest or goal. The common objective is one of the prerequisites for cooperation. The specialization of the core ontology for resource communication through online community is represented in the ontology slice (Fig. 3).

---

[5] https://www.w3.org/TR/owl-features/.

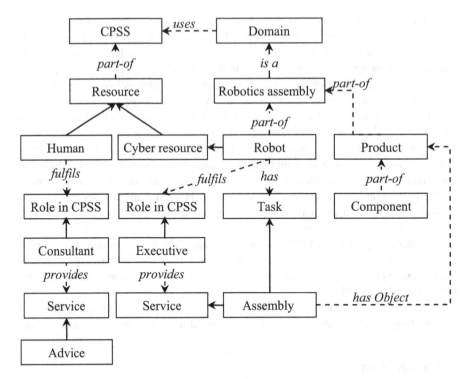

Fig. 2. Ontology for robotics assembly

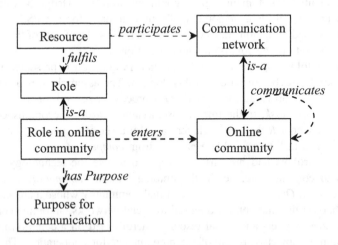

Fig. 3. Ontology specialization for online communities

The ontology (Fig. 2) distinguishes two categories of resources' roles: role in the CPSS and role in the communication network (not shown in the figure for its simplicity). For the CPSS, the role of *executives* for robots and the role of *consultants* for humans are provided for. In the online community, robots may fulfill the roles of *knowledge recipient* and *knowledge providers*; the humans' role is *knowledge provider*.

In the exemplified scenarios, robots have a task to assemble the word "ITMO" from mosaic Russian 3D characters (Fig. 4). The characters are scattered along the robots' ways. Each character is of a unique color because of the robots cannot identify types of the characters (letters), but they can recognize colors. The word "ITMO" is specified as an instance of the concept *Product* in the ontology; the characters are instances of the concept *Component* (Fig. 5). The robots are capable to search for, pick up, and relocate characters.

Fig. 4. Robots assemble "ITMO" word

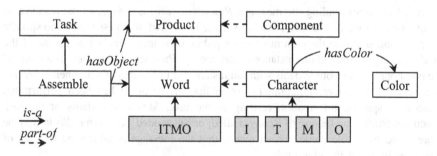

Fig. 5. Specialization of robotics assemble ontology

The robots' knowledge is represented in their own ontologies. The assembly task in these ontologies is specified as a sequence of actions (services in terms of the CPSS ontology). Each action is characterized by preconditions (inputs) for the start of the action and effects (outputs) the action results in. The sequence of action for the considered task is "Search for a characters → Character recognition → Character relocation". The action of characters recognition assumes recognition of the type of the found character and determination if this character belongs to the word being assembled. If the word does not include the character, the following action is "Search for a characters" again.

In the scenarios, robots and humans are participants of a special organized online community. They are jointed the community automatically with roles of *knowledge providers* for humans and *knowledge recipients* for robots.

4.1 Robot-Robot Cooperation

Two robots with the same functionality participate in the scenario of robots cooperation. Initially, the assembly task does not imply cooperation. The process of assembling is distributed between the robots as follows. Each robot knows the character which it should search for and relocate, and the spot for this character in the word being assembled.

When a robot puts a found character in its place, it communicates with the other robot to inform it about which character (to be more precise, the character of which color) and in which position is placed. The mutual communications provides the both robots with knowledge about all the characters comprising the word and their positions. As a result the robots become capable of cooperating.

The communication process through the online community is organized as follows. The robot that has fulfilled a part of the task sends an informing message into the community. This robot performs the role of knowledge provider. The ontology vocabulary is used in the message. The message format is

$$< Type,\ Resource\_Send,\ Resource\_Recip,\ Product,\ Component, Service, Content,\ Status > ,$$

where *Type* is a message type, *Resource_Send* is a resource name (an instance of the concept Resource) sending the message, *Resource_Recip* is a name of the resource or to that the message is intended for (if this name is omitted, the message has no specific recipient and sent into the community as a public message), *Product* is a name of the product being assembled (an instance of the concept Product), *Component* is a name of the component the resource deals with (an instance of the concept Component), *Service* is a service, procedure, function, or action that the resource has been performing, *Content* is specific information relating to the task, *Status* is a status of the task execution (status can be one of Ready, Failed, or Suspended). *Resource_Recip* may be represented by a role name, which means that the message is addressed to a set of resources fulfilling the given role.

For the scenario under consideration, a robot informs the online community that it has relocated the character "T" into the position with coordinates XYZ: *<Notify, Robot1, ITMO, T, Character relocation, T, x1, y1, z1, Ready>*. The content of this message (T, x1, y1, z1) represents inputs (T) and outputs (x1, y1, z1) for the action of character relocation. Robots carrying out the task on assembly of the ITMO product read this message and, if the knowledge containing in the message is new for them, they supplement their ontologies with it. When the word has been assembled, all the robots participating in the process (two robots in the given scenario) know the whole procedure of task execution.

In the paper, implicit and explicit forms of robot cooperation scenarios are proposed. The both forms suppose that initially robots are not aware if they have any partners to cooperate.

In the implicit form of the scenario the online community plays a role of black box. A robot moves along its way, finds a character and checks if this character belongs to the assembled word. If the word comprises the found character then the robot picks it up, informs the community that it is going to carry the character to the position designated for it, and does this. The other robot fulfilling the same task becomes aware of the character that has been found and relocated. Going along its way, it selects any character lacking in the word currently and follows the scenario with informing the community appropriately.

In the explicit form, a robot that found an appropriate character, informs the online community about this. If there is a robot that is fulfilling the same task then this robot sends a notification message directly to the first robot. The message contains information which robot is ready to cooperate. Namely, which robot is fulfilling the same task and what it has been doing. Further communications are made between the two robots.

4.2 Human-Robot Cooperation

The scenario of robot-human cooperation supposes that humans support robots in their actions. In this scenario, robots are not aware of characters positions in the word. Humans control the locations of the characters in order to these characters would form the word. When a robot finds a character it recognizes it and asks humans about the character position. If the word being assembled comprises the found character then a human consultant informs the robot about the coordinates where it should put the character. Otherwise, the robot receives a message to go on its way. As soon as the word has been assembled, the robots stop acting.

The communication process through the online community in this scenario is as follows. The robot has the role of knowledge recipient in the online community. It sends a message in the form

$$< Request, Robot1, Consultant, ITMO, T, Character\ relocation,$$
$$T, ?, ?, ?, Suspended >,$$

where *Request* is the message type, *Robot1* is the name of the robot sending the message, *Consultant* is the resource role (the message is addressed to anyone who fulfils the role of consultant), *ITMO* is the product, *T* is the product component, *Character relocation* is the action being performed, *Suspended* status means that the action is stopped for some period. The content in the form *T, ?, ?, ?* informs that component *T* is the input for the action and that values for outputs (coordinates) are the subject of the request.

Using the robotics assembly ontology (Figs. 4 and 5) the message above is transformed into human-readable view as follows. To any consultant from Robot1: Robot1 is assembling the word ITMO. Robot1 is dealing with the character T. Robot1 is ready to start the action "Character relocation". Robot1 asks coordinates x, y, z for the character "T".

According to the scenario, a human consultant (generally, the consultant is not mandatory human) should reply to the robot with coordinate values. In order to the human messages would be understandable by robots, humans are provided with templates. The template is produced based on the robot request. For the request of Robot1 the consultant replies in the following form:

coordinate x for character T is *value*,
coordinate y for character T is *value*,
coordinate z for character T is *value*,

where *value* is the value provided by the consultant. It is assumed here that the consultant is trained for the task in question. He/she uses a special procedure to determine the coordinated. The consultant judges the value of the coordinate y. This value assigns the line along which the word is assembled. The values v_x of the coordinate x are calculated as follows:

$$v_x = x_0 + (i - 1)w,$$

where x_0– the value of the coordinate x corresponding to the location of the first character of the word, i – the position of the character in the word, w – constant ($w = 2w_l$, where w_l– the average width of the characters).

The scenario of the robot-human cooperation was used for ontology validation [32]. The open source Smart-M3 platform [33] served to provide information exchange infrastructure between the user and robots. The messages were formatted as RDF-triples. The form of the messages proposed in this paper can be considered as an RDF-graph decomposable in triples.

5   Conclusion

The paper describes the research on ontology-based cooperation of cyber and human resources in a cyber-physical social system. Although cooperation and collaboration of heterogeneous entities is a focus of many studies, the issue of cooperation of different worlds in a CPSS has not been sufficiently investigated. The distinguishing feature here is equitable cooperation of humans and cyber-physical components. That is, the roles of CPSS' components are not attached to the types of these components. For instance, the human activity can be delegated to cyber resources.

The present research proposes a core ontology for a cyber-physical social system. The ontology models cyber-physical social systems through a set of resources comprising such systems. Three types of resources are distinguished: physical, cyber, and social. The resources act and communicate depending on the roles they have in the current situation. Concept *Role* introduced in the ontology enables to redistribute the resource activities.

The ontology is supposed to be extended and specialized in real-world application domains. One more contribution of the research is a specialization of the proposed ontology for the robotics and automation domain. A product assembly task from this domain is used to demonstrate scenarios of robot-robot cooperation and robot-human cooperation. In the scenarios, the ontology is used for resource communication. A scenario of robot-human cooperation allows ones to make a conclusion about ontology validity.

So far, the proposed ontology has not been grounded in any upper ontology. Grounding this ontology in a foundational ontology, such as SUMO, DOLCE, or UFO, will enable to achieve a good quality ontology [18, 34]. It is a possible future research direction.

Finally, the research contributes to involvement of the technology of online communities in information exchange. The research proposes the resources to communicate through online communities by messaging. The main advantage of this is explicit form of knowledge being communicated. At present, online communications become common human practice. Adaptation of this form of communication to cyber resources allows the resources from different worlds share the common way of communication and enables to avoid recognition of different communication modalities.

Concluding, it should be mention that the common ontology imposes some limitations. The resources have to use the vocabulary of this ontology to be understood by each other. If a resource is new regarding a CPSS, the vocabulary of this resource needs to be matched against the ontology vocabulary. Matching is a time consuming process that requires additional efforts.

Acknowledgments. The research was partly supported by the projects funded through grants 16-29-04349, 17-07-00247, and 17-07-00248 of the Russian Foundation for Basic Research, the research Programs I.31 and I.5 of the Presidium of the Russian Academy of Sciences, and Grant 074-U01 of the Government of Russian Federation.

References

1. Camarinha-Matos, L.M., Afsarmanesh, H.: Collaborative networks: value creation in a knowledge society. In: Wang, K., Kovacs, G.L., Wozny, M., Fang, M. (eds.) PROLAMAT 2006. IIFIP, vol. 207, pp. 26–40. Springer, Boston, MA (2006). doi:10.1007/0-387-34403-9_4
2. Hoffman, G., Breazeal, C.: Collaboration in human-robot teams. In: AIAA 1st Intelligent Systems Technical Conference. AIAA (2004). http://arc.aiaa.org/doi/abs/10.2514/6.2004-6434
3. Herasiuta, S., Sychou, U., Prakapovich, R.: Distributed information system for collaborative robots and IoT devices. In: Ronzhin, A., Rigoll, G., Meshcheryakov, R. (eds.) ICR 2016. LNCS, vol. 9812, pp. 63–68. Springer, Cham (2016). doi:10.1007/978-3-319-43955-6_9
4. Camarinha-Matos, L.M., Afsarmanesh, H.: A comprehensive modeling framework for collaborative networkedorganizations. J. Intell. Manuf. **18**, 529–542 (2007)

5. Barata, J., Camarinha-Matos, L.M.: Coalitions of manufacturing components for shop floor agility – the CoBASA architecture. Int. J. Netw. Virtual Organ. **2**(1), 50–77 (2003)

6. Simões, D., Ferreira, H., Soares, A.L.: Ontology engineering in virtual breeding environments. In: Camarinha-Matos, L.M., Afsarmanesh, H., Novais, P., Analide, C. (eds.) PRO-VE 2007. ITIFIP, vol. 243, pp. 137–146. Springer, Boston, MA (2007). doi:10.1007/978-0-387-73798-0_14

7. Knoll, S.W., Plumbaum, T., Hoffmann, J.L., De Luca, E.W.: Collaboration ontology: applying collaboration knowledge to a generic group support system. In: Proceedings of the 11th Group Decision and Negotiation Conference, pp. 12–26 (2010)

8. Ermilova, E., Afsarmanesh, H.: Systematic analysis of information management challenges within long-term collaborative networks. In: Camarinha-Matos, L.M., Xu, L., Afsarmanesh, H. (eds.) PRO-VE 2012. IAICT, vol. 380, pp. 446–456. Springer, Heidelberg (2012). doi:10.1007/978-3-642-32775-9_45

9. Budkov, V.Y., Prischepa, M.V., Ronzhin, A.L., Karpov, A.A.: Multimodal human-robot interaction. In: 2010 International Congress on Ultra Modern Telecommunications and Control Systems and Workshops (ICUMT), pp. 485–488. IEEE (2010)

10. Rigoll, G.: Multimodal human-robot interaction from the perspective of a speech scientist. In: Ronzhin, A., Potapova, R., Fakotakis, N. (eds.) SPECOM 2015. LNCS, vol. 9319, pp. 3–10. Springer, Cham (2015). doi:10.1007/978-3-319-23132-7_1

11. Lemaignan, S., Ros, R., Sisbot, E.A., Alami, R., Beetz, M.: Grounding the interaction: anchoring situated discoursein everyday human-robot interaction. Int. J. Soc. Robot. **4**, 181–199 (2012)

12. Nirenburg, S., Raskin, V.: Ontological Semantics. MIT Press, Cambridge (2004)

13. Raskin, V., Taylor, J.M., Hempelmann, C.F.: Ontological semantic technology for detecting insider threat and social engineering. In: 2010 New Security Paradigms Workshop, pp. 115–128. ACM, New York (2010)

14. Petrenko, M., Hempelmann, C.F.: Robotic reasoning with ontological semantic technology. In: Kim, J.-H., et al. (eds.) Robot Intelligence Technology and Applications. AISC, vol. 208, pp. 883–892. Springer, Heidelberg (2012). doi:10.1007/978-3-642-37374-9_85

15. Hong, J.H., Matson, E.T., Taylor, J.M.: Design of knowledge-based communication between human and robot using ontological semantic technology in firefighting domain. In: Kim, J.-H., Matson, E.T., Myung, H., Xu, P., Karray, F. (eds.) Robot Intelligence Technology and Applications 2. AISC, vol. 274, pp. 311–325. Springer, Cham (2014). doi:10.1007/978-3-319-05582-4_27

16. Raskin, V.: Theory, methodology, and implementation of robotic intelligenceand communication. Procedia Comput. Sci. **56**, 508–513 (2015)

17. Borgo, S., Leitão, P.: The role of foundational ontologies in manufacturing domain applications. In: Meersman, R., Tari, Z. (eds.) OTM 2004. LNCS, vol. 3290, pp. 670–688. Springer, Heidelberg (2004). doi:10.1007/978-3-540-30468-5_43

18. Guizzardi, G., Wagner, G.A.: Unified foundational ontology and some applications of it in business modeling. In: Proceedings of the Open Interop Workshop on Enterprise Modelling and Ontologies for Interoperability Co-located with CAiSE 2004 Conference. CEUR Workshop Proceedings (2004). http://ceur-ws.org/Vol-125/paper2.pdf

19. Oliveira, F.F., Antunes, J.C.P., Guizzardi, R.S..S.: Towards a collaboration ontology. In: Proceedings of Second Brazilian Workshop on Ontologies and Metamodels for Software and Data Engineering (WOMSDE 2007), pp. 97–108 (2007)

20. Schlenoff, C., et al.: An IEEE standard ontology for robotics and automation. In: 2012 IEEE/RSJ International Conference on Intelligent Robots and Systems, pp. 1337–1342. IEEE (2012)

21. Antonelli, D., Bruno, G.: Human-robot collaboration using industrial robots. In: 2nd International Conference on Electrical, Automation and Mechanical Engineering (EAME 2017). Advances in Engineering Research, vol. 86, pp. 99–102. Atlantis Press (2017)
22. Daoutis, M., Coradeshi, S., Loutfi, A.: Grounding commonsense knowledge in intelligent systems. J. Ambient Intell. Smart Environ. **1**, 311–321 (2009)
23. Nardi, J.C., de Almeida Falbo, R., Guizzardi, G., Pires, L.P., van Sinderen, M.J., Guarino, N., Fonseca, C.M.: A commitment-based reference ontology for services. Inform. Syst. **54**, 263–288 (2015)
24. Wollman, D.A.: Cyber-physical systems framework. NEMA Electroindustry J. **20**(4), 12–13 (2015)
25. Smirnov, A., Levashova, T., Shilov, N., Sandkuhl, K.: Ontology for cyber-physical-social systems self-organisation. In: Proceedings of the 16th Conference of Open Innovations Association FRUCT, pp. 101–107 (2014)
26. Liu, Z., Yang, D.-S., Wen, D., Zhang, W.-M., Mao, W.: Cyber-physical-social systems for command and control. IEEE Intell. Syst. **26**(4), 92–96 (2011)
27. Dey, A.K.: Understanding and using context. Pers. Ubiquit. Comput. **5**(1), 4–7 (2001)
28. Zimmermann, A., Lorenz, A., Oppermann, R.: An operational definition of context. In: Kokinov, B., Richardson, D.C., Roth-Berghofer, T.R., Vieu, L. (eds.) CONTEXT 2007. LNCS, vol. 4635, pp. 558–571. Springer, Heidelberg (2007). doi:10.1007/978-3-540-74255-5_42
29. Baumgartner, N., Gottesheim, W., Mitsch, S., Retschitzegger, W.: BeAware!-situation awareness, the ontology-driven way. Data Knowl. Eng. **69**(11), 1181–1193 (2010)
30. Sanfilippo, E.M., Borgo, S., Masolo, C.: Events and activities: is there an ontology behind BPMN? In: Garbacz, P., Kutz, O. (eds.) Formal Ontology in Information Systems, pp. 147–156. IOS Press (2014)
31. Scherp, A., Saathoff, C., Franz, T., Staab, S.: Designing core ontologies. Appl. Ontol. **6**(3), 177–221 (2011)
32. Smirnov, A., Kashevnik, A., Mikhailov, S., Mironov, M., Petrov, M. Ontology-based collaboration in multi-robot system: approach and case study. In: 11th System of Systems Engineering Conference (SoSE), pp. 329–334. IEEE (2016)
33. Smart-M3 at Sourceforge (2009). https://sourceforge.net/projects/smart-m3/. Accessed 30 May 2017
34. d'Aquin, M., Gangemi, A.: Is there beauty in ontologies? Appl. Ontol. **6**(3), 165–175 (2011)

Auto-Generation of Distributed Automation Software Based on Formal Product Line Specification

Victor Dubinin[1(✉)], Ilya Senokosov[1], and Valeriy Vyatkin[2,3]

[1] Penza State University, Penza, Russian Federation
victor_n_dubinin@yahoo.com, senokosov.i@yandex.ru
[2] Luleå University of Technology, Luleå, Sweden
vyatkin@ieee.org
[3] Aalto University, Helsinki, Finland

Abstract. In this paper we demonstrate how some features of product lines related to the product assembly plan can be modelled in a formal way using finite state machines. Then we introduce a method for automatic generation of automation software that is empowering the production systems to produce the required range of products based on availability of components. We illustrate the concept on a very simple example, where products are limited to ordered tuples of components. The products can have different complexity which is reflected in the variable number of elements in the tuples. Benefits of automatic generation include reduced implementation cycle, along with assurance in abilities of manufacturing lines to produce exactly specified product descriptions.

Keywords: Sorting · Selection · Workpieces sequence · Specification · Finite state machine · Selecting automaton · Token transfer · Graphs inference · Prolog language · Function blocks · Control system · Standard IEC 61499 · Ball sorting system · NxtStudio

1 Introduction

Future manufacturing systems shall be capable to change quickly from production of one product to another. It is often the case that the same manufacturing line is used to assemble a family of products sharing some common features, a.k.a. product line. To handle the complexity of possible feature combinations in the product line by the automation system, a formal method of generating control software from a product line description is required.

In this paper, we investigate a class of product lines where product's assembly plan can be represented as a sequence of symbols, and the entire product line as a finite state machine (FSM) [1] generating all such sequences. As an illustrative example we use a workpiece sorting system, whose product is understood to be a certain sequence of workpieces in an output tray. We demonstrate how the FSM description of the product line can be translated into distributed control logic of the sorting system, represented as a collection of interacting automata, each of which is focused on the selection of "own" specified workpiece sequences.

© Springer International Publishing AG 2017
V. Mařík et al. (Eds.): HoloMAS 2017, LNAI 10444, pp. 80–91, 2017.
DOI: 10.1007/978-3-319-64635-0_7

A separate problem is the generation of an implementation model on the basis of the description of a source specification. In this case, the modern Model Driven Engineering (MDE) approach to software design and its extension for domain specific languages called Model-Integrated Computing (MIC) can be used [2]. The starting point of the design is a source model of the system, and the final result is a target model of the system. The basis of these technologies is the models transformation.

For the design and implementation of distributed industrial automation control systems the international standard IEC 61499 is increasingly used [3]. This standard is of great importance in the building of new generation low-level control systems. At that, the basic design artifacts are function blocks (FBs).

The goal of this paper is to develop methods and tools for the description and synthesis of IEC 61499 FBs-based control systems for workpieces sorting on the basis of specified sequences selection. This paper is structured as follows. Section 2 defines finite automata used for the selection of specified workpiece sequences. In Sect. 3, an approach to implementation of the selecting automata on the basis of IEC 61499 function blocks using a token passing mechanism is considered. Section 4 is devoted to the automatic transformation of automata-based specifications to the structures of FB-based implementation. Graph inference rules and their representation in Prolog are under consideration here as well. In Sect. 5, a ball sorting system on the basis of the selection of specified workpiece sequences is proposed as a running demo. In Sect. 6, a method of translating automata-based specifications to ball sequences sorting system's control on the basis of IEC 61499 function blocks is developed. The Sect. 7 concludes the paper. Here the results are listed and directions of future work are outlined.

2 The Use of Finite Automata for the Specification and Selection of Workpieces Sequences

Finite state machines can be used both to specify the automata languages, and to recognize the input sequences of these languages. The traditional field of application of these recognizers is lexical analysis in compilers [1].

In this paper, finite automaton is suggested to be used to specify and to select sequences of workpieces according to their type (color). Hereinafter, we call such a finite automaton as a selecting finite automaton. Unlike the recognizer the selecting automaton may ignore incoming input symbols if they do not trigger any of its transitions.

We define a selecting finite automaton A (hereinafter, for sake of brevity an automaton A) as the following tuple:

$$A = (Q, T, C, \delta, \varphi, Q_0, F),$$

where Q is a finite set of states;

$T \subseteq Q \times Q$ is a finite set of transitions;
$C = \{c_1, c_2, \ldots, c_m\}$ is a finite set of types (colors) of workpieces;
$\delta : T \to C$ is a function which assigns colors to transitions;

$\varphi : T' \rightarrow N^+$ is a function which assigns the maximum number of allowable workpieces to self-loops from $T' \subseteq T$. The self-loop does not permit to accept more than $\varphi(t)$ workpieces of $\delta(t)$ color;

Q_0 is a set of initial states;

$F \subseteq T$ is a set of final transitions.

Firing a final transition of the automaton means that the previous workpieces sequence is accepted and assembling a new workpieces sequence begins. As a rule, final transitions of an automaton end in the initial state. It simulates the reset of the automaton to its initial state. At the same time, the alternative target states are of interest. In this case, we can assume that a dynamic change of the initial state of the automaton when building a new workpieces sequence is performed. This property can be classified as self-modification property of the formal model. It should also be noted that the above formal definition of the selecting automaton can be extended for a certain class of sorting problems to be solved.

Selecting finite automata can be divided into deterministic and non-deterministic ones. If the condition $\forall (q_a, q_b), (q_a, q_c) \in T \; [(q_b \neq q_c) \rightarrow \delta(q_a, q_b) \neq \delta(q_a, q_c)]$ holds the automaton is deterministic, otherwise it is non-deterministic. In a deterministic automaton there is only one initial state, $|Q_0| = 1$, while in a non-deterministic automaton there may exist several initial states.

A selecting deterministic finite automaton (SDFA) example is shown in Fig. 1, where O (orange), G (grey) и B (blue) are colors of workpieces. The final transition is indicated by a dotted line.

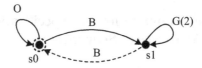

Fig. 1. Example of a selecting deterministic finite automaton

The automaton from Fig. 1 can select, for example, the following sequence of workpieces: BB, BGB, OOBGB, OOOBBBBGGB. If the input chains of workpieces are BG, OOGGGG, or OOOBGG, then the automaton would not select any specified sequence of workpieces from the input chains.

An example of a selecting non-deterministic finite automaton (SNDFA) is shown in Fig. 2(a). An advantage of a SNDFA over the corresponding SDFA is a compact description, and a disadvantage is more complicated implementation.

For description and processing of selecting automata the Prolog language [4] is used. Below is the description of the automaton shown in Fig. 1 in the form of Prolog facts.

```
state(s0).
state(s1).
transition(t1,s0,s1,black,_,ordinary).
transition(t2,s0,s0,orange,999,ordinary).
transition(t3,s1,s1,gray,2,ordinary).
```

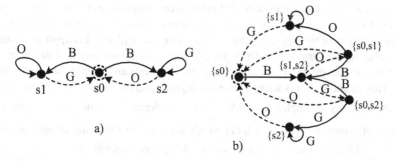

Fig. 2. Example of a selecting non-deterministic finite automaton (a) and the corresponding equivalent selecting deterministic finite automaton (b)

```
transition(t4,s1,s0,black,_,final).
initial_state(s0).
```

In the above description, the following predicates are used:

state is an unary predicate for representing states of the automaton;

transition is a 6-ary predicate to represent the automatons transitions with the following arguments: the first argument is a transitions identifier; second argument is an identifier of an source state; third argument is an identifier of an destination state; the fourth argument is the color of a workpiece; fifth argument is the maximum number of allowable workpieces (for self-loops); sixth argument is the transitions type (ordinary or final);

initial_state is an unary predicate denoting the initial state.

3   Approaches to the Implementation of Selecting Automata on the Basis of Function Blocks

Below approaches to the implementation of selecting automata on the basis of function blocks of the international standard IEC 61499 is considered. In turn, the function block – based implementation of the selecting automata can be easily integrated into general control of a workpieces sorting system based on the same standard.

SDFA can be directly implemented using the Execution Control Chart (ECC) of basic FB. However, the implementation of SNDFA requires more sophisticated approaches. In [5] non-deterministic automata (so-called, "NDA") is treated as a self-contained parallel model with its own rules of functioning. On the other hand, the NDA functioning from [5] can be represented as simulation steps of determinization of a non-deterministic finite automaton in real time. In this case, states of the deterministic finite automaton are implicitly obtained during the NDA functioning as a combination of its active states. The essential point here is the synchronous nature of the NDA functioning. Below we take this approach as a basis.

We can distinguish the following approaches to implement SNDFA on the basis of FB: when (a) transitions, or (b) states of SNDFA are represented as FB. These approaches are inherently equivalent but orientation to transitions is more convenient to represent loops. Moreover, it reduces the number of basic FB types to the number of workpiece colors in the implementation. Therefore, we will use this approach. Due to the synchronous nature of SNDFA functioning a common problem of these two approaches is the problem of conflicts when simultaneously setting/resetting active states. This situation occurs when a state has ingoing and outcoming arcs labeled by the same symbol, for example, $S_1 \xrightarrow[t1]{x} S_2 \xrightarrow[t2]{x} S_3$. At the active state $\{S_1, S_2\}$ the right sequence of transition firing is $(t2, t1)$ which leads to the following change of states: $\{S_1, S_2\} \xrightarrow[t2,t1]{x} \{S_2, S_3\}$. Otherwise, a wrong resulting state is obtained: $\{S_1, S_2\} \xrightarrow[t1,t2]{x} \{S_3\}$. For the sake of brevity, conflicts are not considered hereinafter. It can be only noted that in FB-based implementation the daisy chains can be used for setting an explicit order of transition firing for the priority-based conflict resolution. Further, for the sake of simplicity, we consider mainly the implementation of SDFA. Nuances of SNDFA implementation will be marked separately.

For the simulation of selecting finite automaton's behavior a token passing mechanism is proposed to use. It is a unified approach in relation to both SDFA and SNDFA. The token is a dynamic entity that may be transferred from one FB to another FB. If a FB has a token, it can actively monitor the incoming workpieces, and in the case when a workpiece and the FB itself have the same color, then the FB initiates action to capture the workpiece.

There may be a few tokens in the same time in the different FBs. From the totality of FBs with tokens only FBs, which are configured to receive the workpieces of this type, may accept the current observed workpiece.

Figure 3 shows the structure of a FB-based implementation of the automaton shown in Fig. 1. It is assumed that the information is passed from workpieces color sensor to the FB system via service interface function block (SIFB). The output signal of the FB system is a signal EOS "End of the (selected) sequence".

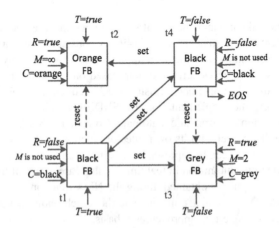

Fig. 3. Structure of FB-based implementation of the automaton shown in Fig. 1

The following elements are used to represent the structure of the FB-based implementation of selecting automata.

- arc *set* for the transfer of a token from the source FB to the target FB;
- arc *reset* for the removal of a token from the target FB;
- hanging input arcs for the setting of the initial values of the following parameters:

  C is the color of a workpiece to be accepted by the FB. In other words, it is a "color of FB". This parameter may not be changed during functioning of the system and installed initially;

  T is a flag of the presence of a token in the FB;

  R is a flag of the iteration. If $R = true$ then the FB performs iteratively gathering of a workpieces chain of the given color. If $R = false$ then the FB is a "transient" one. After the acceptance of one workpiece it moves the token to another FB(s);

  M is the maximum number of workpieces of the given color which may be accepted by this FB before the transfer of the token to another FB(s). This parameter is valid only for FB with $R = true$.

4 Automatic Transformation of Automata-Based Specifications to the Structures of Function Block Networks

For the automatic translation of a selecting automaton to the structure of a FB-based implementation the use of the mechanism of graph transformations is proposed [6]. The advantage of this approach is the visualization, the formality and the availability of tools for transformation. Furthermore, in some cases, direct derivation of elements of a target FB system from elements of a specification is possible. Some rules from the rule set to infer elements of a target FB system from elements of a source selecting automaton is shown in Figs. 4, 5, 6 and 7 below. It should be noted that the restriction in this case is the class of the used automata models which are SDFA and SNDFA without conflicts. For the last class the rule from Fig. 7 should be slightly modified, bearing in mind that FB-transitions with a color which is equal to the current color of workpiece should not be reset.

As can be seen from Figs. 4, 5 and 6, the parameters C and M for the being generated FBs are inferred from the labelling of automaton's transition. The above rules are given for the case of ordinary automaton's transitions and must be slightly modified in the case of final automaton's transitions. The modifications will generally relate to adding the output signal EOS to the generated FB.

Fig. 4. Rule of inferring FB which has the initial token and does not have the iteration

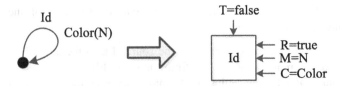

Fig. 5. Rule of inferring FB which does not have the initial token and has the iteration

Fig. 6. Rule of inferring *set* arc

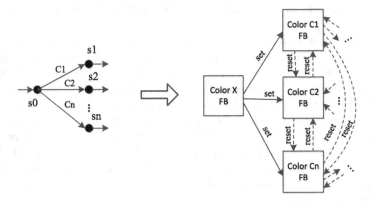

Fig. 7. General rule for transformation of "*Choice*" automata construction

For the inference of the implementing FB system structure a program in the logic programming language Prolog was developed [4]. This language has a powerful built-in inference mechanism. In fact, each rule from the Figures above is represented by a rule in Prolog. In the Prolog program FBs are represented by a 6-arity predicate `function_block`, with the following parameters: FB identifier, the color, the presence of the iteration, the presence of the token, the maximum number of allowable workpieces, the presence of EOS output. For the representation of FB connections a 3-arity predicate `connection` is used which has the following arguments: the identifier of source FB; the identifier of destination FB; the type of a connection arc. Two inference rules in Prolog are given below as an example.

The rule encoding graphical rule from Fig. 5:

```
function_block(Id,Color,true,false,NRep,false):-
transition(Id,State,State,Color,NRep,ordinary),
not(initial_state(State)).
```

The rule encoding upper graphical rule from Fig. 6:

```
connection(T1,T2,set):-
transition(T1,S1,S2,_,_,_),
S1\==S2,
transition(T2,S2,S3,_,_,_),
function_block(T1,_,_,_,_,_),
function_block(T2,_,_,_,_,_).
```

5   Example. Ball Sequences Sorting System

A ball sorting system (BSS) on the basis of the selection of specified workpiece sequences is proposed as a running demo. The system consists of a pusher, three sensors for detecting the type of balls (capacitive, inductive, and optical sensors), two sensors to determine the position of the pusher, a sensor for detecting whether a ball is in the gravity chute; two piston valves for catching balls from the gravity chute to a buffer channel (a storage).

Human Machine Interface (HMI) includes basic static elements of sorting systems, dynamic objects (balls), as well as LEDs for imaging of sensor values and EOS signal (Fig. 8). The HMI of EasyVEEP simulator (www.easyveep.com) for a ball sorting system is used as a prototype for our example.

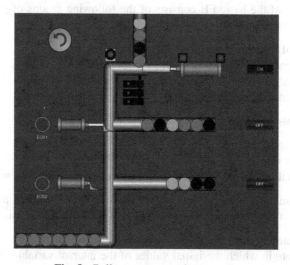

Fig. 8. Ball sequences sorting system.

The sorting system works as follows. Ball sequences determined by the SNDFA from Fig. 2 fall into the first storage while ball sequences selected by the SDFA from Fig. 1 get to the second storage. The balls which do not fall to the first two storages fall into the third storage (for the rejected workpieces).

6   Method of Translating Automata-Based Specifications to Ball Sequences Sorting System's Control

The structures of FB-based implementation used in Sect. 4 do not include all the details of implementation, so there is a need for further refinement theirs in terms of the standard IEC 61499. The FBs used in these structures have the same but adjustable functionality, and differ only in the values of the input parameters. Using them the FB configuration for specific contextual conditions is set. Thus, the same type (of basic) FB (Fig. 9) can be used to represent these FBs.

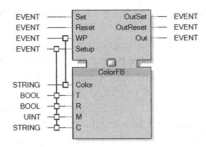

Fig. 9. Interface of basic FB for modelling of the automaton transitions.

The interface of the basic FB consists of the following groups of parameters:
Input signals:

– *Set* is a signal for setting a token in the FB;
– *Reset* is a signal for removal of a token from the FB;
– *WP* is a signal of coming in a workpiece to the sorting system;
– *Setup* is a signal of setting (resetting) the FB initial parameters.

Output signals:

– *OutSet* is a signal setting tokens in other FBs;
– *OutReset* is a signal resetting tokens in other FBs;
– *Out* is a signal indicating that the FB has processed an incoming workpiece.

The input variables correspond to input FB parameters described in Sect. 4.
The execution control chart (ECC) (Fig. 10) of the basic FB consists of six states:

– *Reset* is a state in which the token is reset;
– *Setup* is a state in which the initial values of the internal variables are set;
– *Set* is a state in which the token is set;

- *WP* is a state to which the automaton goes under the following condition: *WP* & (*T1* = *TRUE*) & (*Color* = *C1*). The transition to this state occurs when the incoming workpiece has the color of the FB and the FB has a token;
- *WP1* is a state in which the counter of processed workpieces is incremented. Only FB with *R* = *true* may go to this state. Furthermore, in this state, the output signal *Out* is issued;
- *WP2* is a state in which the removal of the token and issuing all the needed output signals are performed. Only the FB with *R* = *false* or the FB already accepted *M* workpieces of the given color may get to this state.

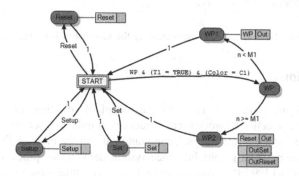

Fig. 10. Execution control chart of the basic FB for modelling of the automaton transitions.

Using the basic FBs a composite FB, which represents an entire automaton selecting ball sequences, is constructed. An example of the composite FB corresponding to the structure from Fig. 3 is shown in Fig. 11. This composite FB is then tested in a closed loop with simulation model and visualization. The scenario is as follows:

First, a ball of a certain color is generated which is detected by sensors and get to the first selecting automaton for analysis. If the ball is suitable then the signal "extend the first gate cylinder (of piston valve)" is transmitted to the model of equipment, and thus the ball falls into the first storage. Otherwise, the signal is transmitted to the second selecting automaton and checked them. As can be seen, the first storage is a higher priority than the second one.

If the ball fits the second selecting automaton then the signal "extend the second gate cylinder" is transmitted to the model of equipment. If the ball does not fit the second selecting automaton then it falls to the third storage for unused balls. When one of the two gate cylinders has been extended but the ball does not fit then it is retracted and lets the ball fall down the gravity chute.

It should be noted that an automatic translator of Prolog-based description of selecting automata to XML-based project of nxtStudio [7] is developed which represents the ball sequences sorting system closed-loop simulation model.

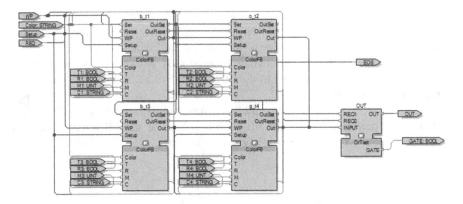

Fig. 11. FB network implementing the automaton from Fig. 1.

7 Conclusion

The developed are as follows: (1) a formal model of selecting finite automata for specification and selection of workpieces sequences in industrial sorting systems; (2) an approach to the implementation of selecting automata on the basis of FB using tokens transfer mechanism; (3) a graphs inference system defining the process of generating structures of IEC 61499 FB systems from finite state machine – based specifications of selectable workpieces sequences; (4) a method of automatic translation of specifications of selectable workpieces sequences to sorting system's control based on IEC 61499 FB.

The proposed approach to the building of workpieces sequences sorting systems is new and has not been used yet in industrial practice. The developed methods and tools for describing and synthesis of FB-based control for workpieces sequences sorting systems are convenient and effective as evidenced by the experience of development and exploitation of appropriate software tools.

The direction of future research are building a class of sorting systems based on selecting pushdown automata and selecting Petri nets as well as the integration and synthesis of selective automata on the basis of the supervisory control theory.

Acknowledgement. The authors are grateful to Andrei Sandru from Aalto University for developing and providing the visual simulation model of the ball sorting system's equipment and the HMI based on FBs.

References

1. Hopcroft, J.E., Motwani, R., Ullman, J.D.: Introduction to Automata Theory, Languages, and Computation, 3rd edn. Pearson, Upper Saddle River (2006)
2. Sami, B., Book, M., Gruhn, V. (eds.): Model-Driven Software Development. Springer, London (2005)

3. Vyatkin, V.: IEC 61499 Function Blocks for Embedded and Distributed Control Systems Design, 3rd edn. Instrumentation Society of America, Pittsburgh (2015)
4. Kloksin, W., Mellish, C.: Programming in Prolog: Using the ISO Standard, 5th edn. Springer, Heidelberg (2003)
5. Vashkevich, N.P., Biktashev, R.A.: Non-deterministic Automata and Their Application for Implementation of Information Parallel Processing. Penza State University Publisher, Penza (2016)
6. Grunske, L., Geiger, L., Zuendorf, A., Eetvelde, N.V., Gorp, P.V., Varro, D.: Graph transformation for practical model driven software engineering. In: Beydeda, S., Book, M., Gruhn, V. (eds.) Model-Driven Software Development, pp. 91–118. Springer, Heidelberg (2005)
7. NxtControl Homepage. http://www.nxtcontrol.com/

Modeling, Simulation and Reconfiguration

Boolean Network Models of Collective Dynamics of Open and Closed Large-Scale Multi-agent Systems

Predrag T. Tošić[1]([⊠]) and Carlos Ordonez[2]

[1] Department of Computer Science, University of Idaho,
Coeur D'Alene / Moscow, ID, USA
ptosic@uidaho.edu
[2] Department of Computer Science, University of Houston, Houston, TX, USA

Abstract. This work discusses theoretical models of decentralized large-scale cyber-physical and other types of *multi-agent systems* (MAS). Arguably, various types of Boolean Networks are among the simplest such models enabling rigorous mathematical and computational analysis of the emerging behavior of such systems and their collective dynamics. This paper investigates determining possible asymptotic dynamics of several classes of *Boolean Networks* (BNs) such as *Discrete Hopfield Networks, Sequential and Synchronous Dynamical Systems*, and (finite, Boolean-valued) *Cellular Automata*. Viewing BNs as an abstraction for a broad variety of decentralized cyber-physical, computational, biological, social and socio-technical systems, similarities and differences between open and closed such systems are rigorously analyzed. Specifically, this paper addresses the problem of enumerating all possible dynamical evolutions of large-scale decentralized cyber-physical, cyber-secure and holonic systems abstracted as Boolean Networks. We establish that, in general, the problem of enumerating possible dynamics is provably computationally hard for both "open" and "closed" variants of BNs, even when all of the following restrictions simultaneously hold: (i) the local behaviors (node update rules) are very simple, monotone Boolean-valued functions; (ii) the network topology is sparse; and (iii) either there is no external environment impact on the system, or the model of the environment is of a rather simple, deterministic nature. Our results provide lower bounds on the complexity of possible behaviors of "real-world" large-scale cyber-physical, socio-technical, social and other distributed systems and infrastructures, with some far-reaching implications insofar as (un)predictability of such systems' collective dynamics.

Keywords: Cyber-physical systems · Multi-agent systems · Boolean Networks · Cellular & network automata · Network dynamics · Systems science

1 Introduction

Network Science and *Agent-Based Modeling* (ABM) have provided useful abstractions, research methodology, as well as mathematical and computational tools for investigating fundamental behavioral properties of a broad variety of physically and

© Springer International Publishing AG 2017
V. Mařík et al. (Eds.): HoloMAS 2017, LNAI 10444, pp. 95–110, 2017.
DOI: 10.1007/978-3-319-64635-0_8

logically decentralized, "networked" systems and infrastructures in engineering, physics, biological sciences and social sciences (see, e.g., [1, 7, 16, 19, 25, 26]). In particular, investigating possible dynamics of discrete, agent-based models has been of a considerable research interest among those studying, designing and/or analyzing various distributed computing infrastructures, as well as various cyber-physical and cyber-secure systems. Both analytical and computational (i.e., simulation-based) studies have been undertaken, often providing valuable insights that would be much harder, or even impossible, to obtain using the "traditional" mathematical and computational methods based on solving appropriate systems of ordinary or partial differential equations analytically whenever possible, or via numerical simulations otherwise.

One important distinction that is often made about such complex distributed systems is, whether a given system is *open* or *closed*. In an open system, there is in general influence of an "environment" external to the explicitly modeled, designed and/or controlled "agents"; and the system designer, who is in charge of controlling or "programing" the behavior of the agents, in general does not exercise control over that environment, how the environment may impact the agents, or indeed how will that environment respond to the agents' actions. In contrast, in a closed system, there is no (relevant) "environment" or other uncontrollable and/or unpredictable sources of impact on the agents in the system, outside of those agents themselves.

Everything else being equal, in general it is easier to design, analyze, and predict or control behavior of agents in a closed environment than in an open environment. Needless to say, however, most if not all "real-world" cyber-physical, socio-technical, biological and physical systems are in reality open, in the sense that it is rather rare that the system designer or the organization deploying a particular engineered multi-agent system has the full control of all relevant entities, interactions within and influences on that system. However, depending on what properties of the system behavior one is interested in, as well as whether and to what extent the actual external factors impact those properties of interest, when modeling cyber-physical, socio-technical and other decentralized multi-agent systems, assuming the system to be (approximately) closed in order to simplify analysis and/or design may still be justifiable.

Distributed computing and distributed AI researchers have extensively studied interactions, emerging behavior, coordination, resource and task sharing, and other important problems formulated in both open and closed system settings. In some circumstances, it may be appropriate to model a particular multi-agent or cyber-physical system as a closed system – for example, when it's justifiable to assume that no "external" aspects of the environment would have any relevant impact on the agents, their resources, decisions, goals or tasks. On the other hand, designing protocols, algorithms, and other techniques for autonomous software or robotic agents in open environments is, as a rule of thumb, both more realistic and more challenging, esp. when possible impact of the environment on agents, their actions and their goals is complex, nondeterministic and/or only partially observable (see, e.g., [14, 17]).

Communicating Finite State Machines (CFSMs) and *Boolean* (or other discrete-valued) *Networks* are among the most popular mathematical formalisms for a broad range of biological, physical, computational, cyber-physical, socio-technical and other decentralized systems and architectures [2, 3, 15–18, 20, 21]. These models allow for crisp formalizations of many properties of such systems' collective and emerging behavior, especially with regards to long-term or asymptotic dynamics [16, 17, 22, 23]. One typical example is formalizing the fairness, liveness, deadlock avoidance and similar properties of interest when it comes to modeling and verification of distributed computing infrastructures, in terms of the fundamental configuration space properties of a formal discrete dynamical system based on CFSMs or Boolean Networks.

The rest of this paper is organized as follows. In Sect. 2 we introduce open and closed distributed multi-agent and cyber-physical systems, as well as how they can be formalized in terms of *Boolean Networks* (BNs). We also outline some MAS applications that could benefit from our theoretical analysis of differences in possible emerging behaviors between open and closed systems. In Sect. 3 we formally define the key configuration space properties of BNs that capture the most important aspects of asymptotic dynamics of those networks. We then focus on the computational complexity of characterizing network dynamics, i.e., answering fundamental questions about those Boolean Networks' configuration spaces. We characterize those problems in both open and closed system settings, and summarize key results for a broad range of sparse BNs with simple local interactions. To the best of our knowledge, no prior work has addressed such comparative analysis of open vs. closed discrete dynamical systems in a formal Boolean Network setting. Last but not least, we summarize the key insights and outline some directions for future research.

2   On the Collective Dynamics of Open and Closed Systems

Our goals in this paper are to, first, mathematically formalize open and closed decentralized information processing systems, and, second, establish some key properties of such systems from a unified standpoint of dynamical system theory and computational complexity/(un)predictability. We would like our framework to be sufficiently abstract yet versatile, so that it provides meaningful insights on a broad variety of decentralized information processing systems and distributed infrastructures, ranging from the classical distributed computing environments and cyber-physical systems to social networks and socio-technical systems to biological systems.

In case of the main results in this paper, these insights will for the most part be in the form of *lower bounds* on complexity of an agent ensemble's collective dynamics. By a unified dynamical systems and computational complexity viewpoint, we mean that we want to understand the dynamics of these complex networks (as our abstraction of the real-world cyber-physical, socio-technical, biological and other systems), and in particular to address the computational complexity (that is, relative hardness or easiness) of characterizing that dynamics.

Our choices of mathematical abstractions for the open and closed distributed multi-agent systems are driven by our interests in agent-based modeling and distributed AI on one hand, and network science, on the other – and esp. the cross-fertilization between these two research areas. In particular, the networks we study are characterized by the following properties: time is discrete (and there is an implicit assumption of the existence of a *global clock*, an important premise discussed in detail, e.g., in [16, 19]). Likewise, the states of the individual agents are discrete. For simplicity, we will assume each agent is *binary-valued*, i.e., it can, at any discrete time step t, be in one of two possible states: 0 or 1. The graph or network structure captures, which (pairs of) agents can potentially directly influence each other. Under these ontological commitments, *Boolean Networks* of interconnected *Finite State Machines* are a natural modeling framework [2, 16, 20]. (Of course, other modeling choices are possible – for example, those in which either time, or states of agents, or both, are continuous as opposed to discrete. Closer to our adopted modeling framework, individual agents or nodes are often allowed to be more general finite state machines, so that, in particular, each node may have more than two states. We prefer the Boolean, i.e., binary-valued model for two reasons: (i) it's the simplest non-trivial model w.r.t. the states of individual nodes or agents, and (ii) binary-valued nodes allow for direct comparisons with the rich existing literature on discrete Hopfield networks, cellular automata and other types of binary-valued *Network Automata*.)

How do we differentiate between open and closed multi-agent systems in this modeling framework provided by *Communicating Finite State Machines* (CFSMs) in general, and *Boolean Networks* as a restricted class of CFSMs, in particular? A closed system can be captured by a Boolean Network in which each node is an agent, whose individual behavior is defined, controlled, or at the very least, well-understood by us. In contrast, in an open system abstracted as a CFSM or a Boolean Network, some nodes correspond to agents, whereas other nodes capture the "environment" that influences the agents, and that we do not have control over. The novelty in the present paper is the explicit differentiation between "open" and "closed" CFSMs and BNA, and how the openness (that is, the presence of an "uncontrollable" environment external to the network of agents) impacts some of these fundamental properties of discrete network's dynamics and their configuration spaces.

An alternative approach, studied by researchers working at the intersection of multi-agent systems and statistical physics, is based on a network of agents operating in an external potential field akin to external electric or magnetic or other force fields studied in physics. We will not discuss this latter class of models; for us, every relevant aspect of the world is a node (finite state machine) in the network, but while we have control over the behavior of certain nodes (namely, those representing our "agents"), we do not have control over others (capturing various relevant aspects of "the environment"). We note that the explicit distinction between open and closed multi-agent systems, and some implications of that distinction, has been studied by the Distributed AI researchers (see, e.g., [1]), although, as far as we are aware, not within our formal modeling framework based on Boolean Networks.

2.1 Some Examples of Open and Closed Cyber-Physical Multi-agent Systems

To provide some real-world "grounding" of the theoretical models of MAS studied in the rest of the paper, we outline some decentralized cyber-physical and/or multi-agent applications in which one can readily differentiate between open and closed systems.

Team Robotics. One popular example is robotic soccer: two teams of robots, each belonging to a different designer, playing soccer against each other. Within a single team, we have a purely cooperative multi-agent system engaging in distributed coordination (see, e.g., [25, 27]). However, from a *Distributed AI* standpoint, the coordination of robots within the same team is more complex than that in purely collaborative, distributed problem-solving settings, as it is done in presence of an adversary – namely, the other team of robots. Importantly, however, the entire "environment" in this application is made of the agents from the two teams of robots (plus the ball, goal posts, and other relevant aspects of the environment that, however, in general do not act deliberately or unpredictably); in particular, there is no "external control" nor an unknown external "environment node" that may unpredictably influence the multi-agent interactions among the robots within a team, or indeed between the two robotic teams. Hence, the robotic soccer is an example of a closed cyber-physical system.

This can be contrasted with, for example, ensembles of autonomous unmanned aerial, underwater or ground vehicles used in a surveillance, search-and-rescue or other type of military or law-enforcement deployment [14, 16, 24]. The physical environments in which such autonomous vehicles operate are, in general, complex and unpredictable; in particular, they often contain other goal-driven agents, possibly including adversarial ones. Unlike with robotic soccer, the behavior of the adversarial and other deliberative and goal-oriented agents is typically not a priori known; likewise, possible impact of external agents and other aspects of the environment on "our" autonomous vehicle agents also in general is not known to the designer of unmanned autonomous vehicles or the organization deploying those vehicles. The natural modeling framework for such ensembles of autonomous unmanned vehicles, therefore, is that of open (cyber-physical, multi-agent) systems.

Traffic Systems. If one considers just the "core infrastructure" such as the signaling system (where it is known, for example, where the traffic lights and other components of a city's traffic signaling system are located, and how all those components function), that would be an example of a closed cyber-physical system. However, when modeling and simulating such traffic systems, the "overall" traffic system is usually considered to also include vehicles, pedestrians and possibly other "agents" whose behaviors, in general, are not a priori known. While one may have a model of possible behaviors, and/or constraints on possible speeds of motion and other relevant aspects of those agents' behaviors, in general, these vehicle and pedestrian agents are more complex and less predictable than say the traffic lights alone. So, in many traffic modeling contexts, the broader traffic system should be considered to be an open system. This is particularly significant when the new agents such as vehicles may unpredictably enter and/or leave the modeled system, thus also making such traffic system open also in the usual distributed computing sense. (We note that the first author's original exposure to the world of agent-based modeling and multi-agent systems, back in the early 2000's, was precisely in the context of defining and analyzing mathematical and computational models for fairly large-scale – ranging from tens to hundreds of thousands of agents – urban/metropolitan area traffic simulations [2].)

Epidemics Propagation. Consider spreading of an epidemic, for example, a flu virus, in a community. Accurate models of epidemics propagation are important in public health domain, as well as for designing the best response when faced with outbreak of massive epidemics or a biological warfare attack. Over the past 20+ years, the classical, continuous mathematics based models (specifically, those based on solving differential equations) have been increasingly being replaced by discrete, agent-based models. For a recent work on agent-based modeling of epidemics, that also provides a good survey of the state of the art and methodology, see, e.g., [28].

Many agent-based models of epidemics propagation assume closed systems (for example, a town or city with a "fixed" population). More realistically, however, on practically any scale larger than that of an individual family, the population(s) that may be affected by the epidemics should be viewed as open systems, since new individuals may enter into the population, some of the existing members may leave it, etc. Depending on the particular aspects of epidemics propagation one wishes to model, however, it may still be justifiable to "treat" the affected population as a closed multi-agent system (with an understanding that, at non-trivial scales, this strictly speaking is hardly ever the case). Therefore, when modeling propagation of epidemics (or opinions, political or social influences, etc.) in a population, sometimes it may be suitable to treat the population in question as a closed system, whereas in other scenarios it is of essence to explicitly take into account the intrinsically open nature of population dynamics problems in most practical scenarios and for all but the smallest of scales (cf. in terms of population sizes).

3 Preliminaries and Definitions

We formulate and then characterize some fundamental properties of *asymptotic dynamics* of open and closed distributed multi-agent systems in the formal setting of *Boolean Networks* and, as their prominent special case, *Discrete Hopfield Networks* [8, 9]. We define those two classes of discrete dynamical systems next.

Definition 1: A *Boolean Network* (also called *Boolean Network Automaton*, or BNA) is a directed or undirected graph so that each node in the graph has a state, 0 or 1; and each node periodically updates its state, as a function of the current states of (some or all of) its neighboring nodes (possibly, but not necessarily, including itself). A BNA dynamically evolves in discrete time steps. If the node v_i has k neighbors denoted v_{i1}, ..., v_{ik} (where this list may or may not include v_i itself), then the next state of vi is determined by evaluating a Boolean-valued function $f_i(v_{i1}, \ldots v_{ik})$ of k Boolean variables; f_i is called the *local update function* or *transition rule* (for the node v_i).

Several comments are in order. First, in general, different nodes v_i may use different local update functions f_i. This applies to *Discrete Hopfield Nets* [4, 5, 8, 9], as well as many other classes of Boolean Networks including those originally introduced by S. Kauffman in the context of systems biology [6, 10], and also several related models proposed in the context of modeling large-scale distributed computing and other decentralized cyber-physical infrastructures [2, 3, 11, 18]. Classical *Cellular Automata* (CA) can then be viewed as a special case of BNA, where all the nodes use the same local update rule f_i [20]. (We note that the underlying graphs in BNA are almost always assumed to be finite, whereas Cellular Automata have been extensively studied in both finite and infinite settings.)

The individual node updates can be done either synchronously in parallel, or sequentially, one at a time (and if so, either according to the fixed update ordering, or in a random order). While other communication models are worth considering [19, 21], the above three possibilities have been studied the most. In this paper, we will focus entirely on the parallel, perfectly synchronous node updates. This means, the next state of the node v_i is determined according to

$$v_i^{t+1} \leftarrow f_i(v_{i1}^t, \ldots, v_{ik}^t) \tag{1}$$

The tuple of all f_i's put together, $F = (f_1, \ldots, f_n)$, denotes the *global map* that acts on (global) configurations of a BNA. When all f_i are the same, the notation in the literature is often abused so that no differentiation is made between the local transition function, acting on a state of a single node, and the global map F, acting on entire configurations of a cellular or network automaton (that is, on all the nodes). In classical CA, all nodes update according to the same local update rule. In most other Boolean Network models, different nodes in general update according to different rules.

Definition 2: A *Discrete Hopfield Network* (DHN) is made of n binary-valued nodes. Associated to each pair of nodes (v_i, v_j) is (in general, real-valued) their weight, w_{ij}. The weight matrix of a DHN is defined as $W = [w_{ij}]_{i,j=1..n}$. Each node also has a fixed real-valued threshold, h_i. A node v_i updates its state x_i from time step t to step $t + 1$ according to a (binary-valued) *linear threshold function* of the form

$$x_i^{t+1} \leftarrow \text{sgn}\left(\sum w_{ij} \cdot x_j^t - h_i\right) \tag{2}$$

where the summation is over $j = 1, \ldots, n$; the term h_i is the *threshold* that the weighted sum needs to reach or exceed in order for the node's state to update to $+1$; to break ties, we define $\text{sgn}(0) = +1$.

The default notation in most of the literature on Hopfield networks is that the binary states of an individual node are $\{-1, +1\}$. In this paper, however, we adopt the Boolean values $\{0, 1\}$ for the states of our nodes, in order to be able to discuss DHNs and our results about them in the broader context of arbitrary types of Boolean Networks (see, e.g., [6, 10, 19]) without the need for cumbersome "translations". Furthermore, in most of the existing literature on DHNs (e.g., [5, 8, 9, 12, 13]), two additional assumptions are usually made, namely, that (i) the diagonal elements of weight matrix W are all zeros: $w_{ii} = 0$; and (ii) the weight matrix is symmetric, $w_{ij} = w_{ji}$ for all pairs of nodes i, j. We will adopt (ii) throughout (we note, this does not affect the main results and insights from them discussed in the next section). As for (i), we will consider two possibilities on the nodes' "memory" (of their own current state, as a part of the local transition rule): either $w_{ii} = 0$ for all nodes v_i, or else $w_{ii} = 1$ for all v_i. The main results in the next section hold under either the *memoryless* ($w_{ii} = 0$) or *with memory* ($w_{ii} = 1$) assumption. Moreover, in the memory case, our results can be readily extended to more general weighing w_{ii} of how is a node's state at time $t + 1$ affected by its own state at time t; these variations will be discussed in an expanded, journal version but are left out of this paper due to space constraints.

We study a variety of Boolean Network models and their asymptotic dynamics. Several of our main results are formulated in the DHN context [22]; some of our prior work was formulated in the context of two other types of Network or Graph Automata (whose nodes' states can but need not necessarily be Boolean-valued), called *Sequential and Synchronous Dynamical Systems* [2, 15]. Hopfield Networks were originally inspired by biology and especially computational neuroscience (in particular, they were introduced as a model of *associative memory* [8]). Subsequently, in addition to theoretical models in computational biology and neuroscience, Hopfield Networks (both discrete and continuous) were used for as a connectionist, self-organizing map model for "learning" and "searching for a solution", i.e., as a powerful tool for various search and optimization problems in computer science, operations research and beyond [9].

We note that some of the earliest Boolean Network models were also originally introduced in the context of theoretical and systems biology, albeit not specifically neuroscience. Indeed, the very name *Boolean Networks* comes from the seminal work in theoretical biology by S. Kauffman [10]. In contrast, Sequential and Synchronous Dynamical Systems (SDS and SyDS, resp.) were specifically introduced in the context of agent-based simulation of complex cyber-physical, socio-technical and engineering systems [3, 11, 15–17]. For clarity and space constraints reasons, we will not formally introduce S(y)DS models here, but rather refer the reader to relevant references. We emphasize that our results in this paper apply to all of the above models (DHNs, SDSs and SyDSs), and indeed most other discrete-time Boolean (or other finite-domain) Networks or BNA found in the existing literature.

Since BNA and DHN are deterministic discrete-time dynamical systems, for any given current configuration C^t at time t, there is a unique next-step configuration C^{t+1}. We can therefore define the BNA or DHN *configuration or phase spaces*, and also various types of *global configurations* (i.e., tuples capturing the states of all nodes in a network) of interest:

Definition 3: A (global) configuration of a cellular or network automaton or a discrete Hopfield Network is a vector $(x_1, ..., x_n) \in \{0,1\}^n$, where x_i denotes the state of the ith node. A global configuration can also be thought of as a function $\gamma: V \rightarrow \{0,1\}$, where V denotes the set of nodes in the underlying graph of a CA, BNA or DHN.

Definition 4: A *fixed point* (FP) is a configuration such that, once a BNA or DHN reaches that configuration, it stays there forever. A *cycle configuration* (CC) is a global state that, once reached, will be revisited infinitely often with a fixed, finite temporal period of 2 or greater. A *transient configuration* (TC) is a global configuration that, once reached, is never going to be revisited again.

Definition 5: Given two configurations C and C' of a CA, BNA or DHN, if F(C) = C' then C' is the *successor* of C (and C is a *predecessor* of C'). That is, configuration C' is reached from configuration C by a single application of the global map.

If the dynamics of a BNA or DHN is deterministic (which we shall assume throughout this paper), then each configuration has a unique successor. However, a configuration may have 0, 1 or more predecessors. By the "pigeonhole principle", it then follows that the global dynamics of a (deterministic) BNA or DHN is invertible iff each configuration has exactly one predecessor.

Definition 6: A configuration with no predecessors is called *Garden of Eden*. Lastly, configuration A is an *ancestor* of configuration C, if starting from A, the dynamics reaches configuration C after finitely many time steps (equivalently, if there exists $t \geq 1$ such that $F^t(A) = C$).

In particular, a predecessor is a special type of an ancestor. Further, "fixed points" are the only type of configurations such that each is its own predecessor. Similarly, each cycle configuration is its own ancestor. In contrast, due to determinism, a TC can never be its own ancestor.

A BNA is called *dense* if the underlying graph on which it is defined is dense. Similarly, a DHN is dense if its weight matrix W is dense, i.e., if W contains many non-zero entries [22, 23]. The natural interpretation of a zero weight $w_{ij} = 0$ in a DHN is that the corresponding nodes i and j do not directly affect each other. (That is, change of state of the ith node does not immediately affect the state of the jth node, and vice versa; of course, they can still indirectly affect each other, via connected paths in the underlying graph whose edge weight products are nonzero). In contrast, we say that a BNA is *sparse* if the underlying network topology (that is, the graph structure) is sparse which, for us, will mean $|E| = O(|V|)$. That is, for our purposes, sparseness means $O(1)$ neighbors per node (alternatively, only $O(1)$ non-zero weights per row of the weight matrix W), on average; equivalently, the total number of edges in the underlying graph (equivalently, the total number of non-zero entries in W) is of the order $O(n)$ where n is the number of nodes.

Further, we call a Boolean Network or a Hopfield Network *uniformly sparse* if every node is required to have only $O(1)$ neighbors (that is, every row/column in W has only $O(1)$ non-zero entries). So, for example, a star or a wheel graph on n nodes would be sparse (the average node degree being $O(1)$ in each case), but neither of those types of networks would be uniformly sparse, as the center of a star or a wheel has $\Theta(n)$ neighbors.

What is the relationship between configuration space properties of a formal BNA, DHN or CA model, and behaviors of real-world cyber-physical and multi-agent systems? Consider, for instance, Gardens of Eden (GEs): these configurations can only occur as initial states of the system. Hence, if one can show that all undesirable or dangerous configurations of, for example, a real-world cyber-secure system are GEs, then, as long as one can ensure that the system does not start in one of those dangerous states, it is safe to assert that the system will never reach any of those "bad" states. Similarly, knowing that all configurations, or more commonly in practice all members of an appropriately defined subset of global configurations satisfying certain pre-specified properties, are actually all recurrent states, would imply that certain fairness and liveness properties for that (sub)set of configurations must hold.

Reachability properties (whether certain types of configurations are reachable from a subset of initial configurations of interest) have been connected to *fairness* in the distributed computing sense. What is also often of interest, is the speed of convergence of a system to its stationary behavior (be it of a temporal cycle or fixed point variety); that speed or rate of convergence can be formally related to the depth of "the basin of attraction" of a fixed point of temporal cycle in question, thus establishing a formal connection between the system dynamics and the distributed computing perspectives. Likewise, enumerating exactly or approximately all "initial states" leading to a given FP or temporal cycle captures the overall size of the basin of attraction.

Last but not least, being able to *enumerate* the total number of (non-trivial) temporal cycles and stable ("fixed point") configurations of a deterministically behaving system is in essence equivalent to knowing in how many ways that system can evolve, for all possible initial configurations. It has been known since the 1990s that certain types of DHNs and CA cannot have non-trivial temporal cycles, implying that the only recurrent states are fixed points. For such systems, enumerating the FPs is therefore synonymous with determining the total number of possible asymptotic behaviors.

4   Configuration Space Properties and Asymptotic Dynamics of Open and Closed Cyber-Physical and Holonic MAS

We now summarize some of the key insights about several fundamental problems about Discrete Hopfield Networks and other types of Boolean Network Automata. Most of these results describe the worst-case computational complexity of determining key configuration space properties of various classes of such networks. Examples of such configuration space properties include: (i) determining the existence of fundamental types of configurations such as stable or fixed-point states (FPs), Cycle Configurations (CCs) or Gardens of Eden (GEs); (ii) determining the exact or approximate number of fundamental types of configurations such as FPs, CCs or GEs; (iii) answering questions about reachability of FPs or of a particular configuration, from a specific initial state or a set of initial states; (iv) answering questions about whether a given DHN's or other BNA's dynamics is invertible. These and related questions about CFSM and BNA dynamics have been studied (by one of the authors as well as other researchers) since at least 2001; we summarize and interpret some of the main results, applied to *closed* cyber-physical and multi-agent systems, in the next subsection.

4.1   Dynamics and Configuration Spaces of Boolean Networks Modeling Closed Distributed Multi-agent Systems

All models of BNA, DHNs and CFSMs we have been studying are deterministic, implying that, regardless of the details of the local update rules, the "underlying topology" (that is, the graph structure), and the particular choice of starting configuration, asymptotically the system will either eventually reach a fixed point or a temporal cycle of length 2 or greater. But can we in general tell which of these two ultimate outcomes will take place? It turns out, differentiating between these scenarios is in general computationally intractable:

Theorem 1: Determining whether an arbitrary Boolean Network or Boolean-valued CFSM, starting from an arbitrary initial configuration, will eventually evolve to a FP or a non-trivial temporal cycle is in general **PSPACE**-complete.

More generally, most non-trivial *Reachability* problems for the sufficiently general classes of BNA (such as the aforementioned SDSs and SyDSs, and other similar classes of Boolean-valued, as well as more general, CFSMs), for sufficiently general local update rules and underlying graphs, are in the worst-case **PSPACE**-complete. The original motivation, formulations and proofs of these reachability results, in the context of (Boolean-valued) Sequential and Synchronous Dynamical Systems as two special subclasses of BNA, can be found in [3] and references there.

Corollary 1: Determining the "ultimate destiny" of a deterministic closed discrete dynamical multi-agent system in which each agent is a 2-state FSM (in terms of differentiating whether that destiny will be stability or oscillation with a fixed periodicity) is **PSPACE**-complete.

Moreover, even answering the basic questions about the existence of FPs and other fundamental types of configurations is, in the worst case, computationally intractable, although these existence problems lie much lower in the computational complexity hierarchy than the related reachability problems:

Theorem 2: Given the description of an arbitrary BNA or CFSM, determining whether it has any FP configurations is **NP**-complete. Similarly, in general, determining if a BNA or CFSM has any non-trivial temporal cycles is **NP**-hard.

Analogous results hold about the fundamental problems about the BNA *inverse dynamics* – that is, about hardness of characterizing dynamical behavior when the direction of time is reversed, as summarized in the next theorem:

Theorem 3: Given the description of an arbitrary BNA or Boolean-valued CFSM, determining whether it has any TC or GE configurations is **NP**-complete. Given such a BNA or CFSM and an arbitrary configuration, determining whether that configuration is a GE is **coNP**-complete.

For proofs of the original formulations of results summarized in Theorems 2–3, see [2] and references therein. Note that in the first part of Theorem 3, the problems about (arbitrary) *Transient Configurations* (TCs) on one hand, and *Gardens of Eden* (GEs) on the other, are fundamentally equivalent: a BNA or CFSM or DHN has a TC if and only if it has a GE [2]. On the other hand, validating whether a configuration is a GE is readily seen to be in class **coNP** (since the complementary problem, viz. whether a given configuration has a predecessor, is clearly in **NP**), whereas determining whether a given configuration is an a TC (but not necessarily GE) is less obvious; however, this problem is certainly **coNP**-hard in the worst-case.

There are, however, important subclasses of both local update rules and underlying graphs, for which the fundamental problems about FPs, CCs, TCs and GEs are actually computationally tractable. In particular, if all nodes of a BNA or a CFSM update according to *monotone* Boolean-valued update rules, then the existence of fixed points is guaranteed:

Theorem 4: If every local update rule in a BNA or CFSM is a *monotone* Boolean-valued function, then the problem of FP existence is computationally easy: such a BNA or CFSM is guaranteed to have at least one FP.

Corollary 2: Discrete Hopfield Networks all of whose edge weights are non-negative are guaranteed to have FPs.

Computational problems about BNA and CFSM configuration spaces that we have investigated in greatest detail pertain to the computational complexity of counting. That counting all FPs or all CCs or all GEs of an arbitrary Boolean Network would turn out #P-hard, is to be expected. What is more interesting, however, is that this hardness of counting remains to hold even for severely restricted classed of BNs and CFSMs, with restrictions applying simultaneously to both the graph structures and the local update rules. In particular, we have the following results:

Theorem 5: Exactly enumerating all FPs of a Boolean Network Automaton (such as Boolean-valued SDSs, SyDSs and DHNs) is #P-complete, even when all local node update rules are symmetric Boolean functions, and the underlying graph is sparse (as in, sparse on average, or even uniformly).

Theorem 6: Exactly enumerating all FPs of a BNA (such as SDSs, SyDSs and DHNs) is #P-complete, even when all local node update rules are monotone functions, and the underlying graph is sparse (on average or uniformly).

For details on various types of BNA with symmetric and/or monotone update rules, and various classes of either sparse-on-average or uniformly sparse underlying network topologies, we refer the reader to [15, 18, 20]. Among the sparse-on-average graphs, we particularly focus on the star and wheel graphs, cf. because of their implications to open systems, that is, BNA embedded in and interacting with an external environment.

Theorem 7: The following enumeration problems are all #P-complete, even when the underlying graphs of a BNA or DHN are restricted to star-graphs (or wheel-graphs), and all local update rules are monotone Boolean functions:

- Determining the exact number of all FPs;
- Determining the exact number of all TCs;
- Determining the exact number of only those TCs that are Gardens-of-Eden;
- Determining the total number of predecessors of an arbitrary configuration.

Detailed discussion and full formal proof of Theorem 7 can be found in [18]. Those results have been further refined and strengthened in [20].

4.2   Dynamics of Boolean Networks Modeling Open Multi-agent Systems

To the extent that cyber-physical systems, multi-agent systems and other decentralized infrastructures can be adequately modeled by these BN and CFSM models, all results in the previous subsection pertain to *closed* such systems or infrastructures: the ones whose behavior isn't affected by anything other than the individual behaviors of agents themselves (i.e., individual nodes' local update rules) and the interaction patterns (i.e., how are these agents interconnected with each other). In contrast, an open system is one in which there's an environment, external to the agents, that in general may also impact the agents' behaviors. From a control theory standpoint, this openness of the system, i.e., a potential impact of an external environment on the agents and their individual and collective dynamics, can be modeled by adding to a BN or CFSM an additional, "environment node" that (in general) is connected to, and therefore may influence, the behavior of all (individual) agent nodes. Assuming "everything else [being] equal", all hardness results about the closed dynamical multi-agent systems in the previous subsection imply similar hardness results for open multi-agent systems. In particular, we have the following results:

Theorem 8: Determining whether an open deterministic multi-agent system will eventually reach stability or non-trivial oscillatory behavior is, in general, **PSPACE**-hard. Moreover, this problem is **PSPACE**-complete if the external control (the "environment node") is behaving according to a deterministic, Boolean-valued function.

Theorem 9: Computational problems of deciding whether an open deterministic multi-agent system's dynamics has any FPs, any unreachable (GE) configurations, or any transient configurations, are in general **NP**-hard. If the environment's behavior is known and can be represented as a deterministic Boolean-valued function, these problems are in the class, **NP** and are therefore **NP**-complete in the worst-case.

Arguably the most interesting consequences of previous complexity hardness results "translated" from closed to open discrete dynamical systems, are those in the context of counting. That is, complexity of counting FPs and other types of configurations in closed discrete dynamical systems, as established in [17, 18, 20], have direct implications for the open distributed multi-agent systems, even those have very restricted agent interaction patterns, such as when the underlying graph is a simple path or ring (i.e., cycle in the graph-theoretic sense). Concretely, the following results hold:

Theorem 10: The following counting problems are all **#P**-complete, even when the underlying topologies of a discrete dynamical system are restricted to simple paths and rings, all agents behave according to monotone Boolean update rules, and additionally, the environment is known to dynamically evolve according to a monotone Boolean function (that, in general, may depend on current states of all individual agents):

- Determining the exact number of all FPs;
- Determining the exact number of all TCs;
- Determining the exact number of only those TCs that are Gardens-of-Eden;
- Determining the total number of predecessors of an arbitrary configuration.

These results are immediate consequences of Theorem 7, when the center of the wheel graph corresponds to the external control (that is, the environment), whereas the peripheral nodes correspond to the agents interconnected with each other into a ring (or path), and so that each agent locally updates according to a monotone Boolean-valued function. The only allowable inputs to each agent's local update rule are the states of the neighboring nodes, possibly the current state of the node in question itself, and the "environment node".

5 Conclusions

In summary, it follows from our results that characterizing most non-trivial properties about possible dynamics of open distributed multi-agent systems is computationally intractable, even for the simplest interaction patterns among the agents, as well as very simple, deterministic local behaviors of individual agents. While intractability holds for many closed systems, as well, in case of the open systems it appears hard to find a non-trivial such system so that its dynamics is tractable, even under considerable restrictions on how can the "environment" influence the agents. The only such systems for which tractability of dynamics has be proven to hold are the CA with restricted types of update rules (such as the simple threshold functions); importantly, in classical (finite) CA, all nodes update according to the same rule. It turns out that adding even a rather modest amount of heterogeneity to local agent interactions (such as, considering BNA whose nodes use two different update rules from the same restricted class of Boolean-valued functions), essentially immediately results in systems whose asymptotic dynamics are in general computationally intractable (see [23] for details).

Moreover, our recent research, and in particular results on the computational complexity of counting fixed points of Discrete Hopfield Networks and related Boolean Network models (see, e.g., [22]), immediately imply that determining the exact or even approximate number of possible asymptotic behaviors of complex networks abstracting various multi-agent, holonic and cyber-physical systems, is in general intractable even when the individual agent behaviors and their interactions are severely restricted – including the allowable models of the environment and its impact on the agents. We suspect most of other fundamental questions about dynamics of open distributed systems are also intractable in the worst-case, likely including some interesting scenarios where those questions are tractable for closed systems.

In particular, we have some evidence to believe that the restricted classes of underlying network topologies studied in [18] provide a good candidate starting point for identifying some of the scenarios that are likely to exhibit a stark contrast in the behavioral complexity between closed and open systems. The networks studied in that paper include star and wheel graphs, as well as other types of network topologies that are sparse-on-average, and based on bipartite and/or planar graphs. Validating this intuition for the non-trivial classes of Boolean Network models whose dynamics in the closed system case are actually tractable (for some examples of closed systems whose practically all interesting aspects of dynamics can be characterized computationally efficiently, see e.g. [19, 21]), yet becomes unpredictable in the open system setting even under very restricted models of the "external environment", is the subject of our ongoing and future work.

References

1. Bandini, S., Manzoni, S., Simone, C.: Heterogeneous agents situated in heterogeneous spaces. Appl. Artif. Intell. Int. J. **16**(9–10), 831–852 (2002). Taylor & Francis
2. Barrett, C., et al.: Gardens of Eden and fixed points in sequential dynamical systems. In: Discrete Mathematics & Theoretical Computer Science (DMTCS), vol. AA, pp. 95–110 (2001)

3. Barrett, C., et al.: Reachability problems for sequential dynamical systems with threshold functions. Theoret. Comput. Sci. **295**(1–3), 41–64 (2003)

4. Davey, N., Calcraft, L., Adams, R.: High capacity, small world associative memory models. Connect. Sci. **18**(3), 247–264 (2006)

5. Floreen, P., Orponen, P.: On the computational complexity of analyzing hopfield nets. Complex Syst. **3**, 577–587 (1989)

6. Graudenzi, A., et al.: Dynamical properties of a Boolean model of gene regulatory network with memory. J. Comput. Biol. **18**(10), 1291–1303 (2011). https://doi.org/10.1089/cmb. 2010.0069

7. Helbing, D.: Social Self-Organization. Understanding Complex Systems. Springer, Heidelberg (2012)

8. Hopfield, J.: Neural networks and physical systems with emergent\collective computational abilities. Proc. Nat. Acad. Sci. **79**, 2554–2558 (1982)

9. Hopfield, J., Tank, D.: Neural computation of decisions in optimization problems. Biol. Cybern. **52**, 141–152 (1985)

10. Kauffman, S.A.: Emergent properties in random complex automata. Phys. D: Nonlin. Phenom. **10**(1–2), 145–156 (1984)

11. Mortveit, H., Reidys, C.: Discrete sequential dynamical systems. Discrete Math. **226**(1–3), 281–295 (2001)

12. Orponen, P.: Computational complexity of neural networks: a survey. Nord. J. Comput. **1**(1), 94–110 (1994)

13. Sima, J., Orponen, P.: General-purpose computation with neural networks: a survey of complexity theoretic results. Neural Comput. **15**(12), 2727–2778 (2003)

14. Tošić, P.T., et al.: Modeling a system of UAVs on a mission, invited session on agent-based computing. In: Proceedings of 7th World Multiconference on Systemics, Cybernetics, and Informatics (SCI 2003), pp. 508–514 (2003)

15. Tošić, P.T., Agha, G.A.: On computational complexity of counting fixed points in symmetric Boolean graph automata. In: Calude, C.S., Dinneen, M.J., Păun, G., Pérez-Jímenez, M.J., Rozenberg, G. (eds.) UC 2005. LNCS, vol. 3699, pp. 191–205. Springer, Heidelberg (2005). doi:10.1007/11560319_18

16. Tošić, P.T.: Cellular automata for distributed computing: models of agent interaction and their implications. In: Proceedings of International Conference Systems, Man & Cybernetics (SMC 2005), pp. 3204–3209. IEEE (2005)

17. Tošić, P.T.: On modeling and analyzing sparsely networked large-scale multi-agent systems with cellular and graph automata. In: Alexandrov, V.N., Albada, G.D., Sloot, P.M.A., Dongarra, J. (eds.) ICCS 2006. LNCS, vol. 3993, pp. 272–280. Springer, Heidelberg (2006). doi:10.1007/11758532_38

18. Tošić, P.T.: On the complexity of counting fixed points and gardens of Eden in sequential & synchronous dynamical systems. Int. J. Found. Comput. Sci. (IJFCS) **17**(5), 1179–1203 (2006). World Scientific

19. Tošić, P.T.: Cellular automata communication models: comparative analysis of parallel, sequential and asynchronous ca with simple threshold update rules. Int. J. Nat. Comput. Res. (IJNCR) **1**(3), 66–84 (2010)

20. Tošić, P.T.: On the complexity of enumerating possible dynamics of sparsely connected Boolean network automata with simple update rules. In: Discete Mathematics and Theoretical Computer Science (DMTCS), pp. 125–144 (2010)

21. Tošić, P.T.: Modeling large-scale multi-agent systems with sequential and genuinely asynchronous cellular automata. Acta Phys. Pol. B (Proc. Suppl.) **4**(2), 217–236 (2011). Polish Academy of Sciences

22. Tošić, P.T.: On simple models of associative memory: network density is not required for provably complex behavior. In: Ascoli, G.A., Hawrylycz, M., Ali, H., Khazanchi, D., Shi, Y. (eds.) BIH 2016. LNCS, vol. 9919, pp. 61–71. Springer, Cham (2016). doi:10.1007/978-3-319-47103-7_7

23. Tošić, P.T.: On phase transitions in dynamics of cellular and graph automata models of sparsely interconnected multi-agent systems. In: ACM Proceedings Autonomous Agents & Multi-agent Systems (AAMAS 2017), Sao Paulo, Brazil, May 2017

24. Tošić, P.T., Agha, G.: Understanding and modeling agent autonomy in dynamic multi-agent, multi-task environments. In: Proceedings of First European Workshop on Multi-Agent Systems (EUMAS 2003), Oxford, England, UK (2003)

25. Tošić, P.T., Ordonez, C.: Distributed protocols for multi-agent coalition formation: a negotiation perspective. In: Huang, R., Ghorbani, A.A., Pasi, G., Yamaguchi, T., Yen, N.Y., Jin, B. (eds.) AMT 2012. LNCS, vol. 7669, pp. 93–102. Springer, Heidelberg (2012). doi:10.1007/978-3-642-35236-2_10

26. Garcia, J., Ordonez, C., Tošić, P.T.: Efficiently repairing and measuring replica consistency in distributed databases. Distr. Parallel Databases 31(3), 377–411 (2013)

27. Vig, L., Adams, J.A.: Issues in multi-robot coalition formation. In: Parker, L.E., Schneider, F.E., Schultz, A.C. (eds.) Multi-Robot Systems: From Swarms to Intelligent Automata, vol. 3. Springer, Dordrecht (2005). doi:10.1007/1-4020-3389-3_2

28. Zhang, M.: Large-scale agent-based social simulation - a study on epidemic prediction and control. Ph.D. dissertation, TU Delft, The Netherlands (2016)

Slicing Simulation Models into Co-simulations

Petr Novák[1,2](✉), Manuel Wimmer[1], and Petr Kadera[3]

[1] Christian Doppler Laboratory on Model-Integrated Smart Production, Business
Informatics Group, Institute of Software Technology and Interactive Systems,
TU Wien, 1040 Vienna, Austria
{petr.novak,manuel.wimmer}@tuwien.ac.at
[2] Czech Technical University in Prague, 16636 Prague, Czech Republic
[3] Czech Institute of Informatics, Robotics, and Cybernetics, Czech Technical
University in Prague, 16636 Prague, Czech Republic
petr.kadera@cvut.cz

Abstract. The emerging generation of large-scale cyber-physical production systems, which represents a backbone of a trend denoted as
Industrie 4.0, broadly adopts fundamentals laid by the multi-agent system paradigm. The joint roots of these concepts bring not only advantages such as flexibility, resilience or self-organization, but also severe
issues such as difficult validation and verification of their behavior. Simulations are a well proven strategy facilitating these issues. Although
simulations as virtual copies of real system behavior are useful test-beds
for various experiments and optimizations along the entire industrial
plant life-cycle, their design and integration are time-consuming and difficult. This paper proposes a new method to facilitate slicing of a monolithic simulation into a co-simulation, which is a simulation consisting
of multiple inter-linked simulation units. The proposed method aims at
specifying interfaces of the simulation units as well as routing signals for
integrating the simulation units. The method improves engineering and
re-design of co-simulations in terms of saving time and effort for creating
and integrating complex co-simulations.

Keywords: Simulation modeling · Modularization and slicing · Holonic
principles for process simulation · Multi-agent systems

1 Introduction

Industrie 4.0 brings a new generation of production systems that are becoming more software-intensive. They are of a cyber-physical nature [6] frequently,
i.e., these systems consist of coupled software and hardware parts. Such cyber-
physical production systems (CPPS) are becoming very complex and their engineering and testing are very complicated and time-consuming tasks, because
the verification cannot be conducted component by component, but the whole
ecosystem of interacting components has to be tested at once. Only such holistic
approach can reveal unintended side effects caused by emergent behavioral patterns. Thus, shifting testing and tuning of industrial plants and their automation

© Springer International Publishing AG 2017
V. Mařík et al. (Eds.): HoloMAS 2017, LNAI 10444, pp. 111–124, 2017.
DOI: 10.1007/978-3-319-64635-0_9

systems from the real world to simulated environments is a part of a "virtualization", which is one of the key movements in emerging areas of *Industrie 4.0* and factories of the future.

Each industrial system should be enhanced with its own virtual copy (a.k.a. virtual twin) for simulating its behavior, testing, optimizing, and virtual commissioning. The vision is that each vendor in the manufacturing value chain produces not only the machinery or the hardware itself, but each semi-product should be accompanied by a virtual twin to simulate it. It can be technically represented for example as a Functional Mockup Unit [1]. Within this vision, simulations should be created by combining and integrating these units in a similar way how products are manufactured along work break down structures.

Although simulation models can significantly ease a detection of weak points in design of CPPS as well as in their control algorithms, the use of simulations is still limited. One reason of their minor penetration into engineering practice is their limited applicability for verification of controllers of large and complex systems. Since one of the common requirements to be verified is the computational power readiness of controllers, real-time simulations of the controlled system have to be used. Because the computational performance of a single CPU is limited by technological limits, slicing a monolithic simulation model into a bunch of co-simulations running in parallel is an enabler of the simulation-based verification method for large systems. This paper contributes to improving the design of co-simulations, which are simulations consisting of multiple inter-linked simulation units. The proposed method can be used for different types of simulations. It is the most advantageous for the continuous-time simulations, because they balance energy distribution in the system transmitting power between system components, which constitutes relatively complicated interfaces and signal relationships between model components. Subsequently, this leads to complicated signal routing in case of continuous-time simulations.

This paper is aimed at improving the engineering of co-simulations for CPPS by facilitating the way how interfaces of individual simulation units are defined and how these emerging units are integrated. The proposed paradigm distinguishes slicing of large-scale simulation models on a junction level and on a connection level. The simulation units themselves can be designed manually or automatically, depending on decisions of simulation project leaders. The benefit of the proposed method is that interfaces of simulation units and their interconnections can be set up first, thus misunderstandings of independent teams or engineers during simulation projects are mitigated. The proposed method solves the problem of simulation unit integration from the structural point of view and timing and synchronization issues are not in scope of this approach.

The remainder of the paper is structured as follows. Section 2 summarizes the state of the art. Section 3 aligns the method within a broader context of co-simulation design and implementation. Section 4 describes how a CPPS simulation can be split into a co-simulation consisting of a set of interlinked simulation units and how the interfaces look like. Section 5 illustrates the method on an example from practice. Finally, Sect. 6 concludes and suggests future work.

2   Related Work

Co-simulation for power systems in terms of technological background and challenges is addressed in [7]. It describes two general-purpose standardized approaches applicable in other domains as well: (i) High-Level Architecture and (ii) Functional Mockup Interface. Beyond these technologies, proprietary approaches can be used as well, but it limits interoperability and maintainability.

On the technical integration level of co-simulation, the High-Level Architecture (HLA) [3] is widely cited. The framework addresses the composition of simulations from sub-models, but it does not address how to get input simulation data and how to store the results. In addition to such an absence of data source management, the shortcoming of this framework is the absence of semantics. The extension of HLA with semantics is proposed in [4].

Functional Mockup Interface[1] (FMI) is a technical solution for composition of simulation models from simulation modules called Functional Mockup Units (FMUs). It targets similar types of problems that are addressed with the older HLA standard, but FMI is more product-oriented in comparison to HLA. The basic idea of FMI is to facilitate co-simulation and model exchange as FMUs are compiled into an executable platform-independent code. Technically, FMUs are ZIP files. Each ZIP file includes the simulation unit itself (i.e., the simulation module), which has an interface in the C language. In addition, each FMU is accompanied with an XML model description annotating the interface of the unit.

The benefits of FMI/FMU are that (i) it enables bridging diverse simulation languages and platforms, as well as (ii) it hinders revealing details how simulation units are implemented. The former aspect is important when integrating units implemented for example in MATLAB-Simulink and Modelica language. The latter aspect is important in simulation projects including several stakeholders in industrial consortium, where intellectual property protection plays a significant role. This situation is frequent for example in automotive industry, where subcontractors deliver products to various competing car manufactures. The FMI technology is well tested, partly adopted by industrial companies, and considered as promising. On the other hand, the FMI does not provide means how to define the size of units, into which a specific large-scale simulation should be split, or how to specify interfaces of these units. Such issues are in the scope of research, see for example [1].

In the area of simulation engineering, bond graphs [2] still play a crucial role. Although they were introduced several decades ago, they provide both generalized and engineering-oriented description of system components that is valid universally across system types and that has not been overcome by another paradigm or method yet. Bond graphs can be considered as a domain-specific language for power flow description in mechatronic systems. Although they were

---

[1] https://www.fmi-standard.org.

introduced for continuous-time physical systems, they can oblige other types of systems as well [11].

In the context of this paper, especially effort $e(t)$ and flow $f(t)$ variables defined by the bond graph theory are important. These variables are called "power variables" as their product is power. They were introduced as abstractions for a unified approach to describe diverse types of systems. For example, the effort variable generalizes voltage in electrical systems, pressure in hydraulic systems, force in mechanical translation system, or concentration in chemical systems. The flow variable generalizes current in electrical systems, flow in hydraulic systems, velocity in mechanical translation systems and molar flows in chemical systems. Another important concept defined by the bond graph theory are 0-junctions for approximating connections with shared effort and 1-junctions approximating connections with the same flow. All these abstractions and correspondences in behavior descriptions across different system types and topologies enable to simplify and to unify mathematical-physical description of various systems in terms of signals and component topologies. Further details are included in the remainder of the paper, but the entire overview can be found in [2].

3   Context of the Proposed Approach

In order to increase the modularity, computational performance, and maintainability of simulations, simulation models have to be split into several simulation units. These units are relatively independent, but can be dynamically coupled. Slicing of complex simulations into a set of coupled simulation units brings the following benefits:

1. Better parallelization of simulation execution
2. Easier maintenance and (re-)design of simulations for complex systems
3. Encapsulation and concealing of intellectual property and business logic
4. Simplified testing of simulation units.

To justify the proposed method into a broader context, the basic scenario of co-simulation design is depicted in Fig. 1. The entry point of the proposed method is a system model, which represents the topology of the real system, signals and variables, connections to the control and automation system, and arbitrarily other pieces of information. In principle, it can be represented in any unambiguous data format, nevertheless, the tested and preferred ones are the XML-based data formats AutomationML [5] or SysML [10]. The system model can be also represented as an ontology, in particular, the authors have proposed the Automation Ontology [8].

The system model is enhanced with a marking of simulation cuts by simulation experts in step 2 of the proposed method depicted in Fig. 1. Although assisted approaches for advising where the real plant topology should be cut can be found in literature, this issue oversizes the scope of this paper and thus it is assumed that the number of cuts and their types are decided by experts.

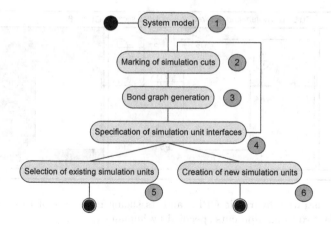

Fig. 1. Context of the method proposed in this paper.

For the given system topology, a bond graph as an abstraction for power flow description can be generated automatically in step 3. The markings of simulation cuts are propagated to the resulting bond graph in order to be consequently used for descriptions of interfaces between simulation units.

Having the selected simulation cuts in the bond graph, this joint information is used for automated generation of simulation unit interfaces and their integration with signals. This is step 4 in Fig. 1. In special cases discussed in details later, an external simulation unit has to be additionally created to efficiently integrate other simulation units. This paper is mainly focused on this step and it proposes a method for designing interfaces of simulation units and their integration. The integration can be solved with adding extra junctions on the simulation unit level and the description of these integration junctions is addressed in this paper as well.

Based on the obtained interface descriptions, either the already existing simulation units are selected, or new simulation units are created in steps 5 and 6. A simulation expert can realize, that the selected cuts lead to an over-complicated co-simulation, therefore, Fig. 1 includes a loop back to the selection of cuts and their types that can be redefined.

From the technical perspective, the proposed approach targets mainly the Functional Mockup Interface (FMI), where co-simulations consist of Functional Mockup Units (FMUs). However, the proposed approach tries to abstract from a specific infrastructure or solution and thus the term co-simulation is used on the level of FMI and the term (simulation) unit is used on the level of FMU.

4   Design of Interfaces for Co-simulation of CPPS

This section addresses step 4 from Fig. 1 in details. It describes how a monolithic simulation can be sliced into a set of simulation units. It specifies emerging interfaces caused by slicing of a monolithic simulation and signal routing between these interfaces, which are the core contributions of this paper.

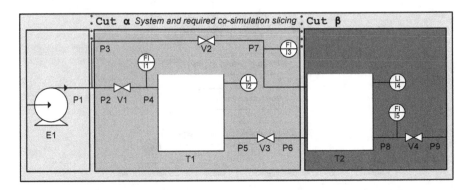

Fig. 2. An illustrative hydraulic CPPS and its slicing into a set of three simulation units given by two simulation cuts specified by human experts.

Two types of cuts can be used for slicing a system topology:

– Cut on the junction level (such as cut α in Fig. 2)
– Cut on the connection level (such as cut β in Fig. 2)

The positions and types of cuts are considered to be specified by human simulation experts in this paper. To illustrate the simulation slicing in practice, an exemplary system of systems is symbolically depicted in the upper part of Fig. 2. The figure shows components within a piping and instrumentation diagram, which is a domain-specific language for describing hydraulic systems. The figure also includes requirements on the decomposition into three simulation units, which is specified by simulation experts according to the simulation project size and requirements. The problems to be solved are the definitions of interfaces of these units and their integration into a co-simulation.

To solve the problem how the interfaces of simulation units created by slicing a monolithic simulation, the well-proven bond graph theory is used. It was selected as a suitable domain-specific language for describing power flows within technical systems. Bond graphs address both of the following aspects systematically: (i) solving which of the energy variables flow and effort is the input one (i.e., an independent variable) and which is the output one (i.e., a calculated/dependent variable); and (ii) assigning positive directions of power.

Although for equation-oriented simulations the signal interfaces need not to be specified in case of monolithic simulations, the situation is different in case of co-simulations. When several equation-based engines have to share data, signal variables have to be assigned a priori. For this reason, the method is suitable not only for signal-oriented simulations such as MATLAB-Simulink, but also for equation-based simulations such as Modelica tools or MapleSim.

Bond graphs are utilized for specifying simulation unit interfaces and their integration in the following way. The positions of given plant cuts are replicated into the bond graph as it is later shown in Fig. 3 on the use-case level. The splitting process depends on the type of each cut, i.e., whether a cut is on a junction or connection level. Both cases are discussed in the following subsections.

4.1   Cuts on the Junction Level

Cuts on the junction level pose a more complex situation, where signals between the sliced units should be added or subtracted according to a considered direction of positive power flows. This case frequently occurs when legacy simulation units or simulation units that cannot be edited easily are used and should be integrated within one co-simulation, such as in the case of locked FMUs. Cutting on the junction level leads to an emergence of a new unit/junction, whose mathematical-physical description is proposed in this section.

As prerequisites for a formal description of bond-graph-based simulation splitting on the junction level, the three predicates are defined:

- $hasStrokeProximity(b, N)$
- $hasPowerIn(b, N)$
- $hasPowerOut(b, N)$

The variable b represents the power bond; the second variable N represents one of the two bond graph nodes that are connected together by this specific power bond b. The predicate $hasStrokeProximity(b, N)$ expresses that the causality stroke at the power bond b is located on the side of the node N. The bond graph theory defines that this predicate holds either for exactly one power bond in case of N is a 0-junction, or for exactly $n - 1$ power bonds in case of N is a 1-junction, where n is number of power bonds $b_i, i = 1, \ldots, n$ connected to this specific node N. The predicate $hasPowerIn(b, N)$ means that the positive value of power represents the direction into the bond graph node N. The predicate $hasPowerOut(b, N)$ is dual, i.e., it holds for positive flow of power outside from the bond graph node N. The bond-graph theory assumes that especially in case of 0-junctions at least one is outgoing and in particular, it is the strong bond (i.e., for the 0-junctions the strong bond is such a bond that has a causality stroke on the side nearby the 0-junction).

Mathematical expressions for specification of the integration of resulting simulation units is based on surrounding bonds, their causality assignments, and utilized power directions. It also differs for cases of 0-junction and 1-junctions. The 0-junctions express parallel connections in non-mechanical systems such as hydraulic, electrical, or mechanical systems. They model serial connections in mechanical systems, but the proposed method brings the main advantage from the user perspective when the slicing is done on a parallel connection level. In case of mechanical systems, the parallel connection is abstracted with 1-junctions.

To remind the basics of the bond-graph theory, the *0-junction* is a junction having the same value of effort $e(t)$ on all connected power bonds and the sum of the directed flows $f(t)$ is zero:

$$e_1(t) = e_2(t) = \ldots = e_n(t) \tag{1}$$
$$f_1(t) + f_2(t) + \ldots + f_n(t) = 0 \tag{2}$$

The indices of the $e(t)$ and $f(t)$ variables are indices of the power bonds considered relatively from the perspective of a specific bond graph junction.

Considering the aforementioned equations, the slicing and integration on the 0-junction level is expressed as:

$$\exists! j (hasStrokeProximity(b_j, N))$$

$$
\begin{pmatrix} eo_1 \\ \vdots \\ eo_{j-1} \\ eo_{j+1} \\ \vdots \\ eo_{n-1} \\ fo_j \end{pmatrix}
=
\begin{pmatrix}
0 & \cdots & 0 & 0 & \cdots & 0 & 1 \\
\vdots & \ddots & \vdots & \vdots & \ddots & \vdots & \vdots \\
0 & \cdots & 0 & 0 & \cdots & 0 & 1 \\
0 & \cdots & 0 & 0 & \cdots & 0 & 1 \\
\vdots & \ddots & \vdots & \vdots & \ddots & \vdots & \vdots \\
0 & \cdots & 0 & 0 & \cdots & 0 & 1 \\
(-1)^{\sigma_1} & \cdots & (-1)^{\sigma_{j-1}} & (-1)^{\sigma_{j+1}} & \cdots & (-1)^{\sigma_{n-1}} & 0
\end{pmatrix}
\begin{pmatrix} fi_1 \\ \vdots \\ fi_{j-1} \\ fi_{j+1} \\ \vdots \\ fi_{n-1} \\ ei_j \end{pmatrix}
\tag{3}
$$

where $\sigma_k = hasPowerOut(b_k, N) + hasPowerIn(b_j, N), k = 1, \ldots, n-1$.

The "+" operator sums Boolean values of both predicates in the algebraic sense; hence, its value set is $0, 1, 2$ in this context. The variables have the following meaning. To the 0-junction N, n power bonds are connected; $b_j(n)$ is a j-th power bond connected to N. The port numbering in the equation respects source plans, but for simplicity reasons, the signal numbering in the junctions realizing this equation is called $eo_1 \ldots eo_{n-1}, fo_n$, respectively $fi_1 \ldots fi_{n-1}, eo_n$.

In case of 1-junctions as integrating junctions on the level of simulation units, the situation is dual. The *1-junction* is a junction having the sum of effort $e(t)$ equal to zero and having the same flow $f(t)$ for all connected power bonds:

$$e_1(t) + e_2(t) + \ldots + e_n(t) = 0 \tag{4}$$

$$f_1(t) = f_2(t) = \ldots = f_n(t) \tag{5}$$

Considering that 1-junctions add/subtract efforts and set the same flows to the connected power bonds according to the aforementioned equations, the following expressions characterize the slicing on the 1-junction level:

$$\exists! j (\neg hasStrokeProximity(b_j, N))$$

$$
\begin{pmatrix} fo_1 \\ \vdots \\ fo_{j-1} \\ fo_{j+1} \\ \vdots \\ fo_{n-1} \\ eo_j \end{pmatrix}
=
\begin{pmatrix}
0 & \cdots & 0 & 0 & \cdots & 0 & 1 \\
\vdots & \ddots & \vdots & \vdots & \ddots & \vdots & \vdots \\
0 & \cdots & 0 & 0 & \cdots & 0 & 1 \\
0 & \cdots & 0 & 0 & \cdots & 0 & 1 \\
\vdots & \ddots & \vdots & \vdots & \ddots & \vdots & \vdots \\
0 & \cdots & 0 & 0 & \cdots & 0 & 1 \\
(-1)^{\sigma_1} & \cdots & (-1)^{\sigma_{j-1}} & (-1)^{\sigma_{j+1}} & \cdots & (-1)^{\sigma_{n-1}} & 0
\end{pmatrix}
\begin{pmatrix} ei_1 \\ \vdots \\ ei_{j-1} \\ ei_{j+1} \\ \vdots \\ ei_{n-1} \\ fi_j \end{pmatrix}
\tag{6}
$$

where $\sigma_k = hasPowerOut(b_k, N) + hasPowerIn(b_j, N), k = 1, \ldots, n-1$.

The "+" operator sums Boolean values of both predicates in the algebraic sense. The variables have the following meaning. To the 1-junction N, n power bonds is connected; $b_j(n)$ is a j-th power bond connected to the junction N. The port numbering in the equation respects the source plans, but for simplicity reasons, the signal numbering in the junctions realizing this equation is called $fo_1 \ldots fo_{n-1}$, eo_n, respectively $ei_1 \ldots ei_{n-1}$, fi_n.

Summarizing both cases of junction-level cuts, the slicing leads to an additional junction where signals are subtracted, added, and propagated through. It is beneficial to use this kind of cut when (i) one needs to abstract the description of individual components from the topology of the rest of the system, (ii) considered simulation units are legacy and provided, for example, by a vendor of a sub-product, and (iii) the co-simulation topology is easier and better maintainable.

4.2   Cuts on the Connection Level

Cutting on the connection level can be also called cutting on the power-bond level, as it was used in [9]. However, a power bond is an artifact that does not exist in the domain of real system descriptions. The authors tend to shift the approach towards the industrial practice as much as possible, hence the term connection level is used in this paper in order to emphasize the principle on the entity existing in a real industrial plan. For the cuts on the connection level, the effort/flow assignment depends on the relative position of the causality stroke only. The direction of the power is not considered as it has been already taken into account when constructing the entire bond graph and specifying sign conventions of signals at junctions located nearby the unit cut.

Whereas in the case of cuts on the junction level, the utilized predicates are useful or even needed for implementation of the extended bond graph method; in case of cuts on the connection level, two further predicates have to be defined:

– $strokeUnitX(b)$
– $strokeUnitY(b)$

Each cut on the connection level separates a simulation model into two units, denoted in general as units X and Y. Since the position of the causality stroke is crucial for cuts on the connection level, these predicates express the position of such a stroke in the relationship to the designated simulation units for each power bond b. The former predicate $strokeUnitX(b)$ holds if and only if the stroke belongs to the unit X, whereas the predicate $strokeUnitY(b)$ holds for those bonds b that have causality stroke as a part of the second unit Y.

To specify the interfaces of the resulting units X and Y as well as their signal mapping, the positions of causality strokes is aggregated into vectors according to the following equations:

$$\boldsymbol{\xi} = \left\{ j : strokeUnitX(b_j) \right\} \tag{7}$$

$$\boldsymbol{\upsilon} = \left\{ j : strokeUnitY(b_j) \right\} \tag{8}$$

The interfaces of the units X and Y sliced on the connection level with the cut c can be described by the following equations, expressing how each signals are mapped/integrated to each other:

$$\left(\begin{pmatrix} X.fo_{\xi,c} \to Y.fi_{\xi,c} \\ Y.eo_{\xi,c} \to X.ei_{\xi,c} \end{pmatrix} \atop \begin{pmatrix} X.eo_{v,c} \to Y.ei_{v,c} \\ Y.fo_{v,c} \to X.fi_{v,c} \end{pmatrix} \right) \tag{9}$$

Since both ξ and v are vectors, the number of items in the matrices can vary according to the specific topology of the system respectively on the given bond graph. The number of rows in the entire signal mapping matrix is twice the number of power bonds that are cut. This is because each power bond is at the end represented by two signals, i.e., one effort and one flow. The operator "$\to$" expresses a signal flow between the interface ports. In an ideal case, both signals affected by this operator should be equal. However, the synchronization of both simulation units causes that the signals can be shifted in time due to the transport delays caused by the communication infrastructure, they can be re-sampled, they can be smoothed or interpolated. All these factors cause that the equality operator cannot be used because of both intended and unintended changes in both signals. The quality of the synchronization can be in layman's words expressed as a distance between the operator "$\to$" and "$=$". However, the metric and manners how to measure and evaluate this distance oversizes this paper and they are a promising issue for future work.

Considering the example depicted in Fig. 2, we can see the case of the connection level as the junction β. The power flows into the 0-junction via a bond from the left 1-junction. Effort is an input of the 0-junction and the junction calculates output flows as the sum of the two flows to the rest of the system on the right-hand side. We can see that the inner implementation of the glue unit depends on neighboring bonds only. However, it is necessary to create the bond graph for the whole system in order to be able to assign causality and power flows correctly.

Cuts on the connection level are suitable when a complex co-simulation is created from scratch, all units of the co-simulation can be edited arbitrarily, and only a limited rate of re-design or re-use of utilized simulation units is expected.

4.3   Mechatronic Components

A mechatronic nature of systems means that various system types interact in the system, such as hydraulic systems are coupled with mechanical ones. When a system is of a mechatronic nature, the energy transformations have to be accompanied with additional signals across these affected system types. For example, a transportation system speed and momentum are influenced by the level of liquid in a transported bottle, because it determines a mass of the entire bottle. By means of bond graphs, the power bonds addressing power flows have to be accompanied with signal bonds modeling additional information needed for proper simulation modeling. Since it is meaningful to slice a simulation exactly at the borderlines between system types, this issue has to be supported by the proposed method. Transformers of the energy types can be modeled according to two basic paradigms:

- A complex mechatronic device in one of the simulation units.
  This choice is characterized by an easier topology, but limited re-use and testing. It is a simulation engineer who tackles the complexity and the proposed approach cannot help him/her significantly.
- Two standard components located in simulation units according to their system types and coupled with one or more signal bonds.
  This leads to a more complex co-simulation topology with a higher number of signals, but it reaches a significantly higher level of re-use and testing. The proposed approach facilitates this choice on the integration level.

The latter case poses a desired solution for industrial practice. Typically it implies that one or more additional signal bonds have to be added to the co-simulation topology for each energy transformation point on the level of simulation unit interfaces.

5 Hydraulic System Use-Case

To illustrate the proposed approach in practice, the utilized system is the hydraulic system with two tanks that is depicted in Fig. 2. The figure includes the positions of cuts as they selected as an example by a simulation expert. The task is to find the input and output interfaces of simulation units and to configure the data exchange.

As the first step, the bond graph for this system has to be generated. The entire bond-graph is depicted in the upper part of Fig. 3, which stresses the positions of cuts for slicing the simulation considered as a human expert entry. We can see that the cut α is of a junction level type and in particular in a 0-junction, whereas the cut β is on the connection level.

Applying the equations proposed in the previous section and considering that the predicate $\exists! j (hasStrokeProximity(b_j, N))$ holds for the power bond on the left-hand side of the cut α, we get the following description for the external 0-junction representation of the cut α:

$$\begin{pmatrix} eo_2 \\ eo_3 \\ fo_1 \end{pmatrix} = \begin{pmatrix} 0 & 0 & 1 \\ 0 & 0 & 1 \\ 1 & 1 & 0 \end{pmatrix} \begin{pmatrix} fi_2 \\ fi_3 \\ ei_1 \end{pmatrix} \tag{10}$$

The signal inter-connection between units A and B implied by the Junction α can be summarized as:

$$\begin{pmatrix} A.eo_{1,\alpha} \rightarrow \alpha.ei_{1,\alpha} \\ \alpha.fo_{1,\alpha} \rightarrow A.fi_{1,\alpha} \\ \alpha.eo_{1,\alpha} \rightarrow B.ei_{1,\alpha} \\ B.fo_{1,\alpha} \rightarrow \alpha.fi_{1,\alpha} \\ \alpha.eo_{2,\alpha} \rightarrow B.ei_{2,\alpha} \\ B.fo_{2,\alpha} \rightarrow \alpha.fi_{2,\alpha} \end{pmatrix} \tag{11}$$

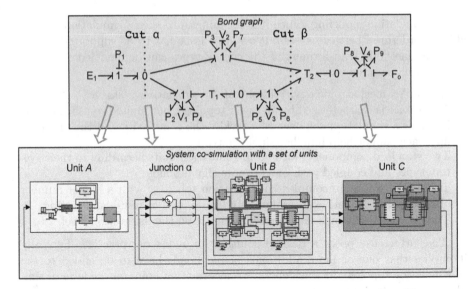

Fig. 3. Bond graph for the hydraulic system including the cuts at the upper part of the figure; and co-simulation with integrated units at the bottom part. In case of unit B, the signals are conditioned by both cuts, but they are handled independently.

In case of the cut β, the situation is easier. Both power bonds have the same positions of causality strokes so that they belong to Unit B on the left-hand side. It means that this cut implies two values of efforts (i.e., hydrostatic pressures of tank T_2) are inputs and two flows are outputs of Unit B (i.e., two flows calculated by valves V_2 respectively V_3). In case of Unit C, the situation is dual. The signal inter-connection between units B and C implied by the Junction β can thus be summarized:

$$\begin{pmatrix} B.fo_{1,\beta} \to C.fi_{1,\beta} \\ C.eo_{1,\beta} \to B.ei_{1,\beta} \\ B.fo_{2,\beta} \to C.fi_{2,\beta} \\ C.eo_{2,\beta} \to B.ei_{2,\beta} \end{pmatrix} \tag{12}$$

For units A and C, the assignment of input and output port numbers exactly correspond to the utilized port numbers, because both units are in scope of just one individual junctions. On the contrary, the unit B participates in both junctions thus the specific port numbers have to respect the merged requirements implied by both cuts. In this particular case, the cut α on the left-hand side was prioritized and signals implied by it are assigned to unit B first, whereas signals implied by the cut B follows as ports 3 and 4.

When doing such slicing, the system has to be simulated with three interconnected simulation units plus one additional junction implementing the 0-junction in the position of the cut α, as it is depicted in the lower part of Fig. 3. It can be implemented either as an ordinary stand-alone unit, or it would be beneficial that the co-simulation platform such as FMI supports making such junctions.

To run the entire co-simulation, it has to be set up with parameter values as well as definitions related to the simulation task such as simulation start time, stop time, time-steps and other settings regarding data and address space. This can be done with the model-based engineering and configuration methods as they were introduced in Fig. 2.

6   Conclusion and Future Work

Although simulations bring a large variety of benefits, they suffer from a time-consuming and error-prone design phase, which limits their use in industrial practice. This paper addresses design and implementation of interfaces of simulation units created by slicing monolithic simulations into a co-simulation consisting of a set of simulation units. The paper addresses the integration of these simulation units as well as it specifies how signal connections are routed and added or subtracted. The proposed method solves the simulation unit integration problem from the structural point of view, hence the timing and synchronization issues are not in scope of this approach. It is assumed that the timing issues are solved by simulation experts configuring the simulation solvers and data transfer frequencies.

The main methodological outcome of this paper is to emphasize the need and the usefulness of additional integration junctions that should be expected and supported by the simulation platform. These junctions are beneficial especially when two or more legacy or locked simulation units are integrated together. It is not efficient to face this problem by re-wrapping one of the simulation units with an upper layer including this junction, because it leads to a more complicated maintainability and a change in one branch of simulation unit topology can violate change requirement in this re-wrapped unit on the other side of the simulation cut. The feature of supporting additional junctions positioned outside of simulation units could be addressed by master algorithms of FMI. It is feasible to support it and it makes sense to implement or to require it from the master algorithm controlling the entire co-simulation, although it is not specified in the current version of the FMI standard.

In future work, we would like to focus on timing of the simulation unit synchronization. Solving the structural aspects and time-synchronization aspects of the simulation slicing are coupled issues that should not be solved independently. The positioning of simulation unit cuts affects the stability and computational performance of co-simulations, hence methodological integration of both aspects poses a promising topic for the ongoing work that is needed by researchers and practitioners.

Acknowledgment. The authors Petr Novák and Manuel Wimmer would like to thank the industrial partners and the Christian Doppler Research Society. This work has been funded by the Austrian Federal Ministry of Science, Research and Economy and the National Foundation for Research, Technology and Development.

The research of Petr Kadera has been supported by institutional resources for research by the Czech Technical University in Prague, Czech Republic.

References

1. Broman, D., Brooks, C., Greenberg, L., Lee, E., Masin, M., Tripakis, S., Wetter, M.: Determinate composition of FMUs for co-simulation. In: Proceedings of the International Conference on Embedded Software (EMSOFT) (2013)
2. Gawthrop, P., Bevan, G.: Bond-graph modeling. IEEE Control Syst. Mag. **27**(2), 24–45 (2007)
3. HLA - High Level Architecture. U.S. Defense Modeling and Simulation Office (2001)
4. Hu, J., Zhang, H.: Ontology based collaborative simulation framework using HLA and Web services. In: Proceedings of the World Congress on Computer Science and Information Engineering, vol. 5, pp. 702–706, April 2009
5. IEC 62714: Engineering data exchange format for use in industrial automation systems engineering - Automation Markup Language
6. Lee, E.A.: Cyber physical systems: design challenges. In: Proceedings of the 11th IEEE International Symposium on Object and Component-Oriented Real-Time Distributed Computing (ISORC 2008), pp. 363–369, May 2008
7. Müller, S.C., Georg, H., Nutaro, J.J., Widl, E., Deng, Y., Palensky, P., Awais, M.U., Chenine, M., Kuch, M., Stifter, M., Lin, H., Shukla, S.K., Wietfeld, C., Rehtanz, C., Dufour, C., Wang, X., Dinavahi, V., Faruque, M.O., Meng, W., Liu, S., Monti, A., Ni, M., Davoudi, A., Mehrizi-Sani, A.: Interfacing power system and ICT simulators: challenges, state-of-the-art, and case studies. IEEE Trans. Smart Grid (99) (2016). http://ieeexplore.ieee.org/document/7444194/
8. Novák, P., Serral, E., Mordinyi, R., Šindelář, R.: Integrating heterogeneous engineering knowledge and tools for efficient industrial simulation model support. Adv. Eng. Inform. **29**(3), 575–590 (2015)
9. Novák, P., Kadera, P., Jirkovský, V., Vrba, P., Biffl, S.: Engineering of coupled simulation models for mechatronic systems. In: Borangiu, T., Thomas, A., Trentesaux, D. (eds.) Service Orientation in Holonic and Multi-agent Manufacturing. SCI, vol. 594, pp. 3–11. Springer, Cham (2015). doi:10.1007/978-3-319-15159-5_1
10. OMG Systems Modeling Language (OMG SysML™). Version 1.4, September 2015. http://sysml.org/docs/specs/OMGSysML-v1.4-15-06-03.pdf
11. Sagawa, J.K., Nagano, M.S.: Modeling the dynamics of a multi-product manufacturing system: a real case application. Eur. J. Oper. Res. **244**(2), 624–636 (2015)

Simulation-Enhanced Development of Industrial Cyber-Physical Systems Using OPC-UA and IEC 61499

Samuli Metsälä[1], Kashif Gulzar[1(✉)], Valeriy Vyatkin[1,2], Laura Gröhn[1],
Eero Väänänen[1], Lauri Saikko[1], and Magnus Nyholm[1]

[1] School of Electrical Engineering and Automation,
Aalto University, 02150 Espoo, Finland
{samuli.metsala,kashif.gulzar,laura.p.grohn,eero.vaananen,
lauri.saikko,magnus.nyholm}@aalto.fi
[2] Luleå University of Technology, Luleå, Sweden
vyatkin@ieee.org
http://elec.aalto.fi/en/

Abstract. This paper presents a case study on simulation enhanced development of a flexible distributed factory automation system with distributed control and wireless communication. The method aims at advanced modular factory automation systems, providing easier behavioural verification, testing, and control in presence of various reconfigurations. The paper presents a model-driven distributed control of IEC 61499 using co-simulation with the system model. It provides the testbench for implementing and developing control and production planning strategies in order to improve system, robustness, reconfigurability and flexibility and security. One particular flexibility aspect implemented is the mechanism for online software updates enabled by the distributed control architecture. Another enabler is wireless communication. The paper discusses the comparison of wired vs. wireless distributed control of a testbed demonstrator.

Keywords: IEC 61499 · Distributed automation engineering · Co-simulation · OPC-UA

1 Introduction

Cyber-physical systems (CPS) based on decentralised control and wireless communication are applied in advanced industrial automation to increase flexibility of the production facilities. Modelling and co-operative simulation (co-simulation) of such automation systems are becoming an advanced trend in industry. The reference architecture of Industrie 4.0 (RAMI4.0) [11] introduces the concept of "digital twin" of a manufacturing system, which includes its simulation software. Simulation provides a platform to experiment with different hypothetical scenarios Garraghan et al. [10]. Co-simulation is a useful tool to

© Springer International Publishing AG 2017
V. Mařík et al. (Eds.): HoloMAS 2017, LNAI 10444, pp. 125–139, 2017.
DOI: 10.1007/978-3-319-64635-0_10

carry out design trade-off studies with different control applications. Nägele and Hooman [13], Hensel et al. [12], Celli et al. [7], Zhabelova et al. [19] and many other researchers have shown its usefulness in different domains. Comparing the real system performance to the simulation can be challenging and requires a right set of software products in a co-simulation environment with a suitable co-simulation interface.

The first step in development of a realistic simulation model that could be connected in the loop with controller is 3D model of the real system. The system model can be built after having all the individual components modelled separately. For creating the 3D model, it is often necessary to measure the real system by hand for all the dimensions, since not always its electronic CAD documentation is available. Integrating the different set of tools requires a standard communication mechanism and synchronization. One such mechanism is the OPC Unified Architecture (UA) machine to machine interface which is widely accepted and used in the automation industry for providing connectivity between various software and hardware platform [3].

In this paper, it is demonstrated how simulation can be applied in process of system transformation for virtual commissioning of the distributed automation system even before the physical system has been completed. A 3D model of a small scale multi-conveyor material handling system demonstrator called EnAS [1] is built in Siemens' Solid Edge ST9 [4], and Festo's CIROS simulation environment. Both central and a distributed control applications are developed using nxtControl's nxtStudio tool following IEC 61499 standard. A co-simulation interface is built to support different application trade-offs and testing of a central and distributed control application. The simulation integrates mechanical design, IEC 61499 based device control configuration with distributed deployments for manufacturing automation systems. The kinematics and signal mapping in these simulations were made after having the overall 3D model of the system. The completely same PLC code was used as with the real system, only a few definitions for the OPC connection was added.

A simulation model was developed to compare the real system with a virtual one from the behavioural perspective. The simulation showed that the real system can be mimicked reasonably well, even though the simulation did not run in real time. The benefit of the simulation model lies in the fact that it can be utilized in designing and testing the system without doing any actual changes, and the simulation could, in fact, be performed in real time.

The PLC code can be created and tested alongside the simulation model with an OPC connection between the software products using co-simulations. At least, a PLC programming software capable of simulating a PLC and a 3D simulation is needed. The software products should have a possibility for OPC communication that is used to send and receive signals from each other. The simulated PLCs (programmed in nxtStudio) were sending output signals to actuators of the simulation model (in CIROS), while the simulation model is reading the values of sensors during simulation and sending corresponding values to inputs of the simulated PLCs.

The paper is organized as follows. Section 1 provides the introduction. Section 2 describes the EnAS demonstrator. Section 3 provides the details about modelling the system in CIROS and the related IO interface provided for OPC connectivity. Section 4 provides additional details about the modelling and co-simulation of the system with nxtControl devices using OPC. Section 7 outlines the concept of on-the-fly updates in a distributed application setup. Section 8 presents the results of work-cycle times for both wired and wireless communication systems. Finally, Sect. 9 concludes this paper.

2   Overview of the EnAS Testbench

The new EnAS system in Fig. 1 is an upgraded version of the testbed developed for the project Autark Energy [1]. It has six conveyors, two jack stations, two grippers and ten optical sensors. The system can be operated in a different sequence actions depending on the product being manufactured. In the current configuration, pallet sections which contain the manufactured cans are transported on three different conveyors. The six distributed nxtControl devices can be connected to a wired or a wireless network configuration. Thus, both central and distributed application architectures can easily be evaluated on this platform.

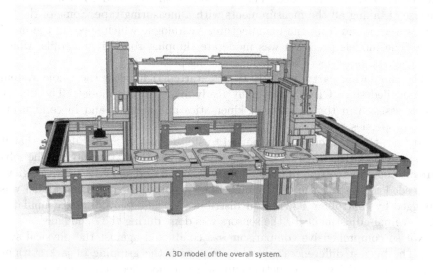

A 3D model of the overall system.

Fig. 1. Upgraded EnAS with simulation model

The individual conveyor belt sections are driven by an electrical motor which moves the pallet in the clockwise direction. The pallet is stopped at the various loading and unloading stations by means of selective switching of the conveyor belt sections. The conveyor belt on each side of the demonstrator consists of three independent conveyors, each driven by a motor with a clockwise rotation on the underside. Thus, the pallet on the conveyor belt always moves clockwise when the motor is activated. Each pallet consists of two small and two large slots. The smaller slots are for the cans and the larger slots are for the covers which sit on top of the cans. The cans and the covers are combined into a closed package. Each pallet can transport a maximum of two aluminium cans and their covers. In the new upgraded version inputs and outputs from the sensors and actuators are interfaced to six nxtSDSMini distributed devices. In the new upgraded architecture, the demonstrated is connected to the six nxtSDSMini devices. The desired control behaviour of this system can be described in many different ways: from monolithic logic to hierarchical modular design proposed by Ferrarini et al. [9]. The following section discusses the central control and a distributed design approach in the context of IEC 61499 standard.

3   Simulation and Modelling in CIROS

The 3D models of the subsystems were created with Siemens' Solid Edge ST9. In Solid Edge, each subsystem (e.g. jack) represents an assembly, and each component (e.g. piston of a cylinder) within that assembly represents a part. The overall system was assembled of subsystems by positioning everything together after every part was modelled. The accuracy of the 3D model is within 2 mm, because of taking all the measurements with a measuring tape. Some of the 3D models were found from the manufacturer's catalogue which sped up the modelling. The models precision was moderate skipping some finer details, which was beneficial in terms of required computing power.

The simulation part with CIROS was started right after the whole system was modelled since CIROS has many ready-made library models. The library models assisted in the creation of kinematics and signals, and in configuring object properties.

At first, the 3D model was exported to step-format in Solid Edge, so that it can be used in CIROS. An OPC connection between the nxtStudio and the software products was tested. In CIROS, an OPC client and an actuator with signals are needed for testing the OPC connection. A complete simulation model was debugged by controlling it with our distributed logic deployed into a simulated PLC. A final adjustment for the sensors was done during the debugging.

Not so comprehensive comparison was conducted against the physical system. The biggest differences seem to occur with the gripping of jack stations because the elasticity of the suction cups was not modelled. The velocities in the simulation can be easily corrected device by device, after measuring all of them within the physical system. Even then some detections of the sensors may lead to an incorrect stoppage position due to the latency of an OPC connection. In the end, the simulation can be used, for example, together with nxtStudio to debug and test a PLC code without any real hardware.

4   Co-simulation

As discussed in Sect. 3 simulation model is created for the EnAS system with CIROS. Each component is modelled so that it can be controlled using co-simulating with nxtStudio. Also, the library models assisted in the creation of kinematics and signals, and in configuring object properties. At first, the 3D model was exported to step-format in Solid Edge, so that it can be opened in CIROS. The simulation model is connected to the OPC-UA server module available for the IEC 61499 device in nxtStudio. Figure 2 shows the co-simulation architecture. Classical OPC-Client has been provided in CIROS which in this configuration is connected to OPC-UA server using the UA-Gateway proxy developed by Unified Automation [2]. Figure 3 shows the OPC-UA connectivity implemented using IEC 61499 FBs'.

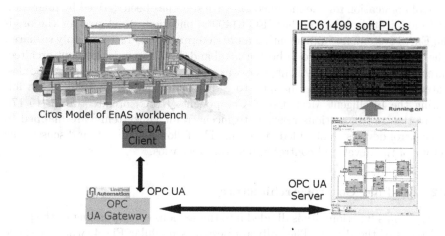

Fig. 2. CIROS nxtStudio co-simulation environment using an IEC61499 soft PLC via OPC/OPCUA communication

The performance and accuracy of the system in the simulation to the behaviour of the physical system is compared at the functional level. The biggest differences in performance seem to occur with the gripping of jack stations because the elasticity of the suction cups is not modelled. Also, the velocities in the simulation can be easily corrected device by device, after measuring all of them within the physical system. Even then some detections of the sensors may lead to an incorrect stoppage position due to the latency of an OPC connection. In the end, the simulation can be used, for example, together with nxtStudio to debug and test a PLC code functionality without the need of EnAS workbench.

4.1   IEC 61499 Control Application

The design patterns for distributed control applications have been extensively studied in the context of IEC 61499 research, in particular in [6,16,20]. The

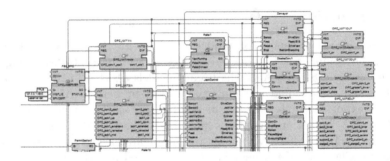

Fig. 3. FB application part related to conveyor 1, jack station1 and pallet with inputs and outputs for OPC-UA connectivity.

control application for the modified EnAS system has been derived by migration and modification from another IEC 61499 application, developed for the original EnAS system, for implementing a pre-determined product assembly scenario. The application was tested in both central and distributed deployment architectures. The central deployment case was using remote input/output modules. Later the application was mapped to a distributed hardware architecture following the Intelligent Mechatronic Components (IMC) architecture [8,15,17], where the control sections relevant to mechatronic subsystems' are mapped to the control devices "embedded" to them. The following subsection discusses the details of the developed control application scenarios.

4.2   Modular Control Architecture

The system's functionality is divided into the sections corresponding to the physical parts of the device. The software design is modular Fig. 4, where a single function block implements the functionality of the section corresponding to the related hardware section. The blocks were defined with an ECC state machine that realized the actions needed for each state and takes care of transiting from one state into another when certain conditions are true. Each of these blocks took the corresponding inputs of the section and execution permissions as inputs and delivered corresponding outputs of the section as well as execution permissions for other sections. The sections are networked with each other by connecting their ready signal output. The ready signal defines whether the section is ready to take a new pallet to the feed and receive inputs of neighbouring sections. It resulted in a structure where, the sections request and feed pallets from the previous section to the next one. Furthermore, OPC-UA server block resides in the device which provides the connectivity to the CIROS OPC client.

Push-buttons are provided for system level functions such as stop, reset and start. In the central control solution, the control logic can't be run on a single PLC since one nxtDCSmini has only 8 input and 8 output pins but we needed 27 inputs and 23 outputs for the whole system to run. For a central control solution, we decided to map all the function blocks responsible for control on a

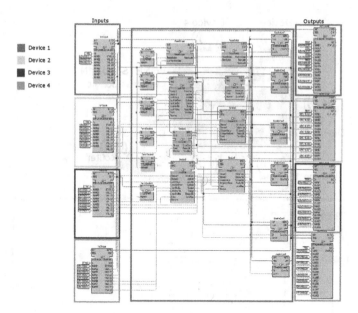

Fig. 4. Central control solution.

single nxtDCSmini and use the other PLCs solely for connecting the remaining inputs and outputs to the program. The central control solution was tested successfully. The main issues arising during the central control phase related to getting desired outcomes with the nxtStudio programming environment, getting all parts functioning based on I/O mappings as well as iteratively configuring and debugging the hardware setup for correct timings at optical sensors.

5 Distributed Architecture with Wireless Communication

Implementation of the application in IEC 61499 drastically simplifies distributed application deployment: each function block in the network in Fig. 4 is mapped to the corresponding PAC device. Figure 5 shows the block mapping to one of the control device attached to the EnAS demonstrator.

The wireless dongles used for establishing communication amongst PAC devices. A WIFI bridge from each PLC to the network are of type VONETS VAP11N [5]. They can either be used in WIFI bridge mode or as a WIFI repeater. To ensure network security, we use the devices in bridge mode so that only the wireless access point will manage the network. The wireless dongles are connected to the PLCs with short RJ-45 Ethernet cables. Input voltage for the dongles is 5 V. The power is provided by a secondary power supply.

The network which all devices are available in is managed by a WIFI wireless access point. The router we used for the project is Asus RT-N12. It operates on 2.4 GHz, supports standards 802.11b/g/n and is capable of handling data rates up to 300 Mbps. We secured the network by WPA2PSK password protection.

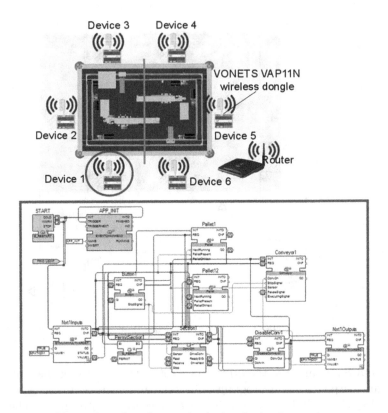

Fig. 5. Distributed control solution device 1 mappings

6   Human Machine Interface

The system has a simplified human machine interface (HMI) using composite automation type (CAT) function blocks telling the user which parts of the system are active at the moment, and also where the pallets are located. The HMI also allows the user to start, pause and reset the whole system.

In addition to these buttons, the system has CAT instances of all the conveyors, pallet locations, jack stations and gripper stations that get signals from the system as inputs and describe their states in the HMI accordingly. The conveyors in Fig. 7 are implemented so that there are several rectangles on top of each other, and the colour of the topmost visible rectangle shows the state of the conveyor. There are also two rectangles in jack gripper Fig. 6, and also, in this case, the colour of the visible one shows whether the Jack/Gripper is executing or not. There are several Pallets CATs. Figure 6 in the HMI to show where the pallets are currently located. The rectangle is either visible or not visible depending on whether there is a pallet or not in the location. The locations are the first sensors of each section and the spaces between them.

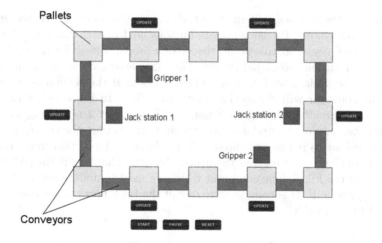

Fig. 6. HMI with all the CAT instances (Color figure online)

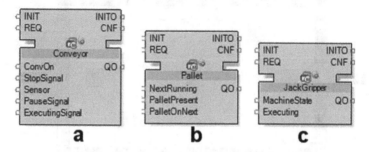

Fig. 7. CATs for: (a) the conveyors, (b) the pallets and (c) the jack and gripper stations (Color figure online)

By using update buttons next to each conveyor, the user can stop the conveyor. The HMI itself doesn't make any updates but prepares the system so that the update could be then made manually. In running HMI the conveyors have four different colours when the system is running: the green when the conveyor is moving, the grey for a stationary conveyor, the yellow is for the system is ready to receive the updates, and the red is the device is updating. Similarly, the jack stations and grippers have two colours assigned: green is for an active station, and grey is for a non-active station. These colours used is demonstrated in the next section.

7 Online Updates

The idea behind the "online software update" is to minimize the production downtime by finding an optimized time slot for the update.

The online updates has a simplified human machine interface (HMI) providing the user with the feedback about the active components where the pallets are located at the running system. The HMI allows the user to start, pause and reset the EnAS system. By using update buttons next to each conveyor, the user can stop the conveyor. At this point, the system prepares itself for the update of that specific location associated device. The associated section can be updated by pushing the update button next to that section. If the section is currently active, the conveyor will change its colour to yellow. In Fig. 8 below the jack station, 2 is currently working with pallet 1. The pallet 2 is waiting for it to finish. But because of the update, after finishing the action, the conveyor 5 will change its colour to red as presented in Fig. 8 below. The section won't receive any pallets until the user releases the update button. That is why the pallets are queued up in the Fig. 9. The computer which we used to update software of the PLCs and provide HMI is connected to one of the LAN ports of the router with a RJ-45 Ethernet cable.

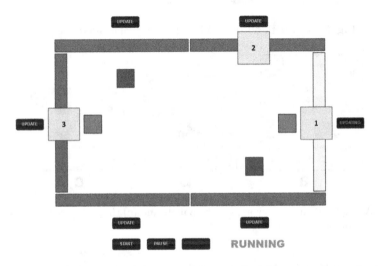

Fig. 8. The yellow conveyor shows that after finishing the current action that section is going to be updated. (Color figure online)

In the future version of this application. The time slot can be derived from data collected by different metrics used for measuring device performance. The software of a production line should be updated without disturbing the manufacturing process itself. The software change could be anything from a simple modification in some code snippet to an urgent firmware update. An update planner can be used for scheduling the software updates based on multiple factors. The importance of the update, as well as factory dependent aspects, are affecting the choice for an optimal time slot. After sufficient data has been gathered from the target production line, priorities between the update process and the manufacturing process can be reported to the update planner. The planner takes into account real-time behaviour and finds the best way to deal with situations ranging from update being critical to cases where the update process is blocked by active manufacturing processes. It watches also for unplanned stops which can show up any time providing quite optimal time slots for updating. The optimization problem can be considered as a process of minimizing waiting time, since other parts of the process may start to wait for the device during the update. Once the update process is ready, any undesirable behaviour in the updated system will lead to a restoration of previous software or repetition of the update process. This implies either downloading the backup of previous software version or running the update process once again.

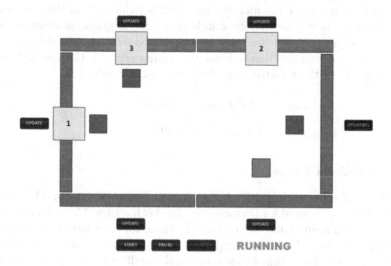

Fig. 9. Section 5 is under update and thus has its conveyor coloured red. (Color figure online)

8   Results

In this section performance have been calculated using the several different metrics for the wireless distributed control against its wired counterpart.

8.1   Overall Equipment Effectiveness (OEE)

Performance can be measured with several metrics. Overall Equipment Effectiveness (OEE) Singh et al. [14] is a standardized metric for the evaluating productivity. It helps to identify the truly productive time of manufacturing activity by using three different factors: availability, performance, and quality. Availability is run time divided by planned production time. The run time is computed by subtracting the duration of unplanned and planned stops from the total time the equipment is supposed to produce. There were no unplanned or planned stops for the measurements taken run time and planned production time are the same.

The performance also takes into account everything that is decreasing the theoretical maximum production speed. Theoretical run time divided by the real run time gives the performance percentage. The theoretical run time is obtained by multiplying the ideal cycle time by the total quantity of produced items. For one work cycle, the theoretical run time is the minimum time for one work cycle. As real run time, the average round time can be used. Therefore, the performance for wireless setup is $58.890/59.335 = 0.993$ and for the wired $58.570/58.882 = 0.995$. Further, quality provides a good measure of system effectiveness. It is a number of good grade items divided by a total number of items. The number of items which do not meet the quality standards is reduced from the total count of manufactured items. No quality standards for the demonstrator was decided but if the workpieces inside the cases are considered as items, the demonstrator produces only good-quality items. Thus, the quality is also 1. OEE score is given by multiplying the three factors together. Hence, the results are,

$$OEE_{Wireless} = 0.9925$$

$$OEE_{Wired} = 0.9947.$$

8.2   Work Cycle Times

Work cycle data was gathered for both wired and wireless setups. The Central controller is not compared for performance. For both setups, 15 work cycles were run and for each round time was taken. The times for each round are presented in the Fig. 10 below. Within 30 rounds and 20 extra rounds, there were to be no such faults. In wireless setup, the number of the faults was four to 30 (the total number of cases the gripper placed) compared to the wired setup's 9 to 30.

8.3   Time for N Rounds of Operation

The alternative way to measure the system performance is to take time for n rounds of operation. It is a metric for benchmarking production time for any given setup. The time elapsed while running the production line for a given amount of through-put was recorded. For 15 rounds the time in wireless setup was 890.03 and in wired 883.23.

8.4   Average Time Between Faults

The another performance measure is an average time between faults. The average time between faults needing human interaction was recorded for a certain time period of operation. This metric can be used to find out differences in the reliability of the given setups. When running the total of 50 rounds, no human interaction was needed. Thus, the average time between faults is infinity.

In comparison to the wireless control system, the wired connection is more reasonable in the sense that deploying the project to the PLCs never failed and the communication between the devices was never lost due to connection issues

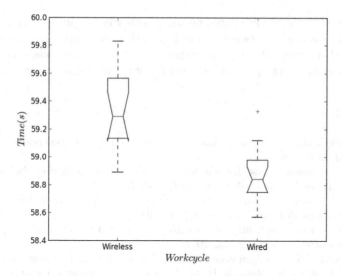

Fig. 10. Comparison of wired and wireless work cycles

when running the system. In other words, there were no contingency factors in the communication within the system when wired connectivity was being used. Moreover, the measured latency when sending a signal from one PLC to another and back was mere 3.36 ms, which means that the communication is faster as compared to a wireless solution.

9   Conclusions

This study demonstrated the integrated development method for industrial cyber-physical systems that uses simulation in the loop, which enhances both development and operation. The potential use of co-simulation of CIROS 3D models with IEC 61499 standard based application in nxtStudio was demonstrated for development and testing of software for flexible manufacturing systems with distributed control. A simulation model was created which can be connected to the planned control software for the behavioural simulations.

The concept of smart updates supported by online co-simulation was also successfully demonstrated. Distributed control and wireless communication makes it possible to considerably decrease the downtime costs in manufacturing factories spent for software updates. The paper also present a comparison between the wired and the wireless solution in a factory-like environment. No visible difference in performance were noticed, however, in spaces with a lot of external wireless traffic wireless system degrades in performance.

The distributed and wireless solutions will be developed further in the future with timestamps [18] to achieve functional accuracy in the demonstration incase of interferences in other channels. This should produce better results, for example, by reducing delay related faults. Another development idea is to optimize sending the events between controllers so that the controllers communicate with each other using different events that are not sent always when a controller reaches new state i.e. the purpose is to get rid of all unnecessary communication.

References

1. Enas-energieautarke aktoren und sensoren. https://www.energieautark.com/. Accessed 20 Feb 2017
2. Building a business case for wireless at your industrial facility. https://www.unified-automation.com/. Accessed 20 Feb 2017
3. Enas-energieautarke aktoren und sensoren. https://opcfoundation.org/about/opc-technologies/opc-ua/. Accessed 7 Mar 2017
4. Siemens'solid edge st9. https://www.plm.automation.siemens.com/en/products/solid-edge/st9/. Accessed 7 Mar 2017
5. Vonets VAP11N. http://en.vonets.es/downloads/. Accessed 14 Mar 2017
6. Cai, X., Vyatkin, V., Hanisch, H.-M.: Design and implementation of a prototype control system according to IEC 61499. In: Proceedings of 2003 IEEE Conference on Emerging Technologies and Factory Automation, EFTA 2003 (Cat. No. 03TH8696), vol. 2, pp. 269–276, September 2003. doi:10.1109/ETFA.2003.1248710
7. Celli, G., Garau, M., Ghiani, E., Pilo, F., Corti, S.: Co-simulation of ICT technologies for smart distribution networks. In: CIRED Workshop 2016, pp. 1–5 (2016). doi:10.1049/cp.2016.0745
8. Dai, W., Vyatkin, V.: Redesign distributed PLC control systems using IEC 61499 function blocks. IEEE Trans. Autom. Sci. Eng. 9(2), 390–401 (2012). doi:10.1109/TASE.2012.2188794. ISSN 1545-5955
9. Ferrarini, L., Veber, C., Lorentz, K.: A case study for modelling and design of distributed automation systems. In: Proceedings 2003 IEEE/ASME International Conference on Advanced Intelligent Mechatronics (AIM 2003), vol. 2, pp. 1043–1048, July 2003. doi:10.1109/AIM.2003.1225486
10. Garraghan, P., McKee, D., Ouyang, X., Webster, D., Seed, J.: A scalable approach for cyber-physical system simulation. IEEE Trans. Serv. Comput. 9(2), 199–212 (2016). doi:10.1109/TSC.2015.2491287. ISSN 1939-1374
11. Hankel, M.: The reference architectural model industrie 4.0 (RAMI 4.0). ZVEI (2015)
12. Hensel, S., Graube, M., Urbas, L., Heinzerling, T., Oppelt, M.: Co-simulation with OPC UA. In: 2016 IEEE 14th International Conference on Industrial Informatics (INDIN), pp. 20–25, July 2016. doi:10.1109/INDIN.2016.7819127
13. Någele, T., Hooman, J.: Co-simulation of cyber-physical systems using HLA. In: 2017 IEEE 7th Annual Computing and Communication Workshop and Conference (CCWC), pp. 1–6, January 2017. doi:10.1109/CCWC.2017.7868401
14. Singh, R., Shah, D.B., Gohil, A.M., Shah, M.H.: Overall equipment effectiveness (OEE) calculation - automation through hardware & software development. Procedia Eng. 51, 579–584 (2013). doi:10.1016/j.proeng.2013.01.082. http://www.sciencedirect.com/science/article/pii/S1877705813000830. ISSN 1877-7058
15. Sorouri, M., Patil, S., Vyatkin, V.: Distributed control patterns for intelligent mechatronic systems. In: IEEE 10th International Conference on Industrial Informatics, pp. 259–264, July 2012. doi:10.1109/INDIN.2012.6301149

16. Vyatkin, V., Hanisch, H.-M., Karras, S., Pfeiffer, T., Dubinin, V.: Rapid engineering and re-configuration of automation objects aided by formal modelling and verification. Int. J. Manuf. Res. **1**(4), 382–404 (2006). doi:10.1504/IJMR.2006.012252. http://www.inderscienceonline.com/doi/abs/10.1504/IJMR.2006.012252
17. Vyatkin, V., Hirsch, M., Hanisch, H.-M.: Systematic design and implementation of distributed controllers in industrial automation. In: 2006 IEEE Conference on Emerging Technologies and Factory Automation, pp. 633–640, September 2006. doi:10.1109/ETFA.2006.355448
18. Vyatkin, V., Pang, C., Tripakis, S.: Towards cyber-physical agnosticism by enhancing IEC 61499 with PTIDES model of computations. In: 41st Annual Conference of the IEEE on Industrial Electronics Society, IECON 2015, pp. 001970–001975. IEEE (2015)
19. Zhabelova, G., Patil, S., Yang, C.-W., Vyatkin, V.: Smart grid applications with IEC 61499 reference architecture. In: 2013 11th IEEE International Conference on Industrial Informatics (INDIN), pp. 458–463, July 2013. doi:10.1109/INDIN.2013.6622928
20. Zoitl, A., Prahofer, H.: Guidelines and patterns for building hierarchical automation solutions in the IEC 61499 modeling language. IEEE Trans. Ind. Inform. **9**(4), 2387–2396 (2013). doi:10.1109/TII.2012.2235449

An Agent-Based Approach for the Dynamic and Decentralized Service Reconfiguration in Collaborative Production Scenarios

Nelson Rodrigues[1,2(✉)], Paulo Leitão[1,2], and Eugénio Oliveira[2,3]

[1] Polytechnic Institute of Bragança,
Campus Sta Apolónia, 5300-253 Bragança, Portugal
{nrodrigues,pleitao}@ipb.pt
[2] LIACC - Artificial Intelligence and Computer Science Laboratory,
Porto, Portugal
eco@fe.up.pt
[3] Faculty of Engineering, University of Porto,
Rua Dr. Roberto Frias s/n, 4200-465 Porto, Portugal

Abstract. Future industrial systems endorse the implementation of innovative paradigms addressing the continuous flexibility, reconfiguration, and evolution to face the volatility of dynamic markets demanding complex and customized products. Smart manufacturing relies on the capability to adapt and evolve to face changes, particularly by identifying, on-the-fly, opportunities to reconfigure its behavior and functionalities and offer new and more adapted services. This paper introduces an agent-based approach for service reconfiguration that allows the identification of the opportunities for reconfiguration in a proactive and dynamic manner, and the implementation on-the-fly of the best strategies for the service reconfiguration that will lead to a better production efficiency. The developed prototype for a flexible manufacturing system case study allowed to verify the feasibility of greedy local service reconfiguration for competitive and collaborative industrial automation situations.

Keywords: Service reconfiguration · Service reconfiguration strategies · Multi-agent systems · Cyber-physical system · Smart manufacturing · Industry 4.0

1 Introduction

Manufacturing industry is facing a continuous evolution, being the implementation of systems exhibiting flexibility and reconfiguration capabilities one of the many challenges of the manufacturing industry in the coming years. Manufacturing companies must be able to react rapidly and cost-effectively to condition changes, in order to overcome the current problems [1]. Aligned with this vision, predictive maintenance plays an important and necessary role to ensure production efficiency although costs become significantly high [2]. To address the mentioned issues and aligned with the vision of Industry 4.0, the employment of reconfiguration mechanisms to dynamically adapt the needed processes and offered services is crucial. Traditionally, service

© Springer International Publishing AG 2017
V. Mařík et al. (Eds.): HoloMAS 2017, LNAI 10444, pp. 140–154, 2017.
DOI: 10.1007/978-3-319-64635-0_11

reconfiguration is performed due to several reasons like, for example, to cope with the unexpected and unpredictable condition changes, to recover from broken processes, to lead to a better production efficiency, to improve the system competitiveness according to the customer's needs and to respond to new business strategies.

Despite the current research efforts, the existing reconfiguration strategies are still too much simple, e.g., components' replacement (to react to the harmful effects or breakdowns) and re-planning (to deal with the modified configurations' requirements) [3]. Additionally, traditional production systems are still lacking automated tools that support the dynamic and runtime reconfiguration strategies by discovering new reconfiguration opportunities and exploring new system configurations.

The majority of the deployed service reconfiguration solutions are manually and reactively executed taking into consideration a centralized perspective. In fact, the decisive actions for the system reconfiguration are made after the occurrence of a failure, which can sometimes involve stopping a running process, diagnosing the failure, reconfiguring and restarting the system/device. In practice, the usual behavior when diagnosing a failure is to select the known recovery action that solves the failure; other possibilities that take more time require the understanding of all possible alternative service configurations' solutions that go beyond the human capacity in an acceptable time. Thus, performing the service reconfiguration manually and, afterward, restarting the system is not enough to address the dynamics of current industrial needs [4]. As a consequence, new reconfiguration strategies are required to support the evolution of the traditional systems by being dynamically performed online and just in time.

This paper describes a flexible and distributed multi-agent system (MAS) approach for the service reconfiguration that allows the proactive and dynamic identification of the opportunities for reconfiguration and the implementation on-the-fly of the best strategies for the service reconfiguration that will lead to a better production efficiency. In the proposed approach, the distributed and autonomous agents embed intelligent mechanisms for the earlier detection of reconfiguration opportunities and the selection of the reconfiguration strategies for improving the service properties or updating the catalog of offered services. In order to avoid conflicts arising from the dynamic reconfiguration of the distributed agents, a collaborative service reconfiguration mechanism was introduced. Information sharing among agents support the identification of the best configurations and avoid redundancies or unnecessary reconfigurations that can lead to poorer system performance. The proposed approach was tested in an experimental flexible manufacturing system, and the preliminary results show the benefits of this dynamic and proactive service reconfiguration.

The remaining of this paper is organized as follows. Section 2 overviews the main concept of service reconfiguration, existing related work and establishes the requirements for a truly dynamic, intelligent and proactive service reconfiguration process. Section 3 presents the proposed multi-agent based approach for the service reconfiguration. Section 4 describes the experimental case study, the implementation details and discusses the preliminary experimental results. Finally, Sect. 5 rounds up the main contributions of the paper with the conclusions and the future work.

2 Related Work

The Service-oriented Architectures (SOA) paradigm [5] is based on the concept of offering and consuming services, each one encapsulating the functionalities of a service provider. The use of service-orientation allows facing interoperability and loose-coupled abstraction in the design of complex systems. In these systems, the concepts of service aggregation, composition, and orchestration are important, to better understand the service reconfiguration concept. Basically, service reconfiguration is related to service adaptation designed to deal with unexpected events, such as failure of a service and loss of the quality of service (QoS) [3].

In this context, several different types of service reconfiguration can be identified:

- *Improvement of the service's behavior and performance*, e.g., changing the calibrating tools and/or switching components of the process to reduce the service's time or improve the service's quality (this can be seen as a weak reconfiguration type).
- *Changing the services' catalog,* i.e. new services are added, and others are removed from the catalog offered by an entity that accommodates the service demand; e.g., offering a new drilling service (this can be seen as a strong reconfiguration service type).
- *Changing the structure of a composed service*, which is built up through the composition of several atomic services, e.g., reorganizing the atomic services by adding some of them and remove others to accommodate better the evolution of the available atomic services (this can be seen as a strong-reconfiguration type).

Aiming to execute a truly dynamic, intelligent, and proactive service reconfiguration, considering the referred reconfiguration types, the following requirements need to be observed:

- R1: The opportunity to execute a service reconfiguration must be identified internally (regarding the system), automatically and at run-time.
- R2: The system needs to have the capacity to select an alternative reconfiguration solution and reconfigure on-the-fly, reducing the perturbation impact.
- R3: Service reconfiguration must be performed in a smooth manner (i.e. avoiding the individual and/or system nervousness).
- R4: Service reconfiguration process should comply with both competitive and collaborative scenarios.

Part of the research that was conducted on the service reconfiguration domain resides in using service composition mechanisms which aim at composing the best service that meets the client's requirements. The process of dynamic service reconfiguration is done according to the following steps [5]:

(a) Discover the services in the central service registry, e.g., UDDI (Universal Description, Discovery, and Integration), by selecting the services that match the requirements.
(b) Select the optimal service candidates, based on filters such as reputation.

(c) Perform the service compositions driven by the QoS, which are the restrictions of the optimization function.

This approach, whenever a disruptive event occurs, conducts a search of appropriate services in a centralized manner (i.e., using the UDDI), to rebuild a composition of services that satisfies the agreed requisites. The structure of the composition is found out by considering a variety of techniques, from optimization techniques that require heuristics algorithms to face the problematic of combinatorial optimization (known to be NP-hard), to an approach that uses Artificial Intelligence (AI) based planning to achieve a near optimal solution and accelerate the execution time. Some authors propose parallelism based on the division of complex tasks into many smaller ones where each sub-task is responsible for a local optimization. Innovative and non-classical solutions, such as the self-organization that was introduced originally by Ashby [6], refer to a cooperation process without any centralized decision. The benefits of decentralization were also investigated in [7], suggesting a decentralization on the service discovery phase by using the social plasticity of the providers. With the aim of improving the system, several authors also suggest an innovative paradigm using integrating agents with SOA to take advantage of agents important features, e.g., loose coupling, decentralization, distribution, and autonomy, to intelligently achieve the client's needs [8].

In addition to the referred works that focus on how to reconfigure the process, a relevant set of methodologies related to defining the moment of change is also proposed, giving relevance to different strategies about (when) reconfiguring. For example, reconfiguring the system due to new consumer policies and requirements [9], when a new service is requested [10] or in the worst cases when an error or disturbance occurs. The work described in [11] covers all undesired events and identifies unexpected opportunities through reactive, predictive, and periodic strategies. Aligned with this trend adoption and with the increasing ˙modification needs, service reconfiguration becomes the *de facto* approach that studies answers to the reconfiguration requirements.

In industrial systems, and in particular in the manufacturing domain, SOA-based paradigms have been proposed for automation and integration of services by extending the SOA paradigm to the domain of embedded low-level devices, such as sensors and actuators [12]. SOA is also used to implement collaborative manufacturing with intelligent Web services [13], and in another work, SOA and MAS are joined to enhance the manufacturing service collaboration as demonstrated in industrial automation [14]. Current trends related to the horizontal and vertical integration is also being faced by using SOA approaches, e.g. to support the increasing or diversity of the system's products or services. In [15], the authors proposed a service model for the dynamic production reconfiguration, in particular to reorganize the machinery in a manufacturing plant to be adapt to a new introduced product.

The service reconfiguration in dynamic environments needs to be quickly adaptable in real time and proactive (as stated in R1). Such dynamism can be monitored by means of existing maintenance strategies (e.g., reactive, preventive and predictive), which are covered by [11] where AI techniques were used to go beyond the traditional operational research by speeding up the generation of potential reconfigurations. However, based on the available service reconfiguration literature in manufacturing domain, the main concern relies on the service integration itself, without mentioning in practice any evidence of service reconfiguration. The majority of the existing reconfiguration solutions are performed manually due to the occurrence of failure events or product changeovers, even when the planners predict the actions to be performed. The reconfiguration is usually also achieved by a centralized composition planner, that does not provide the impact of the proposed new solutions (as stated in R2) and does not take into consideration the need for a smooth reconfiguration in case of change (as indicated by R3). The analysis and execution of the reconfiguration process are usually carried out in an individual way without considering the future impact and without regarding a collaborative analysis (as stated in R4).

Having this in mind, the challenge is to develop an approach that takes a step forward by evaluating potential possibilities in advance, having the capability to self-reconfigure the components without the need to stop or re-program the system, reducing the perturbation impact and decreasing the need for external intervention.

3   Dynamic Multi-agent-Based Service Reconfiguration

The proposed approach for the service reconfiguration aims to comply with the requirements previously described, and considers the use of MAS principles and intelligent algorithms to support the when and how phases of the reconfiguration process.

In this ecosystem, the resource agents (RA) encapsulate every shop floor stations functionalities, as illustrated in Fig. 1, and publish as services the processes they can offer (i.e. each production RA act as service providers).

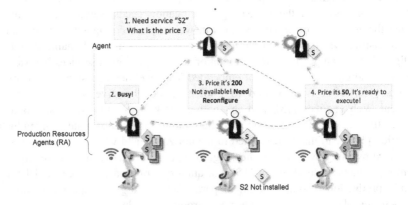

Fig. 1. Multi-agent based cable to perform decentralized service reconfiguration.

The service consumers (such as intelligent products) need to consume the production resources services to meet the production demand for this it is necessary to win an auction, thus based on the RA's local schedule, services performance and availability bid at a certain price that shared provide. From the RA' perspective, they try to get as many services invocations as possible, at the highest price. For this purpose, they are continuously aware of the competitiveness of their services and able to execute a service reconfiguration when an opportunity to improve their services is identified. For this purpose, the resource agents embed several intelligent algorithms to handle the when and the how phases.

3.1 Discovering Opportunities and Determining Reconfiguration Solutions in Automatic Manner

Aiming to face the service reconfiguration, each agent is continuously collecting data and applying actions to maximize its utility under production uncertainty and demand variability. In this context, a crucial issue is to maintain a competitive catalog of services that addresses the customer demands, which is possible by embedding a reconfiguration module that considers the following components [11], as illustrated in Fig. 2: When to Reconfigure (WtR), How to Reconfigure (HtR) and Decide Reconfiguration Solution (DRS).

The dynamic reconfiguration is challenging and can lead to unpredictable opportunities to evolve based on the fact that several variables are unknown, either from the physical perspective (such as the degradation of quality and the unforeseen plug-in of devices) or from the logical viewpoint (such as, the configuration of the manufacturing plant configurations and the scheduling of production orders). In this perspective, predicting these opportunities is wiser than simply reacting, which requires to collect data from the different sources, namely shop-floor and customers, to support the several components of the reconfiguration module.

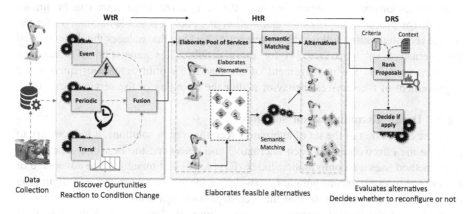

Fig. 2. Service reconfiguration module implemented in each agent.

3.1.1 When to Reconfigure

The first step in the proposed service reconfiguration approach, performed by the WtR component, is related to the monitoring and analysis of the collected data, identifying the triggers or opportunities for the reconfiguration, e.g., a performance or quality degradation, a failure occurrence or the introduction of new products. The WtR model relies on three different triggering strategies to detect possible situations to reconfigure [11]: event, periodic and trend.

The event triggering strategy uses an event-driven approach to detect events related to the system condition changes, e.g., a resource failure, the addition of a new resource/component or the removal of an existing resource/component. This strategy permits a good reaction to facing unexpected events, which is an important feature in dynamic and unpredictable environments.

The trend triggering strategy is responsible for identifying, as earlier as possible, a tendency or pattern in the degradation of a service performance, allowing the earlier implementation of actions to improve its performance or to reconfigure this service by another more useful. Several algorithms can be used to identify these opportunities, namely the anomaly detection, the cluster analysis-based and the structural break [11]. The anomaly detection and cluster analysis-based methods are more appropriate to discover anomalies in patterns [16], and the structural break method is more appropriate to perform a simple trend analysis.

The periodic triggering strategy uses a periodic check to verify the current service performance and decide about the opportunity to reconfigure. The triggering time interval should be dynamically adjusted to better fit the system dynamics, i.e. increasing or decreasing this value, taking into the consideration the application of proper machine learning algorithms. Q-learning [17] is a suitable approach to address this challenge, since it provides a positive/negative reinforcement feedback that handles the system's dynamics, allowing to converge to an optimal value.

3.1.2   How to Reconfigure

After being identified an opportunity to reconfigure, the HtR component is triggered with the responsibility to determine how the service reconfiguration can be implemented. The process comprises the elaboration of a pool of possible alternatives for the service reconfiguration, followed by a semantic checking that reduces the dimension of the alternative solutions (see [4] for more details). The generation of alternative solutions considers the improvement of the resource's utility and consequently the improvement of the services' behavior and/or the changing of the service's catalog.

3.1.3   Decide Reconfiguration Solution

After the calculation of the set of alternative reconfiguration solutions, it is necessary to evaluate the effectiveness of each alternative and determine the best one. The evaluation method uses a reconfiguration index (RI) [4, 18] that quantifies the advantage of performing a certain reconfiguration, considering the ratio between the reconfiguration effort with the expected profit that the reconfiguration can bring [4].

In the end, the several alternative solutions are ranked according to the evaluation method and considering the criteria defined by the system managers.

This component is also responsible for deciding if the best reconfiguration solution should be implemented or not, taking into consideration the nervousness control of the resource. In fact, the system stability is a very important issue, and each resource agent must control its nervousness to avoid falling into a chaotic system. The system should be proactive to identify opportunities for reconfiguration but should not constantly be changing the service reconfiguration because it implies a performance degradation.

3.2   Decentralized Mechanism for Service Reconfiguration

The described proposed approach for the service reconfiguration is carried out in a self-interested, autonomous and competitive way. Each agent, in this competitive situation, is running the service reconfiguration mechanism individually and does not share its objectives with the other agents. However, in collaborative environments, the lack of control or a normative environment using self-interested agents can lead to problematic situations that are damaging to the entire system, namely:

- Conflict situations: conflict of interest among agents have to be managed, e.g., in case several agents want to reconfigure to provide the same service.
- Deadlock situation: simultaneous individual service reconfigurations based on the interest of the most valuable services can lead to situations where no one offers the least profitable but necessary services.

In this sense, the adoption of a decentralized service reconfiguration approach and the design of a well-defined collaborative interaction protocol facilitate the avoidance of deadlocks [19], allowing to reach a mutual agreement that benefits the collaborative system behavior. This will improve the competitiveness of the system and balancing the resources' utilization rate, and avoiding a service reconfiguration carried out in an uncoordinated and chaotic way. To deal with this, an interaction protocol permits to collect the agent's intentions of its interests in adapting/reconfiguring its catalog of services. The protocol works in a synchronous manner by transferring data and control of the reconfiguration design among the agents (rather than using a central agent), to acquire all the data and understand if a global configuration is feasible. In particular, the protocol considers several resource agents, as illustrated in Fig. 3, one acting as an initiator of the interaction (i.e. the one that wants to change its service) and others participating in the collaborative interaction.

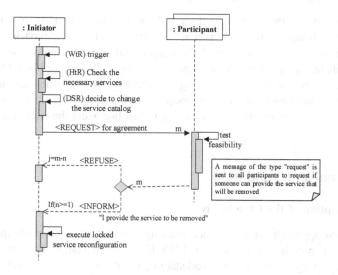

Fig. 3. Collaborative protocol for the interaction among agents.

After identifying an opportunity to reconfigure, the initiator, by using the WtR module that decides to implement a potential service reconfiguration, notifies its intention to implement a service reconfiguration and waits for the non-objection of all participants, aiming to control the system nervousness and to avoid entering into a chaotic situation (e.g., a non-feasible configuration, where no one is providing a necessary service). For this purpose, the initiator sends a "REQUEST" message to all participants, inquiring if someone can provide the service that will be removed. Each participant will reply with "INFORM" or "REFUSE" messages, according to its possibility to provide the service or not.

After, the initiator is waiting for the replies from the participants. If the initiator receives at least one "INFORM" then the system has achieved a feasible collaborative reconfiguration (since at least one participant offers the service that will be reconfigured). Otherwise, the proposed service reconfiguration leads to a non-feasible configuration (in the collaborative perspective), and the initiator will ignore the opportunity to reconfigure. Note that despite being beneficial for one service provider, the reconfiguration is not beneficial for the whole collaborative system, and consequently should not be implemented. The proposed approach considers the individual perspectives and the system as a whole, both with focus on flexibility in many ways:

- The dynamic individual service reconfiguration is directly mapped in competitive situations, where the self-fish behavior of the agents leads to a truly dynamic and decentralized service reconfiguration.
- The decentralized interaction mechanism permits to build a better and more robust reconfiguration approach, and at the same time to smoothly tackle the nervousness problems. By the fact that the conflicts of competition between services are avoided and even if there are several individual service reconfiguration interests, the resource agents decide if they are worth for the system benefits (also avoiding the implementation of non-feasible configuration).

As a drawback, this approach does not ensure the optimality of the service reconfiguration solution. However, as stated by [19], such type of approaches improves the performance regarding increased throughput and lower response. Nevertheless, both methods facilitate scaling the system to new agents. From one hand, they can be non-cooperative perspectives, performing the service reconfiguration autonomously, and from the other hand, they can be cooperative where the overall reconfiguration emerges from the participants without joining in just one agent the entire image of the system.

4   Experimental Validation

4.1   Description of the Case Study

The proposed approach for the service reconfiguration was tested using the flexible manufacturing system AIP-PRIMECA FMS [20], which comprises 5 workstations linked by a conveyor system. The workstations offer a set of services related to the execution of several operations (i.e. sub-products produced in this system, namely the letters A, B, E, I, L, P, and T), which combined can produce the final products BELT and AIP. This case study created based on batch production forcing to set-up and reconfigure the production equipment according to the demand. As illustrated in Table 1, each sub-product has its assembly process plan that needs to be followed to complete its production. For example to generate the sub-product T, the sequence of operations is to load the assembly base plate into the shuttle, followed by assembling 2 Axis, r and L components, performing the inspection and finally unloading the product from the shuttle.

Table 1. Process plans for the catalog of products.

	Product B	Product E	Product L	Product T	Product A	...
1	Loading	Loading	Loading	Loading	Loading	
2	Axis	Axis	Axis	Axis	Axis	
3	Axis	Axis	Axis	Axis	Axis	
4	Axis	Axis	Axis	r_comp	Axis	
5	r_comp	r_comp	I_comp	L_comp	r_comp	
6	r_comp	r_comp	I_comp	Inspection	L_comp	
7	I_comp	L_comp	Screw_c	Unloading	I_comp	
8	Screw_c	Inspection	Screw_c		Screw_c	
9	Inspection	Unloading	Inspection		Inspection	
10	Unloading		Unloading		Unloading	

Table 2 represents the catalog of services offered by each machine, indicating the processing time for each provided service. For example, the "r_comp" service can be executed by the workstation M3 while the workstation M2 offers the service "Axis". Aiming to increase the flexibility of the FMS and to create a richer scenario to test the service reconfiguration approach, a slight change was introduced in the scenario described in [20]. This change is related to expand the number of services provided by the machines, and particularly services that are available but are not currently offered in the machines' catalog. For example, the machines M2 and M3 have the possibility to

Table 2. Catalog of services provided by each machine (processing times in seconds).

Service	M1	M2	M3	M4	M5
Loading	I (10)				
Unloading	I (10)				
Axis		I (20)			
r_comp		NI (20)	I (20)		
I_comp			I (20)		
L_comp			NI (20)	I (20)	
Screw_c				I (20)	
Inspection					I (5)

Legend: I – installed in the catalog; NI – available but currently not offered in the catalog

change their catalog of services by offering, respectively the services "r_comp" and "L_comp". In case the agents decide for the service reconfiguration, a maintenance intervention is required to improve the service performance (taking 20 s) or to change the service provided (taking 30 s).

To simulate realistic scenarios for evaluating the reconfiguration hypotheses the occurrence of disturbances is considered. For this purpose, machines M2 and M3 have a probability of failure of 25% for all services in their catalogs, and when an improvement of the service performance is executed, its failure is reduced by 3%.

The designed MAS was implemented using the JADE framework [21], being the iteration among the agents performed by using FIPA-ACL compliant messages. Each resource agent contains the implementation of the "when" strategies that allow identifying opportunities to reconfigure. In this work, the following strategies of the WtR module were implemented [4, 11]:

- Event: related to the identification of reactive and critical situations, e.g., new production requests and resource/service failures.
- Trend: related to the earlier identification of patterns that result in deviations and anomalies, e.g., loss of quality of a service and decrease of resource usability.

These strategies were implemented on the monitoring behavior of each agent. In respect to the Event strategy, it was triggered by the monitoring procedure that contains the monitoring features to detect new products and disturbances, e.g., service or resource failures. The trend strategy requires more information (i.e., historical and contextual production data) to produce better real-time analysis and statistical computation to support the identification of potential deviations and anomalies patterns. In this case, the algorithms performing data analysis were implemented in R language [22] and accessed by the agents by using the RServe API connected through TCP/IP, which acts as a back-end for web services. From the R-side, the anomaly detection and cluster analysis based methods are continuously running in background to detect the degradation of a service performance. However, when facing production changeover situations, these two algorithms may create some confusion leading to identifying the characteristics of a new product as an outlier that consequently will result in bad configurations. In these cases, the Event module notifies the Trend module about a product change, allowing the adaptation of its trend analysis for a specific product, aiming to perform more accurate predictions.

In the same manner, agents incorporate the HtR module that allows generating potential reconfiguration solutions based on the different types of service reconfiguration, namely weak reconfiguration by improving the service performance, and strong reconfiguration by replacing the service catalog. A special aspect of the HtR algorithm [4] to ensure the feasibility of service reconfiguration solutions is the semantic verification of resources and pool of services, using JENA, to reduce the number of these alternatives.

4.2 Experimental Results

Some testing scenarios were designed to assess the described service reconfiguration approach, exploiting the impact of enabling the individual service reconfiguration performed by the distributed resource agents and enabling the collaborative mechanism to avoid conflicts and chaotic behaviors. In the experiments, the catalog of orders included the production of 20 BELT products. Figure 4 illustrates the experimental results for the different scenarios.

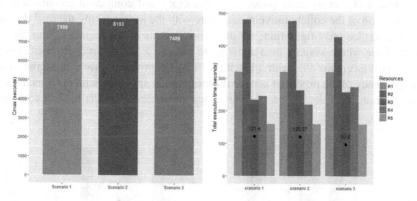

Fig. 4. Experimental results for scenarios with and without service reconfiguration.

Initially, the system was running in normal mode with the service reconfiguration and collaborative mechanisms disabled (scenario #1), measuring the Cmax value (i.e. the makespan that is defined as the total amount of time to process a given manu-facturing order), which is represented in the left graphic of Fig. 4. The right graphic of the same figure represents the standard deviation (σ) of the service utilization for each machine, aiming to verify how well distributed and balanced is the production. In this case, σ values close to zero represent a good balanced production. The scenario #1 presents a value of 7999 s for Cmax and 121.4 s for σ, working as a baseline to compare the proposed service reconfiguration approach.

The second scenario (scenario #2) is related to the enabling of the service recon-figuration mechanism in each resource agent in a self-fish mode, which means that the agents will execute their service reconfiguration individually and without any collab-orative procedure. The results, depicted in Fig. 4, show a decrease of the system performance in 1,8%, reflected in the need to have more 194 s to produce the 20 BELT products, and a slightly more balanced effort among the machines. The small increase in the Cmax may be due to conflict situations since agents are performing service reconfiguration procedures in a self-fish manner in a very typical collaborative envi-ronment, which means that they are reconfiguration to maximizing their individual interests and not the overall system goals.

The third scenario (scenario #3) is related to enabling the collaborative mechanism operating over the decentralized service reconfiguration mechanism being performed individually by the several resource agents. In this case, the results show an increasing of the system performance (illustrated by the reduction of 6,7% of the Cmax), as well as the reduction of the σ value to 97.6 s, which means a better disturbance of the resource utilization. This scenario clearly shows the advantages of applying the collaborative mechanisms to harmonize the service reconfiguration performed individually and in a non-cooperative manner by the distributed agents to reach collaborative environments.

This set of experiments allowed to verify that enabling the individual service reconfiguration, the system production efficiency is slightly improved, which small improvement is due to some possible contradictory and conflictual reconfigurations. The activation of the collaborative mechanism, with the agents taking the final decision about the service reconfiguration, not only considers its own perspective, but also the benefit of the whole system, thus allowing to achieve a higher production efficiency.

A fourth (scenario #4), with a batch of 30 BELT products, was considered to test the dependency of the proposed service reconfiguration approach with the dimension of the production order set. Figure 5 summarizes the achieved results for this scenario.

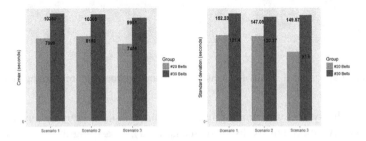

Fig. 5. Experimental results for different batch sizes (20 and 30 batch sizes).

The analysis of the results shows a considerably higher service utilization rate for the batch of 30 BELT, when compared to the batch of 20 BELT, which means that the service reconfiguration considering a proper triggering mechanism represents a wiser and maximized utilization of the services. The makespan value is more dependent on the dimension of the production batch than the standard deviation parameter, being possible to see improvement in the Cmax value for bigger production batch sizes.

5 Conclusions and Future Work

The dynamic service reconfiguration process is, nowadays, a hot topic in manufacturing systems, aligned with the cyber-physical systems context, and particularly with the Industry 4.0 initiative. A literature review on this field shows that the service reconfiguration is usually performed in a manual, offline and centralized manner, and traditionally considers the service integration such as CPS, without mention the truly service reconfiguration.

The proposed approach described in this paper considers the challenge of performing a dynamic, online and decentralized service reconfiguration, where intelligent software agents apply different strategies to identify opportunities to reconfigure proactively. These agents, after identifying opportunities to reconfigure their catalog of services, execute adequate algorithms to determine the alternative possibilities to evolve, and decide for the most promising one. This approach addresses two different situations: a non-cooperative or competitive environment, where the reconfiguration is decided and executed individually by each one of the distributed agents, and a collaborative environment, where the reconfiguration is triggered individually by the distributed agents, but it is only executed if is seen as beneficial for the whole system. A decentralized collaborative mechanism was designed to allow addressing this second situation, avoiding reaching non-feasible configurations and also promoting the balance of the resources utilization.

The proposed service reconfiguration solution was implemented in JADE and tested in a flexible manufacturing system use case. Both in competitive and collaborative scenarios, our service reconfiguration approach has been proven to display better performance than the normal operation, materialized in lower "makespan" (Cmax) values and also the better distribution of the resources utilization. The increase of the batch size also positively affects the use of the proposed service reconfiguration approach. Thanks to the multiagent-based system, the proposed on-the-fly service reconfiguration can be implemented dynamically, automatically and proactively to improve the service profitability, contributing for the beneficial of the individual entities as well as to the entire system (in the case of the collaborative environment).

Future work will be devoted to developing a completely decentralized collaborative mechanism to regulate the service reconfiguration and to develop rules to control the system nervousness avoiding falling into a chaotic situation. This approach, although introducing a higher complexity effort, permits to evolve smoothly easily respond to future disturbances.

References

1. Koren, Y., et al.: Reconfigurable manufacturing systems. CIRP Ann. - Manuf. Technol. **48**(2), 527–540 (1999)
2. Lee, J., Ni, J., Djurdjanovic, D., Qiu, H., Liao, H.: Intelligent prognostics tools and e-maintenance. Comput. Ind. **57**(6), 476–489 (2006)
3. Zeginis, C., Plexousakis, D.: Web service adaptation: state of the art and research challenges. Technical report no. 410. University of Greece, Institute of Computer Science FORTH- ICS (2010)
4. Rodrigues, N., Leitão, P., Oliveira, E.: Dynamic service reconfiguration with multi-agent systems. In: Borangiu, T., Trentesaux, D., Thomas, A., Leitão, P., Oliveira, J. (eds.) Service Orientation in Holonic and Multi-Agent Manufacturing. SCI, vol. 694, pp. 307–318. Springer, Cham (2017). doi:10.1007/978-3-319-51100-9_27
5. Erl, T.: Service-Oriented Architecture: Concepts, Technology, and Design. Prentice Hall/Pearson PTR, Upper Saddle River (2005)
6. Ashby, W.R.: Principles of the self-organizing dynamic system. J. Gen. Psychol. **37**, 125–128 (1947)
7. del Val, E., Rebollo, M., Botti, V.: Combination of self-organization mechanisms to enhance service discovery in open systems. Inf. Sci. **279**, 138–162 (2014)

8. Rodrigues, N., Leitão, P., Oliveira, E.: Dynamic composition of service oriented multi-agent system in self-organized environments. In: Intelligent Agents and Technologies for Socially Interconnected Systems (IAT4SIS 2014), Prague, Czech Republic, pp. 1–6 (2014)

9. Bar-Yam, Y.: Dynamics of Complex Systems. Perseus Books, Cambridge (1997)

10. Maximilien, E.M., Singh, M.P.: A framework and ontology for dynamic web services selection. IEEE Internet Comput. **8**(5), 84–93 (2004)

11. Rodrigues, N., Leitão, P., Oliveira, E.: Triggering strategies for automatic and online service reconfiguration. In: Proceedings of the 11th Iberian Conference on Information Systems and Technologies (CISTI 2016), Gran Canaria, Spain, pp. 76–82 (2016)

12. Cannata, A., Gerosa, M., Taisch, M.: SOCRADES: a framework for developing intelligent systems in manufacturing. In: Proceedings of the IEEE International Conference on Industrial Engineering and Engineering Management (IEEM 2008), pp. 1904–1908 (2008)

13. Shen, W., Li, Y., Hao, Q., Wang, S., Ghenniwa, H.: Implementing collaborative manufacturing with intelligent Web services. In: Proceedings of the Fifth International Conference on Computer and Information Technology (CIT 2005), pp. 1063–1069 (2005)

14. Mendes, J.M., Leitão, P., Restivo, F., Colombo, A.W.: Service-oriented agents for collaborative industrial automation and production systems. In: Mařík, V., Strasser, T., Zoitl, A. (eds.) HoloMAS 2009. LNCS, vol. 5696, pp. 13–24. Springer, Heidelberg (2009). doi:10.1007/978-3-642-03668-2_2

15. Marcos-Jorquera, D., Macia-Perez, F., Gilart-Iglesias, V., Gil-Martinez-Abarca, A.: Service model for the management of industrial environments. Dynamic reconfiguration of production elements. In: Proceedings of the 5th IEEE International Conference on Industrial Informatics (INDIN 2007), pp. 249–254 (2007)

16. Chandola, V., Banerjee, A., Kumar, V.: Anomaly detection: a survey. ACM Comput. Surv. **41**(15), 1–58 (2009)

17. Watkins, C., Dayan, P.: Q-learning. Mach. Learn. **8**(3–4), 279–292 (1992)

18. Neves, P.: Reconfiguration methodology to improve the agility and sustainability of plug and produce systems. Ph.D. dissertation (2016)

19. Chafle, G.B., Chandra, S., Mann, V., Nanda, M.G.: Decentralized orchestration of composite web services. Proceedings of the 13th International World Wide Web Conference on Alternate Track Papers and Posters, pp. 134–143 (2004)

20. Trentesaux, D., Pach, C., Bekrar, A., Sallez, Y., Berger, T., Bonte, T., Leitão, P., Barbosa, J.: Benchmarking flexible job-shop scheduling and control systems. Control Eng. Pract. **21**(9), 1204–1225 (2013)

21. Bellifemine, F., Caire, G., Greenwood, D.: Developing Multi-agent Systems with JADE. Wiley, Hoboken (2007)

22. R Core Team: R: a language and environment for statistical computing. R Foundation for Statistical Computing, Vienna (2015)

Energy Systems

An Integrated Research Infrastructure for Validating Cyber-Physical Energy Systems

T.I. Strasser[1]([⊠])([iD]), C. Moyo[1], R. Bründlinger[1], S. Lehnhoff[2], M. Blank[2],
P. Palensky[3], A.A. van der Meer[3], K. Heussen[4], O. Gehrke[4], J.E. Rodriguez[5],
J. Merino[5], C. Sandroni[6], M. Verga[6], M. Calin[7], A. Khavari[7], M. Sosnina[7],
E. de Jong[8], S. Rohjans[9], A. Kulmala[10], K. Mäki[10], R. Brandl[11], F. Coffele[12],
G.M. Burt[12], P. Kotsampopoulos[13], and N. Hatziargyriou[13]

[1] AIT Austrian Institute of Technology, Vienna, Austria
thomas.strasser@ait.ac.at
[2] OFFIS e.V., Oldenburg, Germany
[3] Delft University of Technology, Delft, The Netherlands
[4] Technical University of Denmark, Lyngby, Denmark
[5] TECNALIA Research & Innovation, Derio, Spain
[6] Ricerca Sul Sistema Energetico, Milano, Italy
[7] European Distributed Energy Resources Laboratories (DERlab) e.V.,
Kassel, Germany
[8] DNV GL, Arnhem, The Netherlands
[9] HAW Hamburg University of Applied Sciences, Hamburg, Germany
[10] VTT Technical Research Centre of Finland, Espoo, Finland
[11] Fraunhofer Institute of Wind Energy and Energy System Technology,
Kassel, Germany
[12] University of Strathclyde, Glasgow, UK
[13] National Technical University of Athens, Athens, Greece

Abstract. Renewables are key enablers in the plight to reduce greenhouse gas emissions and cope with anthropogenic global warming. The intermittent nature and limited storage capabilities of renewables culminate in new challenges that power system operators have to deal with in order to regulate power quality and ensure security of supply. At the same time, the increased availability of advanced automation and communication technologies provides new opportunities for the derivation of intelligent solutions to tackle the challenges. Previous work has shown various new methods of operating highly interconnected power grids, and their corresponding components, in a more effective way. As a consequence of these developments, the traditional power system is being transformed into a cyber-physical energy system, a smart grid. Previous and ongoing research have tended to mainly focus on how specific aspects of smart grids can be validated, but until there exists no integrated approach for the analysis and evaluation of complex cyber-physical systems configurations. This paper introduces integrated research infrastructure that provides methods and tools for validating smart grid systems in a holistic, cyber-physical manner. The corresponding concepts are currently being developed further in the European project ERIGrid.

© Springer International Publishing AG 2017
V. Mařík et al. (Eds.): HoloMAS 2017, LNAI 10444, pp. 157–170, 2017.
DOI: 10.1007/978-3-319-64635-0_12

Keywords: Cyber-physical energy systems · Research infrastructure · Smart grids · Testing · Validation

1   Introduction

Future power systems have to integrate a higher amount of distributed, renewable energy resources in order to cope with a growing electricity demand, while at the same time trying to reduce the emission of greenhouse gases [8]. In addition, power system operators are nowadays confronted with further challenges due to the highly dynamic and stochastic behaviour of renewable generators (solar, wind, small hydro, etc.) and the need to integrate controllable loads (electric vehicles, smart buildings, energy storage systems, etc.). Furthermore, due to ongoing changes to framework conditions and regulatory rules, technology developments (development of new grid components and services) and the liberalization of energy markets, the resulting design and operation of the future electric energy system has to be altered.

Sophisticated (systems and component) design approaches, intelligent information and communication architectures, and distributed automation concepts provide ways to cope with the above mentioned challenges and to turn the existing power system into an intelligent entity, that is, a "Cyber-Physical Energy System (CPES)" (also known as "Smart Grid") [5,13,24].

While reaping the benefits that come along with intelligent solutions, it is, however, expected that due to the considerably higher complexity of such solutions, validation and testing will play a significantly larger role in the development of future technology. As it stands, the first demonstration projects for smart grid technologies have been successfully completed, it follows that there is a high probability of key findings and achieved results being integrated in new and existing products, solutions and services of manufacturers and system integrators. Up until now, the proper validation and testing methods and suitably corresponding integrated Research Infrastructure (RI) for smart grids is neither fully available nor easily accessible [25].

The aim of this paper is to introduce an approach for integrated RI with corresponding CPES-based system-level validation methods that are being currently implemented in the framework of the European project ERIGrid [1].

The remaining parts of the paper are organized as follows: Sect. 2 provides a brief overview of CPES challenges whereas in Sect. 3 the corresponding research needs are outlined. The concept of the ERIGrid integrated RI is introduced in the following Sect. 4. The paper concludes with a discussion about and an outlook on future developments.

2   Higher Complexity in Cyber-Physical Energy Systems

Smart grid systems usually lead to an increased level of complexity within system operation and management as briefly outlined in the introduction. There is an urgent need for the system flexibility to also be increased, in order to avoid dramatic consequences. It also follows that advanced Information and Communication Technology (ICT), distributed automation approaches and power electronic-based grid components are necessary in order to allow a number of important system functionalities (e.g., power/energy management, demand side management, ancillary services) [5,13]. As a consequence of these developments (distributed) intelligence is needed on four different levels in smart grid systems as outlined in Table 1 [23,25].

Table 1. CPES – intelligence on different levels

Level	Implemented intelligence
System	System-wide approaches like power utility automation, coordinated voltage control, demand-side management, energy management, etc. are usually executed in a coordinated way on this level, but also factoring in services of the underlying sub-systems and components. Central or distributed control approaches can be are applied
Sub-system	On this layer the control of the underlying sub-systems or components is carried out. Usually the corresponding functions, services, and algorithms have to deal with a limited amount of components (renewable sources, energy storage system, electric vehicle supply equipment, etc.). Micro-grid control or building energy management are representative examples for this layer. Distributed automation architectures are commonly used
Component	Nowadays, new components like Distributed Energy Resources (DER), energy storages, electric vehicle supply equipment, or tap-changing transformers providing ancillary services are installed on this layer. Intelligence on this level is either used for local optimization purposes (component behaviour) or for the optimisation of systems/sub-systems on higher levels in a coordinated manner
Sub-component	On this level intelligence is mainly used to improve local component behaviour (harmonics, flicker, etc.). Power electronics and the necessary corresponding advanced control algorithms are the main drivers for local intelligence. Component controllers can be considered as examples for sub-components

The top requirements for the realisation of advanced ICT/automation systems and component controllers include flexibility, adaptability, scalability, and autonomy. Open interfaces that support interoperability are also necessary in enabling the above described behaviour [23–25]. As a consequence, the electric power system is moving towards a complex cyber-physical system of systems. Not only the design and implementation, but also the validation and deployment of these systems is associated with increasing both the engineering complexity and total life-cycle costs.

In order to address challenges in CPES, such as network limitations, CPES modeling and computational prediction of system uncertainty [18], multidisciplinary teams that understand the different aspects of CPES and from all layers are needed. CPES research requires control system engineers, engineers familiar with the physical process being controlled (electric generation, electric distribution), communication engineers, and security engineers [19]. The team needs to be assembled based on the particular use case (e.g., modeling/simulation [9,15,20], security [16,21], smart houses/buildings [17,27]).

3   Open Issues and Future Research Needs

To facilitate in the understanding of future CPES validation needs, an illustrative example will be introduced. Figure 1 shows a coordinated voltage control application in an active power distribution grid. Reactive and active power control provided by DER and electric storage units, together with an On-Load Tap Changing (OLTC) transformer, are used to keep the voltage in the grid in defined boundaries [22]. The control application has to calculate the optimal position of the OLTC and to derive set-points for reactive and active power which is communicated over a communication network to the DER and storage devices.

In order to guarantee the safe and secure operation of this CPES application various tests need to be carried out before installing it in the field. This includes the validation of the different components (including local control approaches and communication interfaces for the DER, storage, and OLTC devices) on the sub-component and component levels. Nevertheless, the integration of all components and sub-systems is also still one of the most important issues. The proper functionality of all components is not a guarantee that the whole system will behave as expected. A system-level validation of the actual behaviour is necessary in order to prove that the whole CPES application, together with the ICT devices, works properly.

Up to now, there is no integrated approach for analysing and evaluating smart grid configurations addressing power system, as well as information, communication and automation/control topics that is available [25]. The integration of cyber-security and privacy issues is also not sufficiently addressed by existing solutions. In order to guarantee a sustainable and secure supply of electricity in a smart grid system, with considerably higher complexity and also support the expected forthcoming large-scale roll out of new technologies, a proper integrated RI for smart grid systems is necessary [25]. Such an infrastructure has to support system analysis, evaluation and testing issues. Furthermore, it would foster future innovations and technical developments in the field.

In summary, the following open issues have been identified and need to be addressed in future research and development [3,6,7,12,25]:

– A cyber-physical, multi-domain approach for analysing and validating CPES on the system level is missing today; existing methods are mainly focusing on the component level - system integration topics including analysis and evaluation are not yet addressed in a holistic manner.

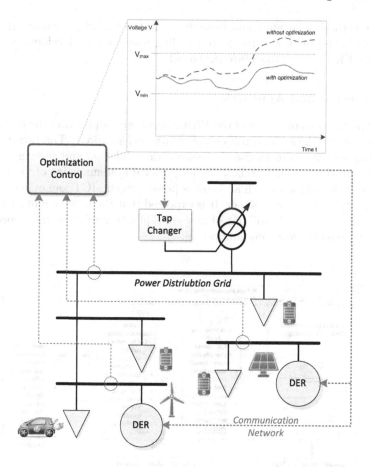

Fig. 1. CPES example – voltage control in an active power distribution grid

- A holistic validation framework (incl. analysis and evaluation/benchmark criteria) and the corresponding RI with proper methods and tools needs to be developed.
- Harmonized and standardized evaluation procedures need to be developed.
- Well-educated professionals, engineers and researchers that understand smart grid systems in a cyber-physical manner need to be trained on a broad scale.

4   ERIGrid Smart Grid Research Infrastructure

In order to tackle the above aforementioned research needs, a Pan-European RI is currently being realized in the European ERIGrid project that will support the technology development as well as the roll-out of smart grid solutions. It provides a holistic, CPES-based approach by integrating European research centres and institutions with outstanding lab infrastructure to jointly develop common methods, concepts, and procedures. In the following sections, the main idea behind everything and the corresponding research and development activities of the ERIGrid approach are explained.

4.1 Overview and Approach

Figure 2 provides an overview of the ERIGrid concept supporting the technology development, validation and roll out of smart grid solutions. The target of this integrating activity is to realise the systematic validation and testing of smart grid configurations from a holistic, cyber-physical systems point of view. It follows a multi-domain approach and covers power system, ICT and cyber-security topics in a cyber-physical manner. It is expected that the provision of support to the upcoming large-scale roll out of new concepts, technologies and approaches will also be possible fostering innovation.

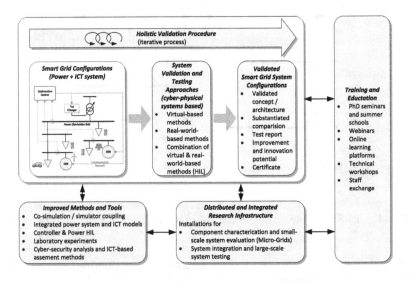

Fig. 2. Overview of the ERIGrid approach

The main research activities are related to the development of a formalized, holistic validation procedure, simulation and laboratory-based testing methods, and the provision of an integrated RI. Additionally, training and education concepts are also being developed.

4.2 Research and Development Directions

(a) Holistic Validation Procedure
Validating smart grid technologies and developments is a task that requires a holistic treatment of the overall process since the entire domain spectrum of

CPES solutions has to be considered. This consideration has to be carried out alongside the technical components such as the grid infrastructure, storage, generation, consumption, etc. it also comprises customers, markets, ICT, regulation, governance, and metrology to name a few of them. It is clear that the full development process has to be covered. This includes design, analysis, testing, verification (even certification), as well as deployment. Furthermore, the whole range of aspects that are of interest and relevant to a stable, safe and efficient smart grid solutions have to be regarded. Thus, small-signal stability together with large-scale scenarios, short-term impacts and long-term sustainability, economic feasibility/profitability, and cyber-security have to be analysed. In fact, since all these topics are dependent upon each other, they have to be analysed in an integrated way. Finally, a holistic approach demands integrating all prospective R&D sites and stakeholders, e.g. hardware/software simulation labs as well as academic and industrial research [25].

Comparable processes have been successfully implemented in other application domains like automotive, consumer electronics, mechanical/chemical engineering (albeit on an arguably less complex level) [11,14]. In order to realize a sustainable and cost effective holistic procedure in smart Grid system validation, two major challenges have to be addressed: *(i)* formalized scenario design and *(ii)* model exchange. These will ensure guaranteed comparability between experiments of different setups and designs. They will also facilitate subsequent re-utilization of experimental results from different stakeholders, as the basis for continuative experiments. Utilising the two aforementioned capabilities, use cases can then be defined with respect to the actual system requirements and with the best setup available. The huge amount of possible scenarios and experiments has to be narrowed down to a valid set of experiments in such a way that yields statistical aspects and reproducible results. Quantifying both the errors and significance of these experiments is of high importance. A consistent methodology for model exchange facilitates coordinated smart grid experiments (of representative scope and scale) within ERIGrid and beyond. It also aids the comparability between experiments, and furthermore to conduct consecutive, continuative, and parallel experiments for the re-utilization and subsequent use of results. In Fig. 3, the holistic validation process is outlined [25].

In detail, the process is divided into the following seven steps [10]:

1. *Scenario Description*: It is important to decide on the system boundaries for each smart grid scenario. It imperative to define which parts of the overall system are being considered and to what level of detail. Thus, the use cases will be derived accordingly. The specific systems configuration will be described within each testcase.

2. *Research Infrastructure Capabilities Profiling*: In order to take advantage of the best suitable infrastructure setup for each use case, all ERIGrid installation (hardware and simulation-based labs) will be profiled. The capabilities of each lab installation will be analysed, documented and published. This will facilitates optimal use of capabilities provided by the existing hardware and software.

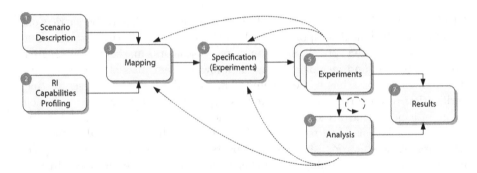

Fig. 3. Different steps for carrying out a holistic validation of CPES

3. *Mapping*: Optimal mapping will be carried out based on both the scenario descriptions and partner profiles. The partner profiles will be analysed, with the goal of identifying which ERIGrid partner(s) is(are) best suitable for realizing each part of the defined use cases and especially the validation of the appropriate test cases. Particular attention will be paid to the interfaces between the various hardware and software components, while still ensuring that the mapping follows a cyber-physical systems approach.

4. *Specification of Experiments:* After the determination of the best partner(s) setup (who), for the test cases (what), the concrete experiments will then be specified (how). In order to realize a use case the interfaces between the necessary hardware/software will be implemented based on the requirements imposed on the corresponding test cases. In addition, the available tool support will be analysed and taken into account. During this step missing models are expected to come to light, triggering the initialisation of their development.

5. *Conducting Experiments:* After the experiments are specified they will be conducted following a consortium-wide specification. Here, it is highly important to identify the right amount and variations of experiments. This step is closely related to the next step addressing analysis tasks.

6. *Analysis:* The step is interrelated to the previous step. Each experiment will be analysed and afterwards iteratively refined in order to meet the test case requirements. This cyclic process allows for the development of high quality experiments. Experimental results may be used to generate surrogate models of certain phenomena/aspects, that can be efficiently computated, and may (if necessary in a virtual manner) be "plugged into" other partners setups.

7. *Test Results:* In the last step the final reports will be compiled as summaries and analysis of the experiments. Certificates will be given to components such as controllers that have been tested successfully against requirements that were defined in reference scenarios and systems. Based on experimental finding, improvement potentials as well as further innovation-related activities will be identified.

(b) Improved Methods and Tools

The current development in the smart grid field shows that future systems will contain a heterogeneous agglomeration of active power electronics and passive network components coupled via physical processes and dedicated communication connections to automation systems (SCADA, DMS) [25]. In order to analyse and evaluate such a multi-domain configurations, a set of corresponding methods and tools is necessary. In the context of smart grids the following possibilities exist [25]:

- Pure virtual-based methods and tools (mainly simulation-based),
- Real-world-based methods (laboratory and demonstration-based), or
- A combination of both (hardware-in-the-loop based).

Figure 4 provides an overview of the methods and tools which will be applied in ERIGrid. The goal is to use all three above mentioned possibilities in order to cover the whole range of opportunities in a cyber-physical manner that is essential for addressing system integration and validation questions. Usually, pure virtual-based methods are not always sufficient for validating CPES since the availability of proper and accurate simulation models cannot always be guaranteed (e.g., inverter-based components are sometimes very complex to model or it takes too long to get a proper model). Also laboratory-based testing approaches and a combination of both (hardware-in-the-loop based) have to be applied.

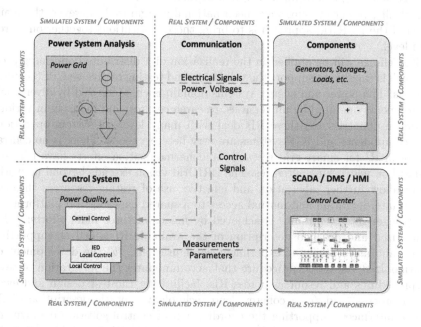

Fig. 4. Improved methods and tools for smart grid validation – possibility to combine virtual (simulated) and real components [25]

ERIGrid follows an approach where the following methods, models and corresponding tools are being improved for component characterization, system integration and validation:

- Co-simulation (simulator couplings covering the power system, components, communication, control system and SCADA),
- Integrated power system and ICT models,
- Controller & Power Hardware-in-the-Loop (HIL),
- Laboratory experiments, and
- Cyber-security analysis and ICT-based assessment methods.

It is usually not possible to test the whole power system infrastructure in a lab environment and also pure simulation-based methods are sometimes not precise enough. A very important issue in ERIGrid approach is that parts of the smart grid system can be available as a physical component (in a laboratory environment), as a simulation model or even as a combination of both.

Further research is necessary in order to combine all three validation approaches in a flexible manner (based on the testing needs of a specific CPES application). In the ERIGrid context this includes the coupling of software tools and simulators, the model exchange between them as well as the provision of necessary component models. The coupling of simulation systems with laboratory equipment is also in focus so as to facilitate the above outlined flexible interaction between hardware and software components (see Fig. 4).

(c) Distributed and Integrated Research Infrastructure
Historically, power systems have been nationally organized, however, the main vision of the ERIGrid approach is to bring those institutions together on European level.

Key efforts will be applied in the realization of a distributed and integrated RI which is capable to support the validation and testing of diverse CPES configurations. The power and energy systems domain is characterized by diverse lab environments operated by universities, research centres, and industry in various European countries. As these RIs deal with many levels of system operation, their components and ICT systems are very heterogeneous. There is no central European RI for smart grid research, and harmonization efforts have till now focussed on networking activities. The ERIGrid vision extends beyond networking to allow further integration and effective use of testing resources through human interoperation and mutual access to a shared experimental platform.

Stronger interoperability is achieved by means of three main efforts: *(a)* a harmonized and detailed description of the available RI aimed at supporting the collaborative design of experiment configurations, *(b)* the development of a harmonized validation procedure that accommodates the integration of testing procedures and resources across RIs, facilitating the test design and evaluation process, and *(c)* a coherent and technology-agnostic description of RI control interfaces, supporting the coordination of control software deployment across RIs. The harmonized RI description *(a)* will soon be available as a publicly accessible database whereas the harmonized validation procedure *(b)* is still under development, but has been outlined in [10].

The coherent RI control interface description *(c)* resulted in a taxonomy as illustrated in Fig. 5. The five control levels are marked C1 ... C5. Local controllers have been assigned the levels D1 ... D5, corresponding to their associated control levels, while external controllers are denoted X1 ... X5. Communication between the local controllers, i.e. communication links which are considered to be part of the laboratory infrastructure, are enumerated L1 ... L4, while those communication links which enable the interaction between the laboratory and external controllers, have been assigned the identifiers E1 ... E12. This taxonomy establishes a combination of structural and functional criteria that can be applied across smart grid laboratories to map the local architecture into a common framework, much like the Smart Grid Architecture Model (SGAM) plane serves that purpose for smart grid standardisation [26].

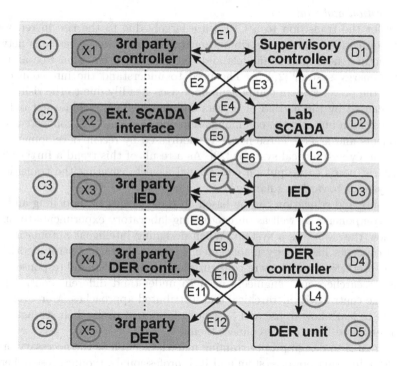

Fig. 5. Harmonized control interfaces

This model outlines a number of possible interactions for external control software deployment, six of which are of particular interest for CPES scenarios:

1. Communication interfaces provided by a lab-internal DER controller, allowing an external Intelligent Electronic Device (IED) to control the DER (E11).
2. Communication interfaces provided by a lab-internal IED, allowing an external IED to influence the behaviour of the internal IED (E7).

3. Communication interfaces provided by a lab-internal IED, allowing the IED to be remotely operated through an external SCADA system (E6).
4. Communication interfaces provided by a lab-internal SCADA system, allowing an external SCADA system to receive and/or send data to laboratory devices through the internal SCADA system (E4).
5. Communication interfaces provided by a lab-internal SCADA system to an external controller (E3).
6. Communication interfaces provided by a lab-internal supervisory controller to an external controller (E1), for example to allow the external controller to influence the control behaviour of the supervisory controller.

Other interactions are possible, however they are considered to be of less interest for the ERIGrid case.

(d) Education and Training

Drivers for the transition to a CPES are largely due to the rise in renewable energy sources, e-mobility, distributed energy storages, more resilient network infrastructure, new market models and the goal of an emission free and sustainable energy system [2,4,5]. The need to understand the interconnections between the power system components increases steadily due to the rising complexity caused by the myriad of players and actors. This includes not only the physical system but also the communication and the control of connected power components and assets. These needs are addressed by recent developments and research in cyber-physical systems [23]. As a result of this trend a further focus in ERIGrid needs to be put on educational aspects covering the transition in power systems towards a smart grid.

Training and education can be based on the concepts of modelling and simulating components as well as on conducting laboratory experiments to understand how they work as a system. When designing intelligent automation and control concepts like energy management systems, voltage control algorithms, dynamic protection, topology re-configuration as well as demand response mechanisms, researchers and engineers need to understand different control paradigms, like centralized, hierarchical and distributed approaches. Moreover, they also have to learn how to use and be aware of different tools; their strengths and weaknesses, and how to interconnect them.

The goal is to design proper training material as well as the necessary procedures for educating power system and ICT professionals, (young) researchers as well as students in the domain of smart grid system integration and validation.

5   Conclusions and Outlook

A large-scale roll out of smart grid solutions and corresponding technologies and products is expected in the upcoming years. The validation of such complex CPES needs attention since available testing approaches and methods are mainly focusing on power system and ICT components. An integrated, cyber-physical systems based, multi-domain approach for a holistic testing of smart grid solutions is currently still missing.

Four main research priorities have been identified and prioritized in context of the European project ERIGrid in order to overcome the shortcomings in the validation of today's smart grid systems. The focus of the future research lies in the development of a holistic validation procedures and corresponding formalized test case descriptions as well as the improvement of simulation-based methods, hardware-in-the-loop approaches, and lab-based testing (incl. a flexible combination of them). In addition, the integration and harmonization of nationally organized labs into a distributed and integrated RI is a further priority. Last but not least, the education and training of researchers and power system professionals on these extended and harmonized testing possibilities is another field of action.

Acknowledgments. This work is supported by the European Communitys Horizon 2020 Program (H2020/2014-2020) under project "ERIGrid" (Grant Agreement No. 654113).

References

1. European Research Infrastructure supporting Smart Grid Systems Technology Development, Validation and Roll Out (ERIGrid). https://www.erigrid.eu. Accessed 07 Apr 2017
2. Strategic Research Agenda for Europes Electricity Networks of the Future. European Commission (EC) - Directorate-General for Research (2007)
3. 10 Steps to Smart Grids - EURELECTRIC DSOs Ten-Year Roadmap for Smart Grid Deployment in the EU. Eurelectric (2011)
4. Smart Grid Mandate - Standardization Mandate to European Standardisation Organisations (ESOs) to support European Smart Grid deployment. European Commission (EC) (2011)
5. Technology Roadmap: Smart Grids. International Energy Agency (IEA) (2011)
6. International Smart Grid Action Network (ISGAN) Annex 5: Smart Grid International Research Facility Network (SIRFN). International Energy Agency (IEA) (2013)
7. SmartGrids SRA 2035 Strategic Research Agenda, Update of the Smart Grids SRA 2007 for the needs by the year 2035. European Technology Platform Smart Grids (2013)
8. Climate Change 2014: Mitigation of Climate Change. IPCC Working Group III Contribution to AR5 (2014)
9. Al Faruque, M.A., Ahourai, F.: A model-based design of cyber-physical energy systems. In: 19th Asia and South Pacific Design Automation Conference (ASP-DAC), pp. 97–104 (2014)
10. Blank, M., Lehnhoff, S., Heussen, K., Bondy, D.M., Moyo, C., Strasser, T.: Towards a foundation for holistic power system validation and testing. In: 2016 IEEE 21st International Conference on Emerging Technologies and Factory Automation (ETFA), pp. 1–4 (2016)
11. Bringmann, E., Krmer, A.: Model-based testing of automotive systems. In: 2008 1st International Conference on Software Testing, Verification, and Validation, pp. 485–493 (2008)

12. Brunner, H., Bründlinger, R., Calin, M., Heckmann, W., Bindner, H., Verga, M.: Proposal for a coordinated investment planning of the future European smart grid research infrastructure. ELECTRA IRP, Deliverable D2.2 (2016)
13. Farhangi, H.: The path of the smart grid. IEEE Power Energ. Mag. 8(1), 18–28 (2010)
14. Fouchal, H., Wilhelm, G., Bourdy, E., Wilhelm, G., Ayaida, M.: A testing framework for intelligent transport systems. In: 2016 IEEE Symposium on Computers and Communication (ISCC), pp. 180–184 (2016)
15. Ilic, M.D., Xie, L., Khan, U.A.: Modeling future cyber-physical energy systems. In: Power and Energy Society General Meeting-Conversion and Delivery of Electrical Energy in the 21st Century (2008)
16. Khan, U.A., Stakovic, A.M.: Security in cyber-physical energy systems. In: Workshop on Modeling and Simulation of Cyber-Physical Energy Systems (MSCPES) (2013)
17. Kleissl, J., Agarwal, Y.: Cyber-physical energy systems: focus on smart buildings. In: 47th Design Automation Conference, pp. 749–754 (2010)
18. Macana, C.A., Quijano, N., Mojica-Nava, E.: A survey on cyber physical energy systems and their applications on smart grids. In: IEEE PES Conference on Innovative Smart Grid Technologies (ISGT Latin America) (2011)
19. Morris, T.H., Srivastava, A.K., Reaves, B., Pavurapu, K., Abdelwahed, S., Vaughn, R., McGrew, W., Dandass, Y.: Engineering future cyber-physical energy systems: challenges, research needs, and roadmap. In: North American Power Symposium (NAPS) (2009)
20. Palensky, P., Widl, E., Elsheikh, A.: Simulating cyber-physical energy systems: challenges, tools and methods. IEEE Trans. Syst. Man Cybern.: Syst. 44(3), 318–326 (2014)
21. Sridhar, S., Hahn, A., Govindarasu, M.: Cyber-physical system security for the electric power grid. Proc. IEEE 100(1), 210–224 (2012)
22. Stifter, M., Bletterie, B., Brunner, H., Burnier, D., Sawsan, H., Andrén, F., Schwalbe, R., Abart, A., Nenning, R., Herb, F., Pointner, R.: DG DemoNet validation: voltage control from simulation to field test. In: 2011 2nd IEEE PES International Conference and Exhibition on Innovative Smart Grid Technologies (ISGT Europe), pp. 1–8, December 2011
23. Strasser, T., Andrén, F., Kathan, J., Cecati, C., Buccella, C., Siano, P., Leitao, P., Zhabelova, G., Vyatkin, V., Vrba, P., Marik, V.: A review of architectures and concepts for intelligence in future electric energy systems. IEEE Trans. Industr. Electron. 62(4), 2424–2438 (2015)
24. Strasser, T., Andrén, F., Merdan, M., Prostejovsky, A.: Review of trends and challenges in smart grids: an automation point of view. In: Mařík, V., Lastra, J.L.M., Skobelev, P. (eds.) HoloMAS 2013. LNCS, vol. 8062, pp. 1–12. Springer, Heidelberg (2013). doi:10.1007/978-3-642-40090-2_1
25. Strasser, T., Pröstl Andrén, F., Lauss, G., et al.: Towards holistic power distribution system validation and testing–an overview and discussion of different possibilities. e & i Elektrotechnik und Informationstechnik 134(1), 71–77 (2017)
26. Uslar, M., Specht, M., Dänekas, C., Trefke, J., Rohjans, S., González, J.M., Rosinger, C., Bleiker, R.: Standardization in Smart Grids: Introduction to IT-related Methodologies, Architectures and Standards. Springer, Heidelberg (2012). doi:10.1007/978-3-642-34916-4
27. Wu, W., Aziz, M.K., Huang, H., Yu, H., Gooi, H.B.: A real-time cyber-physical energy management system for smart houses. In: IEEE PES Innovative Smart Grid Technologies Asia (ISGT) (2011)

Simulation-Based Validation of Smart Grids – Status Quo and Future Research Trends

C. Steinbrink[1], S. Lehnhoff[1], S. Rohjans[2], T.I. Strasser[3(✉)] ⓘ, E. Widl[3],
C. Moyo[3], G. Lauss[3], F. Lehfuss[3], M. Faschang[3], P. Palensky[4],
A.A. van der Meer[4], K. Heussen[5], O. Gehrke[5], E. Guillo-Sansano[6],
M.H. Syed[6], A. Emhemed[6], R. Brandl[7], V.H. Nguyen[8], A. Khavari[9],
Q.T. Tran[10], P. Kotsampopoulos[11], N. Hatziargyriou[11], N. Akroud[12],
E. Rikos[13], and M.Z. Degefa[14]

[1] OFFIS e.V., Oldenburg, Germany
cornelius.steinbrink@offis.de
[2] HAW Hamburg University of Applied Sciences, Hamburg, Germany
[3] AIT Austrian Institute of Technology, Vienna, Austria
thomas.strasser@ait.ac.at
[4] Delft University of Technology, Delft, The Netherlands
[5] Technical University of Denmark, Lyngby, Denmark
[6] University of Strathclyde, Glasgow, UK
[7] Fraunhofer Institute of Wind Energy and Energy System Technology,
Kassel, Germany
[8] G2Elab, University Grenoble Alpes, Grenoble, France
[9] European Distributed Energy Resources Laboratories (DERlab) e.V.,
Kassel, Germany
[10] Commissariat à l'énergie atomique et aux énergies alternatives, Chambery, France
[11] National Technical University of Athens, Athens, Greece
[12] Ormazabal Corporate Technology, Bilbao, Spain
[13] Centre for Renewable Energy Sources and Saving, Athens, Greece
[14] SINTEF Energy Resarch, Trondheim, Norway

Abstract. Smart grid systems are characterized by high complexity due to interactions between a traditional passive network and active power electronic components, coupled using communication links. Additionally, automation and information technology plays an important role in order to operate and optimize such cyber-physical energy systems with a high(er) penetration of fluctuating renewable generation and controllable loads. As a result of these developments the validation on the system level becomes much more important during the whole engineering and deployment process, today. In earlier development stages and for larger system configurations laboratory-based testing is not always an option. Due to recent developments, simulation-based approaches are now an appropriate tool to support the development, implementation, and rollout of smart grid solutions. This paper discusses the current state of simulation-based approaches and outlines the necessary future research and development directions in the domain of power and energy systems.

© Springer International Publishing AG 2017
V. Mařík et al. (Eds.): HoloMAS 2017, LNAI 10444, pp. 171–185, 2017.
DOI: 10.1007/978-3-319-64635-0_13

Keywords: Co-simulation · Cyber-physical energy systems · Hardware-in-the-loop · Modeling · Real-time simulation · Smart grids · Validation

1 Introduction

Due to the interactions between the traditional passive network and also of active power electronic components via dedicated communication networks, smart grids tend exhibit a high degree of complexity [10]. Sophisticated automation and information technology, corresponding control algorithms and data analytics methods are also of high importance for the reliable operation and optimization of such cyber-physical energy systems. This is so as to cope with a high(er) penetration of fluctuating renewable generation and controllable loads. As a result of these developments the validation on the system level, i.e., the testing of the integration and interaction of the connected components and algorithms, becomes today much more important during the whole engineering and deployment process [27,41]. In earlier development stages and for larger system configurations laboratory-based testing is not always an option. Simulation in the domain of power systems is fundamental in order to understand system behaviour under normal but also in emergency situations. It also avoids costly and time-consuming real-world laboratory testing or field trials [41]. Due to recent developments, simulation-based approaches are an important tool in the development, implementation, and roll-out of smart grid solutions [29].

This paper provides a comprehensive discussion of the current state of simulation-based validation approaches in the domain of power and energy systems and addresses smart grid validation needs. It identifies shortcomings in today's practice and outlines the necessary future research and development steps.

The rest of this paper is organized as follows: Sect. 2 briefly outlines main challenges in the validation of smart grid systems. A comprehensive overview of simulation-based smart grid development and validation approaches is given in Sect. 3.2 followed by a discussion of future research needs and directions. Section 5 concludes the paper with the key findings.

2 Validation Challenges

Traditionally, the separate domains of power system and Information and Communication Technology (ICT)/automation have been analysed individually. In the context of the smart grid advancement, and for the first time, new requirements now demand simultaneous coverage of both domains in a comprehensive system-level validation. As already pointed out in the introduction, simulation-based approaches play a vital role in enabling this [27,29].

Figure 1 shows the state-of-the-art in smart grid simulation and corresponding validation. The system complexity grows with the extension of the analysed network part. Smart grid systems will demand modelling of the interaction of different network levels but also the integrated analysis of ICT issues.

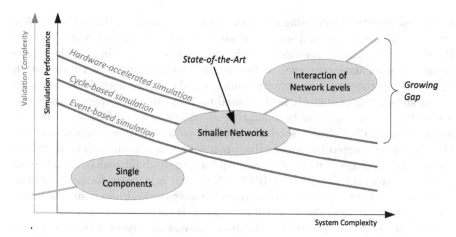

Fig. 1. Growing gap between system complexity and performance of simulations

A fast growing gap can be observed between the system complexity and the performance of known methods for system simulation (see Fig. 1). It still remains that for the hardware-accelerated simulation, a feature of real-time hardware-in-the-loop simulations, the interaction of network levels can only be analysed at very coarse granularity. Todays tools still stem from the phase where single domains were in the focus. As soon as they get coupled with tools from other domains (ICT/automation, energy markets, customer behaviour, etc.), the performance is usually considerably reduced due to the necessary data exchange and format conversion.

In the following sections an overview of different simulation approaches is provided and future research needs and directions are derived in order to overcome the above mentioned gap.

3 Simulation-Based Validation Approaches

Simulation approaches used in the power and energy domain can generally be divided into the following three areas: *(i)* multi-domain simulation, *(ii)* cooperative simulation (also known as co-simulation), and *(iii)* real-time simulation and hardware-in-the-loop. An overview of all these approaches is given below.

3.1 Multi-domain Simulation

Pure simulation tools are suitable in the early development stages for concept design and proof-of-concept validation. Purely analytical or numerical tools are suitable for concept analysis, but if there is no clear separation of the solution (e.g., an embedded control system) the simulation results cannot serve as a means of validation. The validation of embedded systems solutions will require the integration of heterogeneous simulation components as both the systems complexity and heterogeneity is increasing and specialized and validated simulation models are typically developed in a single domain. The simulation framework Ptolemy II [8] offers a rigorous solution to this integration by focusing on the determinism of simulation outcome – a feature particularly important for validation purposes. Another important multi-domain simulation has been developed with the Modelica language [9]. It is also based on first principles approaches in the declaration of models, strictly separating an object and interface-oriented approach to "modelling" from "solving", which is performed in a compilation step. Modelica is supported by both active open source development [11] as well as commercial packages. The third example for a purpose-built multi-domain simulator for smart grid algorithms is IPSYS [5,17] and it is meant for performance-assessment of hybrid power system control strategies. Multi-domain simulators are each built on generalized principles of interaction.

Despite the powerful uses in performance assessment, system-level validation is questionable, as a multi-domain simulator typically requires the candidate system to be adapted or even reformulated to comply with the respective simulator architecture.

3.2   Co-simulation

Overview and Distinction with Other Simulation Types
Co-simulation is defined as the coordinated execution of two or more models that differ in their representation as well as in their runtime environment [37]. Representation in this context means the underlying modelling paradigm. For example, models may be represented as differential equation systems, discrete automata, etc. A runtime environment is a software system that solves model equations or generally allows the model execution. The models in a co-simulation system, therefore, have been developed as well as implemented independently. A number of simulation concepts are related to co-simulation, but differ slightly in their definitions [12]. Setups with combined development and implementation of all model systems are used for "classic" simulation. If models are developed jointly but are then separated into different runtime environments, one speaks of distributed or parallel simulation. Joint implementation and execution of models with different representation is sometimes called hybrid or merged simulation. The different types of simulation are depicted in Fig. 2.

It is important to note that co-simulation implies the interaction of hardware and software components in some domains. In general, all components of a co-simulation setup may be either hardware or software. If hardware/software co-simulation is conducted for hardware testing, it is typically called "Hardware-in-the-Loop" (HIL) [16].

The major benefit of co-simulation is the separation of the modelling and simulation processes. Different researchers or even institutes may develop and implement simulation models representing different systems. Co-simulation users may then employ these models to analyse the dynamics of larger "systems of systems". In other words, co-simulation supports reuse of simulation models.

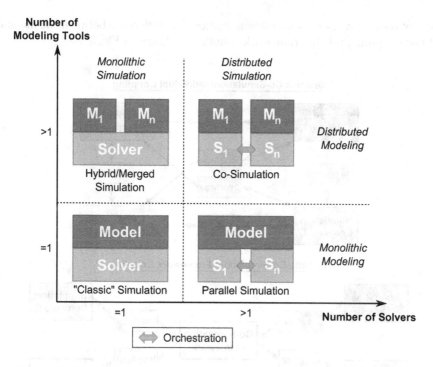

Fig. 2. Distinction between co-simulation and other simulation types [12,37]

Ideally, these models have been created by experts of the particular domain, are properly validated, and thus acknowledged.

Generic vs. Specific Co-simulation

The driving force behind co-simulation is the fact that the involved subdomains already utilise numerous established technologies and simulation tools. Independently, the interactions of each subdomain are not yet fully understood. Many co-simulation approaches feature manual coupling of a small number of tools ad-hoc. Mainly power system and communication network simulation frameworks are regarded [13,14,20,23] since they are considered the major determining factors in smart grid dynamics.

Other co-simulation projects, however, support a more generic approach with a stronger inclusion of different system components. Generic co-simulation approaches involve a middleware that is responsible for data exchange and temporal synchronization of several models. A software fulfilling these tasks is called a co-simulation framework. It typically provides a set of interfaces that may be implemented to establish a connection between the framework and a given model. A connected model can then indirectly exchange data with all other connected tools. The frameworks synchronization algorithm provides a common time frame for this exchange. Therefore, individual coupling between simulation tools is not necessary. This greatly reduces the likelihood of coupling errors and allows easy reuse of tools in various co-simulation studies. The difference between the manual ad-hoc coupling and the framework coupling is shown in Fig. 3.

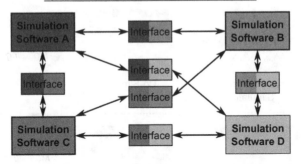

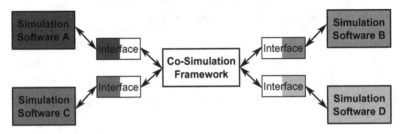

Fig. 3. Difference between specific and generic co-simulation [39]

Model Instantiation

An important concept in co-simulation is model instantiation. That means that several virtual objects are derived from the same model to simulate the behaviour of a number of similar systems. Such an object is called entity or instance. One example is that of several virtual Photovoltaic (PV) panels that are all derived from the same simulation model. The instantiation is important since each entity might receive different inputs from a spatial resolved solar irradiation model. In other words, instantiation is used in co-simulation to account for complex inputs and boundary conditions affecting relatively simple component models. Sometimes, however, the implementation of a simulation tool does not allow for multiple instantiation of it's models. These models are then called singletons.

Interfaces for Simulator Abstraction

Next to software for co-simulation orchestration and execution, interfaces for simulator abstraction are an important concept in co-simulation research. The most popular standard in this context is the Functional Mockup Interface (FMI) [6]. It has been defined in the industrially led MODELISAR project in coordination with the modelling language Modelica. Thus, FMI is supported by Modelica environments like Dymola [7] or SimulationX [26], but also by independent tools and languages like Matlab and Python. Some tool-specific co-simulation approaches employ FMI as well for interface descriptions in order to facilitate future extensibility of their setups [3]. The FMIs benefit is not just given by its formalism in model description. The standard allows users to make their models and simulation tools accessible in the form of so-called Functional Mock-up Units (FMU) that contain an FMI-based formalization as well as some form of representation of the tool in question. This representation depends on the type of FMI employed. The FMI standard is divided into two main parts: *(i)* FMI for Model Exchange and *(ii)* FMI for Co-Simulation. The essential difference is that FMUs of the former standard expect to be solved by a given master algorithm. FMUs of the latter standard, on the other hand, contain a solver so that the master algorithm is only required for the coordination of data exchange. In other words, models standardized with FMI for Co-Simulation are co-simulation-ready components while those standardized with FMI for Model Exchange are not.

All in all, it can be said that co-simulation frameworks (popular tools are Mosaik [34, 38], Ptolemy II [30], and C2WT-TE [24]) and standards are subjects to active, ongoing research. Many tools and concepts already exist with varying foci, features, and degrees of usability and popularity.

3.3   Real-Time Simulation and Hardware-in-the-Loop

A simulation where a fixed time-step of the simulator, required for achieving a solution and performing I/O activities, is equal to the actual wall-clock time is commonly referred to as a real-time simulation. For validation purposes, the real-time simulation is commonly coupled with a Hardware-under-Test (HUT), adding the complexity of the hardware to the assessment procedure [16]. This advanced testing method, HIL, allows for an extensive analysis of the HUT while under a simulated broad range of operating conditions, reducing the risk associated with performing tests on an actual network and at the same time reduces the cost and time required for performing validation of power system components and energy systems.

Depending on the characteristics of the HUT and the properties of interface between HUT and the real-time simulation, HIL can be classified as controller or power HIL (shown in Fig. 4).

- *Controller-HIL (CHIL)*, the HUT exchanges low voltage signals $(+/-10\,V)$ with the real-time simulation. The HUT in CHIL is typically a controller device, although real-time simulations coupled to other devices such as relays, PMU or monitoring components are usually classified as CHIL. This devices are validated in a closed-loop environment under different dynamic and fault conditions, therefore enhancing the validation of control and protection systems for power systems and energy components [40].
- *Power-HIL (PHIL)*, the exchanged signals between simulation and HUT are of high power and therefore a dedicated power interface for amplifying the exchanged signals and injecting or absorbing power is required for coupling high power HUT with software simulation. Different approaches can be

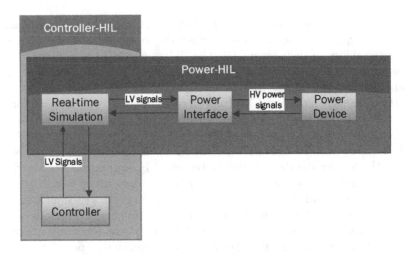

Fig. 4. Overview of the CHIL and PHIL simulation concepts

selected for exchanging the signals, known as interface algorithms, depending on the application and the compromise between stability and accuracy of the simulation [33]. The addition of the power interface introduces inaccuracies into the process as the power interface cannot achieve unity gain with infinite bandwidth and zero time delay, therefore the stability and accuracy of PHIL experiments needs to be assessed before an experiment takes place. A number of compensation methods for improving the stability and the inaccuracies are frequently used within PHIL simulations [15,42]. Hardware components without detailed simulation models are now capable of being tested through PHIL simulations.

CHIL techniques have been successfully used for testing protection relays [1], novel control algorithms for power system devices [21], PMU and other low power devices. However, sometimes the fidelity to represent the dynamics of complex power components such as power electronics converters have to be compromised due to the fixed time-step of real-time simulatons, limiting the size of the simulations and the transient performance [19]. For this purpose, PHIL simulations have been carried out for testing the integration of converter connected generation into power systems or validating novel power converter structures [18].

4   Future Research Needs and Directions

Simulation techniques are essential in the engineering and validation of smart grid system development. As outlined above, different approaches are useful for different design stages. However, there are still several open issues related to the usage of simulations in the domain of power and energy systems. In the following, the most important research needs and target directions are discussed.

4.1   Representative Models and Model Exchange

One of the main challenges the research community faces with respect to single and multi-domain simulations is the availability of representative validated models. It is crucial that the models utilized for the purpose of simulation (offline or real-time) are validated against their representative behaviour. Most domain specific simulation tools offer elementary components required in the development of complex models. These are used by the research community to develop more complex models and novel control solutions. However, the following two challenges need to be addressed:

– *Interoperability:* Such validated models made available within one simulator cannot be utilized within other simulation tools. This often requires rebuilding the same model for each of the simulation tools by the prospective user.
– *Intellectual Property (IP):* More often than not, validated models are not shared with the wider research community due to the IP issues involved. This acts as a setback to the general progress of research.

FMI provides a potential solution to both the above challenges. FMI for Model Exchange (ME), as a standard, offers a way to develop models independent of the simulation tool, where a model is converted into a C-code, compiled, supplemented with XML-schema representing the model interactions and made available for use. As most simulation tools utilize C as their lower level language, this allows for the developed models to be imported and simulated. Furthermore, it allows for models to be exported as a black-box, protecting the IP. Although FMI-ME is well accepted within the automotive industry, at this present day, many proprietary power systems simulation tools are still yet to incorporate the FMI-ME standard. Furthermore, although the models exported from simulation tool A can be run within simulation tool B (assuming simulation tool A and B support FMI-ME), it requires both simulation tool A and B to be installed on the recipient computer, limiting the capabilities of FMI-ME.

The practice of making a software open source is widely exercised within energy domains, however libraries of models are rarely open source. Open source does provide a variety of advantages that include, but are not limited to, encouraging quality and identification of prospective collaborations.

4.2   Co-simulation

In research, the following topics need to be addressed to meet current and upcoming requirements for co-simulation based validation of smart grid systems:

– *Automated Scenario Generation/Scenario Formalization:* Sets of scenarios need to be generated automatically from a relatively high-level description, if employed simulators and parameter values are known. A close-to-reality formalisation of smart grid scenarios, that can be translated into executable co-simulation scenarios (incl. validation of scenario completeness, coherence, etc.), needs to be developed.

- *Simulation Interface/Description Standard:* A semantic description of a simulator needs to be specified. A promising interface standard is already given in form of FMI, but an additional layer providing a more direct mapping to the real world would allow automated scenario validation.
- *Additional Research Domains:* More research needs to be carried out in terms of integration of communication systems, economic dynamics, social/psychological effects and dynamics, security-related issues, and environmental factors/dynamics into the co-simulation setup. The latter may even lead to a need of spatially resolved, GIS-based co-simulation.
- *Performance Optimization:* The execution of different simulators in a single experiment needs to be distributed onto several machines. Parallelization of a co-simulation execution without the requirement of a single common "data hub" in the form of a machine that runs the scheduler needs to be realized. The design of co-simulation scenarios should allow for a formal method to select simulators with a performance as high as possible and an output accuracy as high as necessary. Surrogate modelling should facilitate the automated creation of surrogate replacements of computationally expensive simulators for performance increase.
- *Data Management:* Data stream management should allow for analysis, aggregation and monitoring of co-simulation output during the simulation process. Through big data storage, efficient long-term storage of large data sets should be enabled, allowing for data mining operations.
- *Visualization:* Improved tools for easy on-line monitoring and demonstration of co-simulation scenarios should be developed. Solutions for feeding co-simulation output into a control room/SCADA setup for the sake of training, testing or development should be realized.
- *Uncertainty Quantification (UQ):* The effect of the coupling of different UQ approaches handling different simulators in a co-simulation setup should be researched. Approaches for UQ should be developed, focused on uncertainty sources related with simulator interaction (e.g. different resolutions, data transformation, instable data exchange, etc.). Moreover, useful aggregation and depiction of the output of UQ studies need to be developed.

4.3 Real-Time Simulation and Hardware-in-the-Loop

Offering a wide range of possibilities for validation and testing of smart grid systems, current HIL technology still has several limitations. In the European project ERIGrid[1], a survey was addressed at the experts in 12 top European research institutions about current limitations and mandatory future improvements of HIL technology (PHIL and CHIL). Current open issues can be classified into four categories:

- Limited capacity of HIL simulation for complex systems (computing power, complexity and synchronization) and for studies of non-linearity, high harmonics and transient phase.

---

[1] https://www.erigrid.eu.

- Limited capacity of remote HIL and geographically distributed HIL for joint experiments, mostly due to synchronization (CHIL and PHIL) and power interface stability and accuracy with respect to loop delay (PHIL).
- Difficulty in integration of HIL technology to the communication layer, particularly related to the synchronization of real-time and offline simulation, as well as continuous and discrete timelines.
- Lack of a general framework to facilitate the reusability of models, information exchange among different proprietary interfaces or among different partners of a joint HIL experiment.

Due to the aforementioned issues, HIL technology needs several aspects to be improved. Overall, the following research trends can be observed and need to be addressed:

- *Integration of Co-simulation and HIL:* It is expected that integrating HIL technology into co-simulation frameworks is an important contribution toward a holistic approach for experimenting with cyber-physical energy systems. Combining the strengths of both approaches, multi-domain experiments can be studied with realistic behaviours from hardware equipment under a variety of complex environments, co-simulated by appropriate and adapted simulators from the relevant domains. It will enable a complete consideration of the electrical grid to be interconnected with other domain. Until now, this is still limited. Most of the current work involving integration of HIL and co-simulation uses only a direct coupling with the real-time simulator [4] or a CHIL setup [36].
- *Remote and Geographically Distributed HIL:* Latency strongly influences the accuracy (HIL) and the stability (PHIL) of a HIL test. Moreover, random packet loss due to network congestion outside of LAN may alter the information and cause malfunction at the real-time simulator, including any connected hardware [31]. Up-to-now scientists have investigated the possibility of extending PHIL beyond laboratory geographical boundaries, and mostly, for latency tolerant applications (e.g., monitoring) [22,28]. These developments could be a first step in enabling the possibility of remote HIL and geograhically distributed HIL.
- *Interoperability and Standardization:* Within a HIL-co-simulation test it is crucial to ensure seamless communication among the individual components and simulators. Additionally, when the experiments involve multiple domains or multi-laboratories, it is required to have strong interoperability between different partners [25]. A common information model is necessary to enable seamless and meaningful communication among applications. First attempts have been made towards creating a common reference model to improve interoperability and reusability of HIL experiments [2]. With these efforts towards harmonization and standardization of HIL technology, a standardized and general framework for HIL experiments can be established.
- *Power Interface Stability and Accuracy:* Basically, the challenge here is to synchronize and compensate the loop delay, in order to stabilize the system

and increase the accuracy of a test. The first step should be selection of appropriate interface algorithms and power amplification. Recommendations from [16] should be used. Secondly, a time delay compensation method could be considered, such as introducing phase shifting, low-pass filter to the feedback signal [18], extrapolation prediction to compensate for time delays [32], phase advance calibration [35] or multi-rate real-time simulation [42].

5   Conclusions

The ongoing transition towards smart grids implies significant changes in the overall energy system's architecture and infrastructure. A newly arising issue is the continuously increasing level of the system's complexity, i.e., growing number of components in various subsystems that are interrelated to each other. In order to manage, analyse and understand this novel smart grid system, simulation approaches have to be adopted.

As outlined in the paper mainly three different simulation approaches – multi-domain, co-simulation, and real-time hardware-in-the-loop – are suitable tools for analysis and validating smart grids during various development steps. Despite achievements that have been made in this area, a lot issues are yet to be solved.

The main research directions related to co-simulation can be summarized as usability improvements, standardized interfaces, performance optimization, data management, and visualization. In the domain of real-time simulation and HIL, future research should address PHIL interface improvements, remote HIL, standardization and coupling with co-simulation. In summary, there remains ample space for future research in simulation-based smart grid system validation.

Acknowledgments. This work is supported by the European Communitys Horizon 2020 Program (H2020/2014–2020) under project "ERIGrid" (Grant Agreement No. 654113).

References

1. Almas, M.S., Leelaruji, R., Vanfretti, L.: Over-current relay model implementation for real time simulation & Hardware-in-the-Loop (HIL) validation. In: IECON 2012–38th Annual Conference of the IEEE Industrial Electronics Society, pp. 4789–4796 (2012)
2. Andrén, F., Lehfuss, F., Jonke, P., Strasser, T., et al.: DERri common reference model for distributed energy resources - modelling scheme, reference implementations and validation of results. e & i Elektrotech. Informationstechnik **131**(8), 378–385 (2014)
3. Bastian, J., Clauß, C., Wolf, S., Schneider, P.: Master for co-simulation using FMI. In: 8th International Modelica Conference, pp. 115–120 (2011)
4. Bian, D., Kuzlu, M., Pipattanasomporn, M., Rahman, S., Wu, Y.: Real-time co-simulation platform using OPAL-RT and OPNET for analyzing smart grid performance. In: 2015 IEEE Power and Energy Society General Meeting, pp. 1–5 (2015)

5. Bindner, H., Gehrke, O., Lundsager, P., Hansen, J., Cronin, T.: IPSYS - a simulation tool for performance assessment and controller development of integrated power system distributed renewable energy generated and storage. In: European Wind Energy Conference and Exhibition (EWEC), pp. 128–130 (2004)
6. Blochwitz, T., Otter, M., Arnold, M., Bausch, C., et al.: The functional mockup interface for tool independent exchange of simulation models. In: 8th International Modelica Conference, pp. 105–114 (2011)
7. Brück, D., Elmqvist, H., Mattsson, S.E., Olsson, H.: Dymola for multi-engineering modeling and simulation. In: 2nd International Modelica Conference (2002)
8. Davis, J., Galicia, R., Goel, M., Hylands, C., Lee, E.A., et al.: Ptolemy II: heterogeneous concurrent modeling and design in Java. University of California, Berkeley, Technical report, UCB/ERL M 99 (1999)
9. Elmqvist, H., Mattsson, S.E.: An introduction to the physical modeling language Modelica. In: 9th European Simulation Symposium (ESS), vol. 97, pp. 19–23 (1997)
10. Farhangi, H.: The path of the smart grid. IEEE Power Energ. Mag. 8(1), 18–28 (2010)
11. Fritzson, P.: Modelica - a cyber-physical modeling language and the OpenModelica environment. In: 2011 7th International Wireless Communications and Mobile Computing Conference (IWCMC), pp. 1648–1653 (2011)
12. Geimer, M., Krüger, T., Linsel, P.: Co-simulation, gekoppelte simulation oder simulatorkopplung? O+P Ölhydraulik und Pneumatik 50(11–12), 572–576 (2006)
13. Georg, H., Müller, S.C., Dorsch, N., Rehtanz, C., Wietfeld, C.: INSPIRE: integrated co-simulation of power and ICT systems for real-time evaluation. In: 2013 IEEE International Conference on Smart Grid Communications (SmartGridComm), pp. 576–581 (2013)
14. Godfrey, T., Mullen, S., Griffith, D.W., Golmie, N., Dugan, R.C., Rodine, C.: Modeling smart grid applications with co-simulation. In: 2010 IEEE International Conference on Smart Grid Communications (SmartGridComm), pp. 291–296 (2010)
15. Guillo-Sansano, E., Roscoe, A., Jones, C., Burt, G.: A new control method for the power interface in power hardware-in-the-loop simulation to compensate for the time delay. In: 2014 49th International Universities Power Engineering Conference (UPEC) (2014)
16. de Jong, E., de Graaff, R., Vaessen, P., Crolla, P., Roscoe, A., Lehfuß, F., Lauss, G., Kotsampopoulos, P., Gafaro, F.: European white book on real-time power hardware-in-the-loop testing. DERlab report (2011)
17. Kosek, A., Lnsdorf, O., Scherfke, S., Gehrke, O., Rohjans, S.: Evaluation of smart grid control strategies in co-simulation - integration of IPSYS and mosaik. In: 2014 Power Systems Computation Conference (PSCC) (2014)
18. Kotsampopoulos, P., Kleftakis, V., Messinis, G., Hatziargyriou, N.: Design, development and operation of a PHIL environment for Distributed Energy Resources. In: IECON 2012-38th Annual Conference of the IEEE Industrial Electronics Society, pp. 4765–4770 (2012)
19. Kotsampopoulos, P.C., Lehfuss, F., Lauss, G.F., Bletterie, B., Hatziargyriou, N.D.: The limitations of digital simulation and the advantages of PHIL testing in studying distributed generation provision of ancillary services. IEEE Trans. Ind. Electron. 62(9), 5502–5515 (2015)
20. Lin, H., Sambamoorthy, S., Shukla, S., Thorp, J., Mili, L.: Power system and communication network co-simulation for smart grid applications. In: 2011 IEEE PES Innovative Smart Grid Technologies (ISGT) (2011)

21. Loddick, S., Mupambireyi, U., Blair, S., Booth, C., Li, X., Roscoe, A., Daffey, K., Rn, L.J.W.: The use of real time digital simulation and hardware in the loop to de-risk novel control algorithms. In: 2011 IEEE Electric Ship Technologies Symposium, pp. 213–218 (2011)

22. Lundstrom, B., Chakraborty, S., Lauss, S., Brndlinger, R., Conklin, R.: Evaluation of system-integrated smart grid devices using software- and hardware-in-the-loop. In: 2016 IEEE Power Energy Society Innovative Smart Grid Technologies Conference (ISGT), pp. 1–5 (2016)

23. Mets, K., Verschueren, T., Develder, C., Vandoorn, T.L., Vandevelde, L.: Integrated simulation of power and communication networks for smart grid applications. In: 2011 IEEE 16th International Workshop on Computer Aided Modeling and Design of Communication Links and Networks (CAMAD), pp. 61–65 (2011)

24. Neema, H., Sztipanovits, J., Burns, M., Griffor, E.: C2WT-TE: a model-based open platform for integrated simulations of transactive smart grids. In: Workshop on Modeling and Simulation of Cyber-Physical Energy Systems (MSCPES) (2016)

25. Nguyen, V.H., Tran, Q.T., Besanger, Y.: Scada as a service approach for interoperability of micro-grid platforms. Sustain. Energy Grids Netw. **8**, 26–36 (2016)

26. Noll, C., Blochwitz, T., Neidhold, T., Kehrer, C.: Implementation of modelisar functional mock-up interfaces in SimulationX. In: 8th International Modelica Conference, pp. 339–343 (2011)

27. Palensky, P., van der Meer, A., Lopez, C., Joseph, A., Pan, K.: Cosimulation of intelligent power systems: fundamentals, software architecture, numerics, and coupling. IEEE Ind. Electron. Mag. **11**(1), 34–50 (2017)

28. Palmintier, B., Lundstrom, B., Chakraborty, B., Williams, T., Schneider, K., Chassin, K.: A power hardware-in-the-loop platform with remote distribution circuit cosimulation. IEEE Trans. Ind. Electron. **62**(4), 2236–2245 (2015)

29. Podmore, R., Robinson, M.: The role of simulators for smart grid development. IEEE Trans. Smart Grid **1**(2), 205–212 (2010)

30. Ptolemaeus, C. (ed.): System Design, Modeling, and Simulation using Ptolemy II. Ptolemy.org (2014)

31. Ren, L., Manish, M., Mayank, P., Rob, H., Anurag, S., Siddharth, S.: Geographically distributed real-time digital simulations using linear prediction. Int. J. Electr. Power Energy Syst. **84**, 308–317 (2017)

32. Ren, W., Sloderbeck, M., Steurer, M., Dinavahi, V., Noda, T., Filizadeh, S., Chevrefils, A., Matar, A., Iravani, R., Dufour, C., Belanger, J., Faruque, M.O., Strunz, K., Martinez, J.A.: Interfacing issues in real-time digital simulators. IEEE Trans. Power Deliv. **26**(2), 1221–1230 (2011)

33. Ren, W., Steurer, M., Baldwin, T.L.: Improve the stability and the accuracy of power hardware-in-the-loop simulation by selecting appropriate interface algorithms. IEEE Trans. Ind. Appl. **44**(4), 1286–1294 (2008)

34. Rohjans, S., Lehnhoff, S., Schütte, S., Scherfke, S., Hussain, S.: Mosaik - a modular platform for the evaluation of agent-based Smart Grid control. In: 4th IEEE/PES Innovative Smart Grid Technologies Europe (ISGT EUROPE) (2013)

35. Roscoe, A.J., Mackay, A., Burt, G.M., McDonald, J.R.: Architecture of a network-in-the-loop environment for characterizing ac power-system behavior. IEEE Trans. Ind. Electron. **57**(4), 1245–1253 (2010)

36. Rotger-Griful, S., Chatzivasileiadis, S., Jacobsen, R.H., Stewart, E.M., Domingo, J.M., Wetter, M.: Hardware-in-the-loop co-simulation of distribution grid for demand response. In: 2016 Power Systems Computation Conference (PSCC), pp. 1–7 (2016)

37. Schloegl, F., Rohjans, S., Lehnhoff, S., Velasquez, J., Steinbrink, C., Palensky, P.: Towards a classification scheme for co-simulation approaches in energy systems. In: International Symposium on Smart Electric Distribution Systems and Technologies (EDST) 2015, pp. 516–521 (2015)
38. Schütte, S., Scherfke, S., Tröschel, M.: Mosaik: a framework for modular simulation of active components in smart grids. In: IEEE First International Workshop on Smart Grid Modeling and Simulation (SGMS), pp. 55–60 (2011)
39. Steinbrink, C.: A nonintrusive uncertainty quantification system for modular smart grid co-simulation. Ph.D. thesis, University of Oldenburg (2016)
40. Steurer, M., Bogdan, F., Ren, W., Sloderbeck, M., Woodruff, S.: Controller and power hardware-in-loop methods for accelerating renewable energy integration. In: Power Engineering Society General Meeting, pp. 1–4. IEEE (2007)
41. Strasser, T., Pröstl Andrén, F., Lauss, G., et al.: Towards holistic power distribution system validation and testing–an overview and discussion of different possibilities. e & i Elektrotech. Informationstechnik 134(1), 71–77 (2017)
42. Viehweider, A., Lauss, G., Felix, L.: Stabilization of power hardware-in-the-loop simulations of electric energy systems. Simul. Model. Practi. Theory 19(7), 1699–1708 (2011)

Prediction Models for Short-Term Load and Production Forecasting in Smart Electrical Grids

Adriano Ferreira[1,3(✉)], Paulo Leitão[1,2], and José Barata[3]

[1] Polytechnic Institute of Bragança, Campus Sta Apolónia,
5300-253 Bragança, Portugal
{a.ferreira,pleitao}@ipb.pt
[2] Artificial Intelligence and Computer Science Laboratory,
4169-007 Porto, Portugal
[3] Faculty of Sciences and Technology, New University of Lisbon,
Quinta da Torre, 2825-114 Caparica, Portugal
jab@uninova.pt

Abstract. The scheduling of household smart load devices play a key role in microgrid ecosystems, and particularly in underpowered grids. The management and sustainability of these microgrids could benefit from the application of short-term prediction for the energy production and demand, which have been successfully applied and matured in larger scale systems, namely national power grids. However, the dynamic change of energy demand, due to the necessary adjustments aiming to render the microgrid self-sustainability, makes the forecasting process harder. This paper analyses some prediction techniques to be embedded in intelligent and distributed agents responsible to manage electrical microgrids, and especially increase their self-sustainability. These prediction techniques are implemented in R language and compared according to different prediction and historical data horizons. The experimental results shows that none is the optimal solution for all criteria, but allow to identify the best prediction techniques for each scenario and time scope.

Keywords: Multi-agent systems · Prediction models · Microgrids sustainability

1   Introduction

The recent "green power trend" propelled by the commitment signed in the Treaty of Lisbon, pushed the development of more sustainable models compatible with environmental protection. This change in the power generation paradigm allied to the resilience and robustness requirements, triggered the transition from the traditional power grids towards smart grids. This change in the power grid paradigm is also aligned with the Distributed Renewable Energy Generation (DREG), Distributed Energy Resources (DER), smart appliances, storage

© Springer International Publishing AG 2017
V. Mařík et al. (Eds.): HoloMAS 2017, LNAI 10444, pp. 186–199, 2017.
DOI: 10.1007/978-3-319-64635-0_14

facilities, and Electric Vehicles (EVs). This evolution also stimulates the use of decentralization, where the components of the network are spread across the grid and are able to operate autonomously.

Electrical microgrids are small-scale power systems comprising DERs [1], both related to energy consumption (e.g., factories and households) and energy generation (e.g., photovoltaic panels (PV), wind turbines, fuel cells and diesel generators. These microgrids have suitable control systems that allow to work in both grid-connected and islanded operating modes.

In islanded microgrids, the achievement of self-sustainability is a challenging topic, being defined as "the ability to the degree at which the system can sustain itself without external support" [2]. This issue is especially hard in microgrids comprising RES and limited resources, where important loads have to be attended with the addition of the users momentary will. Table 1 characterizes the assumptions, requirements and challenges related to the self-sustainability in electrical microgrids, considering the two operating modes: permanent stand alone and temporary stand alone.

Table 1. Characterization of the self-sustainability problem in smart electrical microgrids

	Operating in permanent stand-alone mode	Operating in temporary stand-alone mode
Assumptions	- Forced islanding due to geographical isolation or to community will - Always disconnected from the main utility	- In case of failure in the supply from the main utility - Works temporarily disconnected from the main utility to keep its full functionalities
Requirements	- Continuously optimize the balancing between production and demand - Minimize the utilization of non-renewable generation sources - Ensure high levels of QoS	- Optimize the production resources to ensure the full operation of priority loads - Maintain the QoS
Challenges	- Storage and management of EVs - Dynamic change of loads priorities - Accurate short term prediction (few days) for both energy demand and generation - Weather volatility influencing the forecasting results	- Dynamic change of loads priorities and schedule - Accurate very short term prediction (few hours) of both energy demand and generation

Under the permanent stand-alone operation, the microgrid is isolated, e.g., due to geographical reasons, with the need to attend the maximum number of loads maintaining the high levels of QoS. This requirement imposes the need to have a proper classification and selection of the momentary priority loads, the efficient management of the available storage devices and the accurate prediction of demand, production and weather profiles. On the other hand, the temporary islanding, e.g., due to a failure in the main utility grid, needs to ensure the full operation during the failure period through the optimization of the available resources with minimum impact in the QoS. This process will imply an adjustment of the loads priorities and an accurate short term prediction of the generation and demand profiles. In order to face these challenges, a proper vision of the upcoming events is needed in order to provide schedules for different scenarios and time horizons. Additionally, the unpredictability associated to the weather increases the complexity, requiring a flexible and dynamic control that is able to predict, anticipate, regulated and control the microgrid in order to extend its sustainability.

In this scenario, a decentralized and intelligent approach is required to cope with inherent complexity required to manage dynamic, heterogeneous and distributed electrical components. Multi-Agent System (MAS) [3] is a good candidate to implement such approach, providing important features, namely modularity, decentralization, flexibility, robustness, autonomy and adaptability. The distributed agents, along with their reasoning, communication and intelligence capabilities, can be enriched with prediction capabilities to forecast the energy demand and generation. Additionally, these prediction models can contribute to mitigate the unpredictability introduced by the use of some renewable energy sources, which are strongly dependent of the weather uncertainty.

Having this in mind, this paper studies the existing prediction algorithms that will fit the requirements imposed by the dynamic characteristics of demand and production profiles in microgrids operating conditions. The study will evaluate these algorithms based on the accuracy for both very short and short term, as well as considering the computation time across different scenarios. The selected prediction algorithms were implemented in R language and evaluated under several scenarios created using the Gridlab-D tool. At the end, the best prediction techniques for the prediction of demand and prediction of production, and for the permanent and temporary operation situations, were identified.

This paper is organized as follows. Section 2 overviews the multi-agent system approach for self-sustainable electrical micro grids, and Sect. 3 describes the related work related to the use of prediction techniques for forecasting the energy production and demand in electrical microgrids. Section 4 presents the experimental case study and Sect. 5 analysis the achieved results. Finally, Sect. 6 rounds up the paper with the conclusions and states the future work.

2   Multi-agent System Approach for the Self-sustainable Electrical Microgrids

MAS have already proven its capabilities across several application domains, namely manufacturing control, dynamic product routing, production planning, logistics, aerospace, and many others [4]. In terms of electrical power grid systems, MAS have being applied in a wide range of areas, such as diagnosis, market simulation, power grid monitoring and power systems automation [5].

The distributed capabilities of MAS enables the high performance required to prevent or contain rapidly evolving adverse conditions. In [6], a MAS based architecture focusing the self-sustainability in electrical smart microgrids is described. This architecture considers 3 types of agents that represent the different types of entities presented within the electrical microgrid, namely:

- Consumer agent (CA): representing the controllable loads and responsible for the management of their consumption according to their needs, priorities and state of the grid.
- Producer agent (PA): representing the producers of energy, e.g., photovoltaic panels and wind generators, and responsible to manage the produced power.
- Storage agent (SA): representing the storage units and electric vehicles, and responsible to manage their charging and discharging cycles.

The global system behavior emerges from the interaction among the distributed agents, sharing and combining knowledge and skills in order to achieve the local and global optimums. Figure 1 illustrates the MAS architecture, and particularly represents the interactions among the agents in order to accomplish their individual goals. This exchange of information, according to different cooperation patterns, assumes critical importance under stressed moment where the global optimum arises. Therefore, each agent is endowed with local autonomy and intelligence required to dynamically adapt to changes in the system.

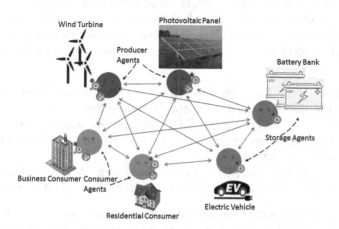

Fig. 1. Multi-agent system architecture for the intelligent micro-grid management

Additionally, each agent is endowed with prediction models that allows to forecast the energy production and demands for the future, which is a crucial issue in microgrids operating in isolated mode, and particularly relevant when the objective is to improve its sustainability. In fact, the agents are able to dynamically anticipate upcoming events that could affect the sustainability of the microgrid.

For this purpose, the prediction methods embedded in each agent are dependent of their performance regarding the following aspects: (i) type of prediction, i.e. prediction of energy production or energy demand, and (ii) forecasting horizon, which can vary from hours to months, and (iii) the computational time to execute the prediction. These aspects are also constrains that are used as selector for the prediction method, meaning that in some particular cases a less accurate but faster technique is more adequate than a more accurate but slower technique. This means that a study of the available prediction techniques that better matches the requirements of the several agents in the microgrid management is required.

3   Related Work

This section provides an overview of the prediction methods as well as their classification within the forecasting horizon. The application of these prediction methods within the smart grid paradigm is also discussed.

3.1   Prediction Techniques

With the integration of intelligence at the various levels of the electrical system (e.g., transportation and more recently distribution), allied with emergent decentralized paradigms (e.g., smart grids and smart buildings), the new generation of electrical power system are more complex and unpredictable.

Nevertheless, forecasting is a deeply investigated field across the different sectors from electric power systems to logistics and factory plants. Several review papers provide a good overview on prediction methods, namely [7–10]. In this field, and dependent of the prediction horizon, three sub-fields can be identified [11]:

- Very Short-Term Load Forecasting (VSTLF): ranging from seconds or minutes to hours, and used to control the power flow.
- Short-Term Load Forecasting (STLF): ranging from hours to weeks, and usually used to predict upcoming generation and demand, aiming to update the market prices accordingly.
- Medium-Term and Long-term Load Forecasting (MTLF/LTLF): ranging from months to years, and usually used to predict the plant asset utilities.

Regardless of the model the main difference among them is the range of the input variables, which ranges from minutes or hours in the VSTLF models up to weeks or months in the MTLF/LTLF models. In our work, the focus is in VSTLF and STLF models, which algorithms have been widely used over the past decades with a myriad of approaches. Kyriakides and Polycarpou compiled the VSTLF and STLF prediction methods as follows [9]: (i) Regression models such as the Seasonal Decomposition of Time Series by Loess (STL) that uses local regression to remove irregularities from data. The STL method is very versatile method that handles any type of seasonality, not only monthly and quarterly data, that allows to control the seasonal component and rate of change over time. (ii) Linear time series models, namely auto-regressive moving average (ARMA) [12] and auto-regressive integrated moving average (ARIMA) that is a generalization of an ARMA model, that can be viewed as a filter that aims at separate the signal from the noise, then extrapolating the signal into the future to obtain forecasts. (iii) State-space models (SSMs), that are filtering-based techniques such as the Holt-Winters (HWT) that is also known as Triple Exponential Smoothing seasonal method, recursively applying as many as three low-pass filters with exponential window functions. (iv) Nonlinear models namely machine learning approaches, such as neural networks that are based on simple mathematical models of the brain, they can be thought of as an organized network of neurons. The predictors/inputs form the bottom layer, and the forecasts/outputs form the top layer, the intermediate layers contain the hidden neurons. Simpler networks do not contain hidden layers, being these equivalent to linear regression.

3.2 Application of Forecasting in Smart Grids

Regarding the application of the afore mentioned methods and techniques there are several techniques aiming to address different issues in the demand and production forecasting applied to the smart grid domain.

Bessa et al. presented a spatialtemporal forecasting method that combines observation of the solar generation retrieved from the smart meters and distribution transformer controllers to forecast 6-h-ahead residential solar photovoltaic and medium-voltage substation levels [13]. An ARMA model was used in [14] to predict the future solar generation in a laboratory-level microgrid. Charytoniuk and Chen presented an VSTLF prediction model based on Artificial Neural Networks (ANNs) to model the load dynamics in changing environments using five different networks that calculated five time intervals with 10 min spacing [15]. A Wavelet Artificial Neural Network (WANN) with pre-data filtering was used to forecast the consumption values for the horizons of up to one hour [16]. Asber *et al.* investigated methods to forecast MTLF models and demonstrated how one can utilize a general load-modeling framework to extract the essence of specific modeling problems and achieve practical models [17].

Kandil *et al.* [18] presented an approach that implements a knowledge-based system to perform decision support of the most suitable forecasting model for M/LTLF power system planning. The system knowledge-base consists on static historical data (e.g., load patterns, economics and weather) and dynamic data (e.g., load and energy attributes, losses and estimation errors). A regression ANN was used in [19] and [20] by Zhang and Ye for STLF and LTLF respectively, using historical data from the previous years to train the model and predict into the future. Two models for LTLF were presented by Daneshi et al. [21], where the first applies a linear regression method to obtain the regression model equation, and the second model applies fuzzy sets to ANN to model long-term uncertainties and compare the enhanced forecasting results with those of traditional methods.

Enel the Italian energy company monitor over 32 million smart meters and use the recovered data predict upcoming demand values and use this forecast to leverage customized hourly-based tariffs [22]. Joe-Wong et al. presented an algorithm to estimate day-ahead and device usages prices based upon historical data, l allowing the service provider to adjust the offered electricity prices based on users behavior [23]. Borges et al. [24] present a methodology that sums the forecasts on the compounding individual loads to perform load forecasting in large power systems.

A Plug-in Hybrid Vehicles (PHEVs) charging scheme based upon price prediction is presented in [25]. The proposed scheme uses generation and demand forecast to predict the upcoming price schemes, avoiding peak hours that would a severe impact in the price.

All the previously referred techniques address specific challenges, applying the same technique to static forecasting and historical data horizons. A combination of the best suited prediction techniques allied with the intelligence of MAS provides the necessary reasoning capacity to perform the selection of the ideal prediction method. This selection is impacted by the precision and calculation times of each prediction method, this way a study of available prediction method is needed in order to selected the most suitable ones.

4   Experimental Case Study

This section presents the case study focusing a small electrical microgrid as well as the chosen forecasting and evaluation methods.

4.1   Description of the Case Study

The case study scenario considers a small 4 person family house inserted within a small microgrid, with incandescent illumination, electric water heater and other loads (e.g., refrigerators, electric heating and television). Additionally, the house comprises an independent solar panel that can either feed power to the grid or be used as house supplier.

As distributed energy resources are the core part of a microgrid, each profile will be unique and important for the common wealth of the power community. For this purpose, the input dataset was generated using the smart grid simulation tool GRIDLAB-D [26], where the demand and photovoltaic (PV) production profiles were generated with 5 min interval, with an entire year corresponding to 105410 samples. Additional simulated samples will serve as validation data serving as an independent measure of the performance of the methods.

The winter demand and production simulated profiles are presented in Fig. 2. As it is noticeable from the figure, there are clear consumption peaks near the

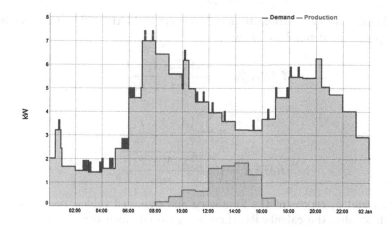

Fig. 2. Profiles of the energy demand and production

wake-up times and dinner. The winter season and center-European/north American longitudes prone shorter periods of sun light and cold temperatures influence the photovoltaic production capabilities resulting less power produced per m^2 of panels installed.

4.2 Selection of Prediction Methods to Be Analyzed

Depending on the type of models and length of the forecast window, each method will produce faster/slower, more/less accurate results, which means that the case study will need to support the analysis of the prediction techniques for different historical data sets and prediction windows. A total of four methods were evaluated, namely ARIMA, ANN, STL and HWT, these four were picked as they are some of the most used algorithms to VSTLF and STLF. Each one of these methods were used through the existing libraries of the R platform [27] and run in the same machine under certain conditions regarding historical data size and prediction horizons. For the demand forecasting:

- Historical data size: 2 days (576 samples), 2 weeks (2016 samples), 2 months (17856 samples) and 1 year (105410 samples).
- Prediction horizon: 1 h, 1 day, 1 week and 1 month.

For the generation forecasting:

- Historical data size: 3 days (864 samples).
- Prediction horizon: 1 h, 2 h, 4 h, next morning, next day.

The prediction accuracy is an important criterion to evaluate the forecasting techniques. In this study, three statistical measures are used to determine the prediction accuracy, namely: root-mean-square error (RMSE), mean absolute error (MAE) and mean absolute percentage error (MAPE). The three measures are, respectively, defined as follows:

$$MAPE(\%) = \frac{100}{n} \sum_{t=1}^{n} \left| \frac{A_t - F_t}{A_t} \right| \tag{1}$$

$$MAE = \frac{1}{n} \sum_{t=1}^{n} |A - t - F_t| \tag{2}$$

$$RMSE = \sqrt{\frac{\sum_{t=1}^{n}(A_t - F_t)^2}{n}} \tag{3}$$

where A_t and F_t represent the foretasted and observed values, respectively.

Additionally, the calculation time is measured since the speed of the algorithm execution is relevant in dynamic prediction systems as the recalculation and adjustment procedures often need quick response times.

Each prediction method was executed six times to ensure accurate values during the evaluation procedure, being calculated the average of the experiments. In this way, sporadic events were absorbed providing smother and more consistent results.

5   Analysis of Results

This section presents and discusses the achieved results for the selected prediction methods, considering the energy demand and production curves.

5.1   Prediction Models for the Energy Demand

The evaluation of the selected prediction methods using the afore mentioned evaluation methods is summarized in the Table 2.

As it is presented in the table, the precision of the algorithms, shown in the MAPE and RMSE columns, varies with the historical data size and prediction horizon. This variation is depicted in Fig. 3, where it is presented the evolution of MAPE across the historical data and prediction horizon. The statistical model ARIMA, the only auto-regressive method presented, stays accurate during the bigger historical data sets although it starts getting good accuracy when the size of the data set decreases. This usually happens due to underestimation, since the ARIMA model uses past values in the regression equation, the low amount of past values affects the capability to predict future events. Despite the accuracy loss in the smaller horizons with smaller sized historical data, it is a very responsive method capable to provide fast forecasts.

The HWT model performed similarly to the ARIMA model, although with better accuracy with smaller historical data sizes, decreasing the calculation time as the data set size also decreases. These results make this prediction method as a good choice to provide an accurate forecast although it requires longer periods

Table 2. Results of the prediction methods for the energy demand

Historical Data Size	Horizon	ARIMA				HWT				NN				STL			
		Error			Speed	Error			Speed	Error			Speed	Error			Speed
		MAE	MAPE	RMSE	(s)	MAE	MAPE	RMSE	(s)	MAE	MAPE	RMSE	(s)	MAE	MAPE	RMSE	(s)
1 Year	1 Month	0,571	13,483	0,829	7,98	0,636	15,630	0,857	538,14	1,689	53,738	2,130	2963.46/13,99	0,428	10,586	0,589	7,19
	1 Week	0,841	13,923	0,841	9,56	0,621	14,676	0,845	49,42	1,336	38,425	1,778	3,34	0,522	10,608	0,590	6,01
	1 Day	0,473	11,199	0,706	7,94	0,489	4,367	0,662	6,6	0,790	18,460	1,044	0,65	0,429	2,020	0,590	6,04
	1 Hour	0,108	5,557	0,122	8,06	0,039	1,986	0,044	1,37	0,036	1,976	0,050	0,65	0,072	3,709	0,080	6,07
1 Month	1 Month	0,525	13,755	0,715	0,86	0,696	13,897	0,917	447,21	1,642	51,879	2,028	322,48/12,58	0,428	10,586	0,587	2,03
	1 Week	0,538	13,972	0,720	0,81	0,796	21,289	1,002	23,03	1,353	37,856	1,755	2,87	0,428	10,586	0,587	2,04
	1 Day	0,439	11,208	0,581	0,79	0,564	15,557	0,745	1,68	0,725	17,504	0,918	0,41	0,429	10,611	0,588	1,78
	1 Hour	0,082	4,628	0,120	0,85	0,195	10,637	0,245	0,67	0,080	4,173	0,093	0,42	0,071	3,694	0,080	1,81
1 Week	1 Week	0,539	14,040	0,719	0,91	0,556	15,549	0,847	20,31	1,697	51,291	2,093	24.82/6,89	0,428	10,582	0,587	0,92
	1 Day	0,439	11,220	0,580	0,92	0,298	8,453	0,408	1,23	1,031	24,858	1,337	0,93	0,429	10,607	0,588	0,93
	1 Hour	0,081	4,596	0,121	0,98	0,111	5,656	0,146	0,61	0,083	4,426	0,104	0,88	0,071	3,695	0,080	0,96
1 Day	1 Day	0,350	10,146	0,474	0,68	0,230	6,586	0,430	1,15	0,266	7,215	0,429	0.92/0,36	0,226	1,348	0,368	0,67
	1 Hour	0,273	14,623	0,293	0,66	0,141	7,696	0,244	0,61	0,099	5,551	0,147	0,41	0,124	6,425	0,139	0,83

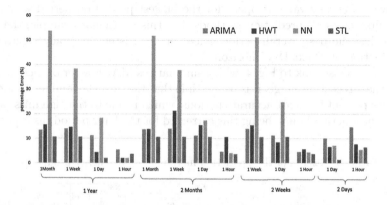

Fig. 3. Comparison of the prediction models results for the energy demand

to perform the forecast turning it a second option whenever quicker forecasts are required.

The NN method proves to be the least accurate method where the forecast horizon is bigger, improving its accuracy for shorter horizons. The low values of RMSE can be mistaken as good accuracy when in fact it points to an overfitting problem, related to the size and nature of the training data leading a large numbers of layers containing many neurons. A closer analysis to the achieved results, revealed that the main responsible for the high error values was the undetection of sporadic demand peaks. Although, as the historical data size and prediction horizon decreased the number of sporadic demand peaks decreased, improving this way the accuracy.

The STL method provided slightly better accuracy and calculation times when compared with the ARIMA model as it decomposes the time series in three components, trend, seasonal and remainder, providing a better recognition of the seasonal components presented in the household demand data. Therefore, we could say that the STL and ARIMA methods are complementary, providing the first method good results for longer horizons and the second for shorter horizons.

Taking a roundup of the four analyzed methods, the least prone for a dynamic forecast of the demand would be the neural networks as it as long training times and presented the lower overall accuracy turns-it the least usable. The STL prediction method would provide a better overall accuracy as well as quick calculation times.

5.2   Prediction Models for the Energy Production

Table 3 shows the simulation results of the four prediction methods for the energy production scenario. Similarly to the prediction of the energy demand, the accuracy tends to improve as the forecasting horizon decreases. As it is noticeable, the lowest accuracy value happens for the biggest prediction period with similar results across all prediction methods. For this particular example, the STL method has the best overall performance with consistent accuracy values with the exception of "Next Day" horizon.

Taking a close look to Fig. 4, which summarizes MAPE error of each method across the forecasting range, it is perceptible that the next day and next morning scenarios present the least accurate periods, which is due to the high miss rate in the non-production hours, being this corrected for the later periods as it possible

Table 3. Results of the prediction methods for the energy production

Historical Data Size	Horizon	ARIMA				HWT				NN				STL			
		Error			Speed	Error			Speed	Error			Speed	Error			Speed
		MAE	MAPE	RMSE	(s)	MAE	MAPE	RMSE	(s)	MAE	MAPE	RMSE	(s)	MAE	MAPE	RMSE	(s)
3 Days	Next day	0,278	29,307	0,457	0,640	0,236	23,468	0,323	1,170	0,496	53,375	0,715	4,53/ 0,278	29,307	0,457	0,640	0,236
	Next morning	0,161	28,956	0,246	0,610	0,173	36,713	0,212	0,740	0,363	49,666	0,572	0,161	28,956	0,246	0,610	0,173
	4 Hours	0,459	12,584	0,615	0,710	0,076	2,066	0,126	0,680	0,132	4,008	0,169	0,459	12,584	0,615	0,710	0,076
	2 hours	0,297	11,157	0,364	0,680	0,128	3,544	0,176	0,560	0,124	4,626	0,167	0,297	11,157	0,364	0,680	0,128
	1 Hour	0,426	17,730	0,472	0,640	0,044	1,268	0,100	0,550	0,169	7,172	0,216	0,426	17,730	0,472	0,640	0,044

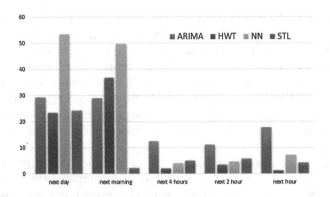

Fig. 4. Prediction models accuracy comparison for the production curves

verify in Table 3. This is especial prone to happen as solar radiation is directly dependent to the weather conditions, which makes the trend analysis of the historical data harder to be identified.

In this case, the calculation time is negligible as all the methods present fast prediction performances (under 5 s), similarly to the behavior presented in the demand forecasting, the STL method proved to be the most consistent method across the forecasting horizon.

6 Conclusions

Self-sustained micro grids require an efficient management of the available energy resources to face the energy demands. A particular challenge is to predict the upcoming patterns of demand and generation of energy in order to anticipate unexpected events. This paper described the evaluation of four prediction methods (ARIMA, HWT, NN and STL) running in different scenarios, for both energy production and demand and using simulated data generated by the smart grid simulator Gridalb-D. The programing language R as well as its available libraries were used to implement these simulation tests and run the evaluation procedure.

In the case of the prediction of the energy demand, the achieved results showed that there is no method that clearly outperforms the others. The results are ranging from the average of 7.31 MAPE (STL) to 24.41 (NN) across all scenarios. The accuracy showed to be lower than expected, due to the added noise and influence of users in the overall behavior. The peak estimation is essential as part of a proper estimation of the demand profile, as the demand tend to be more and more a discrete chart instead of a linear curve. In conclusion, a combination of several methods depending on the computational resources and available time to execute the forecast can provide better overall results than using a single algorithm. Combining the STL method for the longer forecasting periods and the HWT method for the shortest would result a better accuracy across the forecasting range.

Analyzing the results for the prediction of the energy generation, it is possible to state a difference across the evaluated prediction methods, where the differences are not related to the performance as they present similar results, but in terms of accuracy. In this field it is clear that the STL method is most consistent showing better accuracy across the different forecasting horizons.

Microgrids in full islanding have fewer resources, translating into higher number of adjustments this way they would benefit from a combination of the STL and HWT as this combination cover with the higher accuracy multiple prediction horizons. Microgrids in temporary islanding run the forecasting algorithm in the islanding moment in order to anticipate the needs until the moment of reconnection, needing this way a quick method and accurate for longer periods such as the STL.

The future work is related to the combination of these results with learning techniques in order to implemented an intelligent selection of the prediction methods according to the forecasting horizons and data size.

References

1. Colson, C., Nehrir, M.: A review of challenges to real-time power management of microgrids. In: 2009 IEEE Power & Energy Society General Meeting, pp. 1–8. IEEE, July 2009
2. Menasche, D.S., Rocha, A.A.A., e Silva, E.A.d.S., Leao, R.M., Towsley, D., Venkataramani, A.: Estimating self-sustainability in peer-to-peer swarming systems (2010)
3. Wooldridge, M.: An Introduction to MultiAgent Systems. Wiley, New York (2002). ISBN 978-0471496915
4. Leitao, P., Vrba, P., Strasser, T.: Multi-agent systems as automation platform for intelligent energy systems. In: IECON 2013–39th Annual Conference of the IEEE Industrial Electronics Society, pp. 66–71. IEEE, November 2013
5. McArthur, S.D.J., Davidson, E.M., Catterson, V.M., Dimeas, A.L., Hatziargyriou, N.D., Ponci, F., Funabashi, T.: Multi-agent systems for power engineering applications part I: concepts, approaches, and technical challenges. IEEE Trans. Power Syst. $22(4)$, 1743–1752 (2007)
6. Ferreira, A., Leitão, P., Barata Oliveira, J.: Formal specification of a self-sustainable holonic system for smart electrical micro-grids. In: Borangiu, T., Trentesaux, D., Thomas, A., Leitão, P., Barata Oliveira, J. (eds.) Service Orientation in Holonic and Multi-Agent Manufacturing. SCI, vol. 694, pp. 179–190. Springer, Cham (2017). doi:10.1007/978-3-319-51100-9_16
7. Feinberg, E.A., Genethliou, D.: Load forecasting. In: Chow, J.H., Wu, F.F., Momoh, J. (eds.) Applied Mathematics for Restructured Electric Power Systems, pp. 269–285. Springer, Boston (2006)
8. Hahn, H., Meyer-Nieberg, S., Pickl, S.: Electric load forecasting methods: tools for decision making. Eur. J. Oper. Res. $199(3)$, 902–907 (2009)
9. Kyriakides, E., Polycarpou, M.: Short term electric load forecasting: a tutorial. In: Chen, K., Wang, L. (eds.) Trends in Neural Computation, vol. 418, pp. 391–418. Springer, Heidelberg (2007)
10. Muñoz, A., Sánchez-Úbeda, E., Cruz, A., Marín, J.: Short-term forecasting in power systems: a guided tour. In: Rebennack, S., Pardalos, P., Pereira, M., Iliadis, N. (eds.) Handbook of Power Systems II, pp. 129–160. Springer, Heidelberg (2010)
11. Hippert, H., Pedreira, C., Souza, R.: Neural networks for short-term load forecasting: a review and evaluation. IEEE Trans. Power Syst. $16(1)$, 44–55 (2001)
12. Gross, G., Galiana, F.: Short-term load forecasting. Proc. IEEE $75(12)$, 1558–1573 (1987)
13. Bessa, R.J., Trindade, A., Miranda, V.: Spatial-temporal solar power forecasting for smart grids. IEEE Trans. Ind. Inform. $11(1)$, 232–241 (2015)
14. Huang, R., Huang, T., Gadh, R., Li, N.: Solar generation prediction using the ARMA model in a laboratory-level micro-grid. In: 2012 IEEE Third International Conference on Smart Grid Communications (SmartGridComm), pp. 528–533. IEEE, November 2012
15. Charytoniuk, W., Chen, M.S.: Very short-term load forecasting using artificial neural networks. IEEE Trans. Power Syst. $15(1)$, 263–268 (2000)
16. Guan, C., Luh, P.B., Michel, L.D., Wang, Y., Friedland, P.B.: Very short-term load forecasting: wavelet neural networks with data pre-filtering. IEEE Trans. Power Syst. $28(1)$, 30–41 (2013)
17. Asber, D., Lefebvre, S., Saad, M., Desbiens, C.: Modeling of distribution loads for short and medium-term load forecasting. In: 2007 IEEE Power Engineering Society General Meeting, pp. 1–5. IEEE, June 2007

18. Kandil, M.S., El-Debeiky, S.M., Hasanien, N.E.: Long-term load forecasting for fast-developing utility using a knowledge-based expert system. IEEE Power Eng. Rev. **22**(4), 78–78 (2002)

19. Zhang, H.T., Xu, F.Y., Zhou, L.: Artificial neural network for load forecasting in smart grid. In: 2010 International Conference on Machine Learning and Cybernetics, pp. 3200–3205. IEEE, July 2010

20. Zhang, Z., Ye, S.: Long term load forecasting and recommendations for china based on support vector regression. In: 2011 International Conference on Information Management, Innovation Management and Industrial Engineering, pp. 597–602. IEEE, November 2011

21. Daneshi, H., Shahidehpour, M., Choobbari, A.L.: Long-term load forecasting in electricity market. In: 2008 IEEE International Conference on Electro/Information Technology, pp. 395–400. IEEE, May 2008

22. Gullo, F., Ponti, G., Tagarelli, A., liritano, S., Ruffolo, M., Labate, D.: Low-voltage electricity customer profiling based on load data clustering. In: Proceedings of the 2009 International Database Engineering & #38; Applications Symposium, IDEAS 2009, pp. 330–333. ACM, New York (2009)

23. Joe-Wong, C., Sen, S., Ha, S., Chiang, M.: Optimized day-ahead pricing for smart grids with device-specific scheduling flexibility. IEEE J. Sel. Areas Commun. **30**(6), 1075–1085 (2012)

24. Borges, C.E., Penya, Y.K., Fernandez, I.: Evaluating combined load forecasting in large power systems and smart grids. IEEE Trans. Ind. Inform. **9**(3), 1570–1577 (2013)

25. Erol-Kantarci, M., Hussein, T.M.: Prediction-based charging of PHEVs from the smart grid with dynamic pricing. In: IEEE Local Computer Network Conference, pp. 1032–1039. IEEE, October 2010

26. Chassin, D.P., Schneider, K., Gerkensmeyer, C.: GridLAB-D: an open-source power systems modeling and simulation environment. In: 2008 IEEE/PES Transmission and Distribution Conference and Exposition, pp. 1–5. IEEE, April 2008

27. R Development Core Team: R: A Language and Environment for Statistical Computing. R Foundation for Statistical Computing, Vienna, Austria (2008). ISBN 3-900051-07-0

Validating Intelligent Power and Energy Systems – A Discussion of Educational Needs

P. Kotsampopoulos[1], N. Hatziargyriou[1], T.I. Strasser[2(✉)] (iD),
C. Moyo[2], S. Rohjans[3], C. Steinbrink[4], S. Lehnhoff[4], P. Palensky[5],
A.A. van der Meer[5], D.E. Morales Bondy[6], K. Heussen[6], M. Calin[7],
A. Khavari[7], M. Sosnina[7], J.E. Rodriguez[8], and G.M. Burt[9]

[1] National Technical University of Athens, Athens, Greece
kotsa@power.ece.ntua.gr
[2] AIT Austrian Institute of Technology, Vienna, Austria
thomas.strasser@ait.ac.at
[3] HAW Hamburg University of Applied Sciences, Hamburg, Germany
[4] OFFIS e.V, Oldenburg, Germany
[5] Delft University of Technology, Delft, The Netherlands
[6] Technical University of Denmark, Lyngby, Denmark
[7] European Distributed Energy Resources Laboratories (DERlab) e.V,
Kassel, Germany
[8] TECNALIA Research and Innovation, Bilbao, Spain
[9] University of Strathclyde, Glasgow, UK

Abstract. Traditional power systems education and training is flanked by the demand for coping with the rising complexity of energy systems, like the integration of renewable and distributed generation, communication, control and information technology. A broad understanding of these topics by the current/future researchers and engineers is becoming more and more necessary. This paper identifies educational and training needs addressing the higher complexity of intelligent energy systems. Education needs and requirements are discussed, such as the development of systems-oriented skills and cross-disciplinary learning. Education and training possibilities and necessary tools are described focusing on classroom but also on laboratory-based learning methods. In this context, experiences of using notebooks, co-simulation approaches, hardware-in-the-loop methods and remote labs experiments are discussed.

Keywords: Cyber-Physical Energy Systems · Education · Learning · Smart grids · Training · Validation

1 Introduction

The rise in the extent of renewable energy systems, electrification of transportation, technology improvements to obtain a more resilient network infrastructure and challenges to have emission free and sustainable energy supply are the main drivers for the ongoing transition towards an intelligent energy system [3].

© Springer International Publishing AG 2017
V. Mařík et al. (Eds.): HoloMAS 2017, LNAI 10444, pp. 200–212, 2017.
DOI: 10.1007/978-3-319-64635-0_15

With the surge of complexity due to the myriad of players and actors, the need to understand the interconnections between all energy infrastructure components increases steadily [5]. Technically speaking there is a higher need for the integration and interaction between these actors. This includes not only the grid physics and power devices, but corresponding automation and control systems are becoming more important in the power and energy domain, in the bid to master their complexity [9]. These needs will be addressed by ongoing developments in the area of Information and Communication Technology (ICT). As a result of this trend a strong focus should be put on the further research and even more on educational aspects covering the ever rising complexity in energy systems [3,5,21].

Education and training in the area of intelligent energy systems, especially on smart grids, can be build on communicating the concepts of modelling and simulating components [15] to understand how they work as a system. When engineers design intelligent concepts like energy management systems, voltage control, etc. [20], they need to understand the paradigms of centralized and distributed control, how to use different tools, know their strength and weaknesses and how to interconnect them [10,22].

The main contribution of this paper is a discussion of the challenging needs and requirements for educating current and future researchers and engineers in the domain of intelligent power and energy systems. Corresponding possibilities and necessary tools are described as well, not only focusing on the classroom but also on laboratory-based learning methods. In this context, experiences of using notebooks, co-simulation approaches, hardware-in-the-loop methods and remote labs experiments are discussed.

The following parts of this paper are organized as follows: Sect. 2 briefly explains challenges in intelligent power and energy systems. Education needs and requirements are discussed in the following Sect. 3, whereas corresponding learning approaches and tools are outlined in Sect. 4. The paper is concluded with the main findings in Sect. 5.

2 Intelligent Power and Energy Systems

2.1 Increased Complexity Trough Multi-domain Solutions

Intelligent Power and Energy Systems can be seen as the big brother of smart grids: power systems are not only enhanced with information and communication technology, but they are integrated with other systems such as heat networks, energy markets, electric mobility, or smart city as outlined in Fig. 1. As expected, the injection of information and communication technology at a grand scale has led to the rise of systems and components that are "intelligent" [20,23]. This has major implications on the understanding of system operations and interactions. Decentralised control strategies become more vital, in order to govern behaviour and ensure that the grid can be operated safely both within and even in ranges closer to the limits.

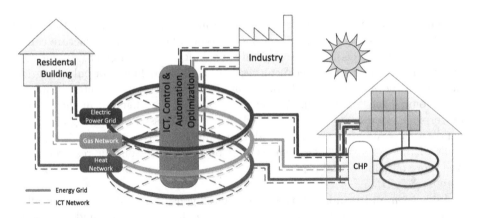

Fig. 1. Illustration of intelligent energy system elements and coupling infrastructures

Additionally, the trans-disciplinary nature of grid systems requires advanced and new types of methods for description, analysis, and optimization. Facilitating a combination of different numerical tools and domain models is the first step towards such a holistic description, but by no means is it sufficient. Non-formalized or inaccessible model information is often "in the brains" of experts, and requirements and constraints often remain "in the hearts or bellies" of stakeholders. It is crucial to put these soft factors into the loop of designing, optimizing and operating such diverse Cyber-Physical Energy systems (CPES).

2.2   Status Quo in Education and Training

The transformation of the traditional energy systems into a more intelligent medium opens new paths and poses new challenges. As intelligent power and energy systems present additional complexity, current and future engineers and researchers should have a broad understanding of topics of different domains, such as electric power, heat and definitely ICT related topics. Appropriate education on modern topics is essential at university level, both for undergraduate and postgraduate studies, so that future engineers will be able to understand and tackle the challenges and propose/implement new methods.

For example, the classic electrical power engineering education usually does not sufficiently cover smart grid topics, posing challenges to young researchers and students and also to the industry. Recently several universities have incorporated new courses in the undergraduate engineering curriculum or have enriched their existing courses with more modern material. Some universities have also created dedicated master courses with relevant topics. The instruction is performed with traditional methods, such as class lectures, but also with programming, advanced simulations [19] and laboratory exercises [2,6], where educational methods such as problem-based learning and experiential learning [8] are applied in some cases.

Moreover, the ongoing training of current professional engineers on modern topics is important. In some cases professionals tend to be hesitant of change, and this can also be evidenced by the reluctance of industry in adopting modern solutions. By proper training, professional engineers can better understand the benefits of modern solutions and ways in which to apply them so as to improve their work. For effective training, the material should be carefully designed, for example by focusing more on the practical aspects than the theoretic background. At this point it is important to highlight that frequently power systems professionals lack thorough understanding of ICT topics. On the other hand, ICT professionals often find it hard to understand the operation of the power system. As these areas (among others) are closely connected due to the emergence of intelligent power and energy systems, it is important to create links between them. Of course, a thorough understanding of all areas (electric power, heat, ICT, automation, etc.) is difficult to achieve, however an understanding of the fundamentals of each area, without sacrificing the expert focus in each particular field, will become more and more important. The same applies to researchers who are working to find solutions beyond the state-of-the art.

3   Learning Needs and Requirements

Intelligent power and energy systems are concerned with the communicative coupling of relevant actors (producers, consumers, network operators etc.) to optimize and monitor their interconnected parts so as to result in efficient and reliable system operation. Additionally, an increasing number of decentralized, renewable energy resources (photovoltaics, wind energy, biomass, heat pumps, etc.) have to be integrated.

The problem is, however, considerably more difficult because only an integrated view of all influencing factors, such as user acceptance, CO_2 emissions or security of this socio-technical system, while still being held in tension by profitability, reliability, and ecological sustainability can produce practically realizable solutions that adequately take into account the complex interrelations.

For this reason, energy informatics and automation not only provides the system intelligence algorithms for adaptive control and continuous dynamic optimization of the complex and very extensive power and energy supply, but also provides the methods to create and orchestrate overall system competences (complexity control through decomposition and abstraction, identifying and focusing on general principles, finding decoupling points for effective governance, avoiding bottlenecks, etc.).

In such complex systems of systems, the design and validation is a multi-stage process, as briefly outlined in Fig. 2. Conceptual development stages already involve rough tests leading to a "proof of concept". When the development subject is refined, so are the tests. This allows for early identification of errors and thus makes the development process more efficient.

The earliest testing stages may often-times be realized by pure mathematical calculations. However, as soon as interactions of different components in

CPES are considered, test cases become too complex for analytical approaches to be feasible. Hardware experiments, on the other hand, excel at reproducing interaction dynamics close to reality – especially if installed in the actual energy system as field tests; however, it is important to bear in mind the possible safety and cost consequences in the event of malfunction affecting hardware. Therefore, hardware setups are only suitable for the late stages of the development and testing process [21].

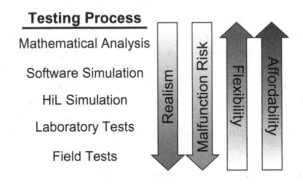

Fig. 2. Steps in the testing process for smart grid components [18]

The harsh trade-offs between analytical assessments and hardware testing underline the increasing importance of software simulation for power and energy systems research and development. Various software tools exist for simulation-based analysis of CPES. Review articles like [11,14,19] typically suggest that different tools are needed for different purposes. Also domains of expertise are wide spread, including electronics, ICT, automation, politics, economics, energy meteorology, sociology and much more. Each domain requires a specialised set of skills, but also the ability to interact and coordinate the solution of trans-disciplinary challenges.

These future experts require the relevant insight and abilities to coordinate and execute design and validation of CPES solutions. These abilities are facilitated by both generic engineering and cross-disciplinary technical competences.

The generic competences include the conception, design and analysis of systems (the CDIO skills catalogue [1]), which can be supported, for example, by project oriented teaching methods. With increasing problem complexity, systems-oriented skills can be strengthened, such as problem decomposition, abstraction and multi-disciplinary coordination of engineering challenges.

Cross-disciplinary learning is also required as the integration and interdependency of software and hardware systems is increased. Engineering students who aim to design and work with CPES solutions like complex control, supervisory and decision support systems, data analytics, require an increased level of programming and systems conceptual design competences, and a pragmatic view on the applicability of methods. This means that some familiarity with domain specific system architectures and description methods is useful (references architectures like SGAM[1] and RAMI[2], use cases, test cases, etc. [4,12]). Basic familiarity with distributed software systems problems is also a present knowledge gap within engineering education.

Complementary in strengthening required competences in CPES education, simulation-based tools are useful for the emulation and experience of physical behaviours and cyber-physical system couplings.

Summarizing, the following needs addressing education in the domain of intelligent power and energy systems have to be addressed:

- Understanding the physical behaviour of CPES and its connected sub-systems and components
- Understanding automation and control systems
- Understanding communication networks
- Understanding advanced control, optimization, and data analytics

Therefore, A holistic understanding of the physical and the cyber part of intelligent power and energy systems is necessary in order to design and develop a reliable and sustainable energy infrastructure of the future.

4 Education Possibilities and Corresponding Tools

4.1 Classroom Education and Training

Given the cross-disciplinary nature of intelligent power and energy systems as outlined above, students learning about this topic are exposed to a wide set of tools and concepts related to different knowledge domains. Thus, new education methods and tools must be developed, which are capable of bringing the different knowledge domains together, and allowing the students to understand the coupling and interaction of elements within intelligent solutions.

It is established in Sect. 3 that simulations will play a role in the testing process of new solutions. It is therefore natural that students learn to use domain-specific simulation tools, both in standalone use cases and in co-simulation setups. From an educational perspective, methods that allow students to understand the coupling of theory and application (through simulation or laboratory experiments) are required.

In the following two very interesting and promising classroom examples are discussed in more detail in order to see how such courses can fulfill the challenging needs in educating about intelligent power and energy solutions.

Example: Jupyter Notebooks
One approach applied at the Intelligent Systems course at the Technical University of Denmark is the use of Jupyter notebooks[3] using an IPython [13] kernel. These code notebooks allow the execution of code cells along with explanatory text, as seen in Fig. 3.

---

[1] Smart Grid Architecture Model.

[2] Reference Architectural Model for Industry 4.0.

[3] http://www.jupyter.org.

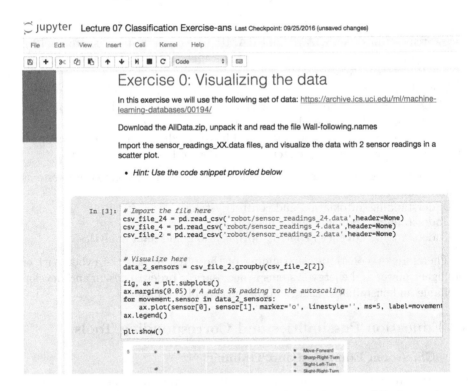

Fig. 3. Example of a Jupyter notebook, where markup language and Python code can be used to showcase complex examples.

The use of these notebooks provide a way to narrow the gap between theoretical concepts and application by setting up code examples where the student is able to able to receive a theoretical explanation followed by simulation results. Notebooks of this kind can be developed to cover a wide spectrum of intelligent energy systems concepts.

Furthermore, we believe that by constructing a framework where students can focus on a problem to solve, instead of dealing with issues related to programming, the students are able to better absorb and understand the core course concepts. So far, students have given positive feedback regarding their learning experience with these notebooks.

The gap between theoretical concepts and simulation can be addressed in the classroom, but it is also important that the students understand the limitations of solutions developed in pure simulation environments. As experiments on hardware are resource intensive, the Intelligent Systems course further employs a rapid prototyping scheme, by employing realistic software emulations of the target controls systems with a simulated back-end. This setup facilitates training on realistic automation software developments, avoiding the resource and time intensive maintenance of hardware platforms in the laboratory. In contrast to simulation-based solutions, the software developed on such platforms can be directly ported to the real hardware setup in the laboratory.

Example: Mosaik-Based Co-simulation

Another approach is taken at the University of Oldenburg as part of the master specialization in energy informatics. In a practical course students learn to plan, execute, and analyse co-simulation-based experiments. The target audience are computer scientists, environmental modelling students and participants of the post graduate programme in renewable energies. They learn how to model controllable and flexible electrical loads and generators, as well as integrating them into smart grid scenarios along with appropriate control and optimization mechanisms.

For this purpose, students should first derive and evaluate the differential equation-based models from the physical models and then transform them into discrete simulation models. Ultimately, they use the smart grid co-simulation framework "mosaik" (which was developed in Oldenburg) to use control and regulation mechanisms [16,17].

One of the main objectives is to have students understand and engineer the function of distributed agent-based control and regulation concepts, as well as algorithms, in decentralized generators and consumers, and all way up to the operation of electrical energy systems – in addition they analyse the requirements for real-time performance, resource utilization, robustness and flexibility.

The students are taught the basics in planning, execution and evaluation of simulation-based experiments. Special focus is put on the trade-off between accuracy and reliability of expected results and the necessary effort (Design of Experiments, Statistical Experimental Planning) to determine, as closely as possible, the interrelationships between influencing factors and observed target variables.

In terms of professional competences, the students learn to

- Evaluate and derive discrete (time-stepped) models from continuous physical models,
- Implement the smart grid co-simulation framework "mosaik",
- Analyse distributed agent-based control concepts and algorithms for decentralized generators and consumers for the operation of electrical energy systems, with regards to the requirements of performance balancing, equipment utilization, robustness and flexibility,
- Design the basis for the planning, execution and evaluation of simulation-based experiments, and
- Recognize the importance of the trade-off between accuracy and reliability of expected results and the effort required (Design of Experiments, statistical experiment scheduling) in order to investigate the interrelations between influencing factors and observed target values with as few attempts as possible – but as accurately as necessary.

Moreover, regarding methodological competences, the students learn to

- Model simple controllable and flexible electrical loads and generators,

- Simulate appropriate control and regulation mechanisms in smart grid scenarios for electrical consumers and generators,
- Apply distributed agent-based control concepts and algorithms for decentralized generators and consumers to electrical energy system operation,
- Evaluate simulation results,
- Research information and methods for implementing the models, and
- Present their own hypotheses and check them with means of experimental planning and statistical scenario design.

Finally, the social- and self-competencies to be imparted are to

- Apply the method of pair programming,
- Discuss the design decisions taken,
- Identify work packages and take on responsibility,
- Reflect on their own behaviour within the limited resource energy, and
- Take criticism and understand it as a proposal for the further development of their own behaviour.

Classroom education and training (as presented in the previous two examples) allow for rapid prototyping of solutions. Yet, the shortcomings of rapid prototyping are in the realistic emulation of the hardware behaviour. A way to bridge the gap between simulation and real-world implementation, through laboratory training, is discussed below.

4.2 Laboratory-Based Training

Laboratory-based training can offer practical experience to power and energy system professionals, ICT engineers, university students and (young) researchers. Such kinds of exercises and courses have been part of the engineering curriculum for decades [7]. However, new material and advanced training methods are necessary to deal with recent developments and new trends like the increased integration of renewables, controllable loads, etc. Therefore, laboratory courses need to be designed and applied in efficient and flexible laboratory environments.

Power and energy system engineering students usually lack the experience of working with real-world examples. For example, a realistic power system with several feeders, loads, transformers, generators is expensive and hard to build (contrary to other fields such as electric machines). Therefore, software solutions are typically used in laboratory exercises to perform power flow calculations, dynamic simulations etc. In some cases, experiments with real hardware are performed, however with low flexibility and typically for dedicated purposes. In the past, laboratory education in the power systems domain was performed with miniature generators and analogue transmission line models [7]. The situation has now changed with the wide deployment of personal computers and the development of suitable software which provides the freedom to model, flexibility and low cost.

Example: Hardware-in-the-Loop Lab Course

Power Hardware-In-the-Loop (PHIL) simulation allows the connection of hardware devices to a real-time simulated system executed in a Digital Real-Time Simulator (DRTS). PHIL simulation presents several advantages for educational/training purposes [8]. The real-time operation (monitor and control) is more realistic for the students. Hands-on experience of using real equipment (renewalbes, controllable loads) can be obtained, whereby actual magnitudes are measured and real equipment is controlled. Morever, equipment that is not available in the laboratory environment can be simulated, which gives freedom to design experiments (see Fig. 4) [8, 16, 19]. In addition, the performance of challenging tests in a safe and controllable environment is possible.

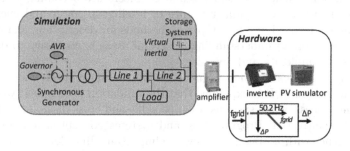

Fig. 4. PHIL-based experimental setup [8]

In this framework, laboratory exercises on modern Distributed Energy Resources (DER) related topics were designed/executed using the PHIL approach for the first time at the National Technical University of Athens [8]. The students (both undergraduate and graduates for their dissertation) highly appreciated real-time simulation as an educational tool. Moreover, it was shown that PHIL simulation can bring the students to the hardware lab, while maintaining the modelling capability of pure simulation approaches.

Outlook – Improvement of Education and Training Material
The above lab course example shows that the coupling of hardware equipment with a real-time simulated power grid provides various possibilities. However, additional work is necessary in order to provide a suitable and sufficient environment for teaching intelligent power and energy systems solutions. In the framework of the European project ERIGrid[4] the following educational activities are currently in progress to address the aforementioned requirements:

– Creation of online databases with educational material,
– Webinars on relevant smart grid topics,
– Development of a remote lab for DER, and
– Creation of virtual labs and online software tools.

---

[4] https://www.erigrid.eu.

In this context a remote lab is being developed that will allow access to the hardware of a microgrid. The users will be able to perform various experiments and corresponding tests within the grid-connected and island operation of the microgrid application. Moreover, voltage control issues (i.e., provision of ancillary services) will be studied and experiments with multi agent systems performed.

5   Conclusions

The emergence of intelligent solutions in the domain of power and energy systems (smart grids, CPES) poses new challenges, therefore appropriate education and training approaches for students and engineers are becoming increasingly important. The trans-disciplinary nature of intelligent power and energy systems requires advanced and new types of methods for description, analysis, and optimization. A broad understanding of several areas is necessary to deal with the increased complexity and diversity.

Challenging education needs and requirements have been identified and analysed in this study. It is explained that the validation of complex systems is a multi-stage process, while systems-oriented skills and cross-disciplinary learning needs to be cultivated. Programming and systems conceptual design competences, together with a pragmatic view are important. In order to cover the distance between theory and hands-on practice, coding and laboratory education is beneficial. The capabilities of advanced tools and methods have been discussed. The use of notebooks bridges the gap between theory and application, allowing the user to focus on solving the problem, instead of dealing with issues related to programming. Planning, executing and analysing co-simulation approaches is taught in a practical course focusing on distributed approaches. The use of PHIL simulation in laboratory education can provide hands-on experience of using real equipment in a highly flexible and controllable environment.

Future work will cover the setup of new courses, summer schools and the creation and collection of corresponding education material.

Acknowledgments. This work is supported by the European Communitys Horizon 2020 Program (H2020/2014–2020) under project "ERIGrid" (Grant Agreement No. 654113).

References

1. Crawley, E.F., Malmqvist, J., Lucas, W.A., Brodeur, D.R.: The CDIO syllabus v2.0. An updated statement of goals for engineering education. In: 7th International CDIO Conference, Copenhagen, Denmark (2011)
2. Deese, A.: Development of smart electric power system (SEPS) laboratory for advanced research and undergraduate education. In: 2015 IEEE Power Energy Society General Meeting, p. 1 (2015)
3. Farhangi, H.: The path of the smart grid. IEEE Power Energ. Mag. **8**(1), 18–28 (2010)

4. Gottschalk, M., Uslar, M., Delfs, C.: The Use Case and Smart Grid Architecture Model Approach: The IEC 62559-2 Use Case Template and the SGAM Applied in Various Domains. Springer, Heidelberg (2017). doi:10.1007/978-3-319-49229-2

5. Gungor, V., Sahin, D., Kocak, T., Ergut, S., Buccella, C., Cecati, C., Hancke, G.: Smart grid technologies: communication technologies and standards. IEEE Trans. Ind. Inf. **7**(4), 529–539 (2011)

6. Hu, Q., Li, F., Chen, C.F.: A smart home test bed for undergraduate education to bridge the curriculum gap from traditional power systems to modernized smart grids. IEEE Trans. Educ. **58**(1), 32–38 (2015)

7. Karady, G.G., Heydt, G.T., Olejniczak, K.J., Mantooth, H.A., Iwamoto, S., Crow, M.L.: Role of laboratory education in power engineering: is the virtual laboratory feasible? Part I. In: 2000 IEEE Power Engineering Society Summer Meeting, vol. 3, pp. 1471–1477 (2000)

8. Kotsampopoulos, P., Kleftakis, V., Hatziargyriou, N.: Laboratory education of modern power systems using PHIL simulation. IEEE Trans. Power Syst. **PP**(99), 1 (2016)

9. Liserre, M., Sauter, T., Hung, J.: Future energy systems: integrating renewable energy sources into the smart power grid through industrial electronics. IEEE Ind. Electron. Mag. **4**(1), 18–37 (2010)

10. Martinez, J., Dinavahi, V., Nehrir, M., Guillaud, X.: Tools for analysis and design of distributed resources - part IV: future trends. IEEE Trans. Power Deliv. **26**(3), 1671–1680 (2011)

11. Mets, K., Ojea, J.A., Develder, C.: Combining power and communication network simulation for cost-effective smart grid analysis. IEEE Commun. Surv. Tutor. **16**(3), 1771–1796 (2014)

12. Neureiter, C., Engel, D., Trefke, J., Santodomingo, R., Rohjans, S., Uslar, M.: Towards consistent smart grid architecture tool support: from use cases to visualization. In: 2014 IEEE PES Innovative Smart Grid Technologies Conference Europe (ISGT Europe) (2014)

13. Pérez, F., Granger, B.E.: IPython: a system for interactive scientific computing. IEEE Comput. Sci. Eng. **9**(3), 21–29 (2007)

14. Pochacker, M., Sobe, A., Elmenreich, W.: Simulating the smart grid. In: IEEE PowerTech Grenoble (2013)

15. Podmore, R., Robinson, M.: The role of simulators for smart grid development. IEEE Trans. Smart Grid **1**(2), 205–212 (2010)

16. Rohjans, S., Lehnhoff, S., Schütte, S., Scherfke, S., Hussain, S.: Mosaik - a modular platform for the evaluation of agent-based smart grid control. In: IEEE/PES Innovative Smart Grid Technologies Europe (ISGT EUROPE) (2013)

17. Schütte, S., Scherfke, S., Tröschel, M.: Mosaik: a framework for modular simulation of active components in smart grids. In: IEEE First International Workshop on Smart Grid Modeling and Simulation (SGMS), pp. 55–60 (2011)

18. Steinbrink, C.: A nonintrusive uncertainty quantification system for modular smart grid co-simulation. Ph.D. thesis, University of Oldenburg (2016)

19. Strasser, T., Stifter, M., Andrén, F., Palensky, P.: Co-simulation training platform for smart grids. IEEE Trans. Power Syst. **29**(4), 1989–1997 (2014)

20. Strasser, T., Andren, F., Kathan, J., Cecati, C., Buccella, C., Siano, P., Leitao, P., Zhabelova, G., Vyatkin, V., Vrba, P., Marik, V.: A review of architectures and concepts for intelligence in future electric energy systems. IEEE Trans. Ind. Electron. **62**(4), 2424–2438 (2015)

21. Strasser, T., Pröstl Andrén, F., Lauss, G., et al.: Towards holistic power distribution system validation and testing—an overview and discussion of different possibilities. e & i Elektrotech. Informationstechnik **134**(1), 71–77 (2017)
22. Vournas, C.D., Potamianakis, E.G., Moors, C., Cutsem, T.V.: An educational simulation tool for power system control and stability. IEEE Trans. Power Syst. **19**, 48–55 (2004)
23. Vrba, P., Marik, V., Siano, P., Leitao, P., Zhabelova, G., Vyatkin, V., Strasser, T.: A review of agent and service-oriented concepts applied to intelligent energy systems. IEEE Trans. Ind. Inf. **10**(3), 1890–1903 (2014)

MAS in Various Areas

Conceptual Model of Complex Multi-agent System Smart City 4.0

Michal Postránecký[1]([⊠]) and Miroslav Svítek[2]

[1] CIIRC Czech Technical University in Prague, Prague, Czech Republic
michal@postranecky.com
[2] Faculty of Transportation Science, Czech Technical University in Prague,
Prague, Czech Republic

Abstract. This paper is introducing a framework of Smart City 4.0 conceptual model, based on adoption and of Industry 4.0 Concept principles, characteristic and integration of computing technologies. Existing city systems are recently upgraded with latest ICT technologies through out of all their levels of infrastructure. New data are collected in big amounts and ability to use them is changing how systems will communicate together, to make cities work better and serve better to their users.

Cities are under continuous development, in relation to attractiveness of city structure, based on all activities and transactions conducted in city area and related surrounding, newly also through connected virtual world. Upgrade of existing cities into Smart city level is necessity for urbanized areas to survive a competition for satisfied client. It means actively acting citizen, as part of multi-agent Cyber Physical System, participating on city development.

Industry 4.0 Concept represents a future upgrade of one of city system segments. Integrating ICT and computing technologies throughout whole production enterprise enable to share data, information, and instructions between all agents during all phases of production value chain, where certain instructions are attached to product. Industry 4.0 concept includes six principles, which are also adopted by Smart City 4.0 concept. To evaluate and understand smartness level of multi agent systems and subsystems of Smart City and relations between them, authors are introducing Triangle Rule Diagram.

Keywords: Smart city · Smart City 4.0 · Cyber physical system · Industry 4.0 · Multi-agent system · Holonic · Complex system

1 Introduction

Cities are recently upgraded due to technical advancement and equipped with new products to acquire data from different sources, combine and analyze them, finding new facts and specifics about all activities and processes in these urbanized areas [18, 20, 26]. It is also a purpose for new techniques to design, build, manage and maintain them.

Smart City concept model is reliant an implementation of latest ICT and advancement in computing technologies. Connecting human to human, humans to machines, and machines to machines, transmitting data with different connectivity requirements through 2G/3G/4G cellular network, Wi-Fi, low throughput network,

© Springer International Publishing AG 2017
V. Mařík et al. (Eds.): HoloMAS 2017, LNAI 10444, pp. 215–226, 2017.
DOI: 10.1007/978-3-319-64635-0_16

LPWAN, LPN, Bluetooth, LoRa, and other technologies, platforms and internet supports a progress of retrofitting activities of existing urban structures (cities, sprawl development around cities, or rural areas), solve problems with overused technical infrastructure of cities or pure connectivity and innovation potential of urbanized elements around rural areas.

All recent city systems are most likely acting as individual silos [1–6] with centralized control management, with only a minimum interaction between each of them. Along with governmental regulations and policies, this creates many barriers in future rehabilitation of existing cities and their non-functional parts and neighborhoods, transportation infrastructure competing with historically grown urban structure (consisting of buildings, open spaces and underground infrastructure), and absence of political or citizens' support for systematic changes.

Development of Internet of Services, Internet of Things, Social Networks are having positive impact on organization of public transportation system, optimization of energy distribution, water and waste distribution management, city infrastructure maintenance, control processes, and peoples' distribution around city, especially in critical situations.

Homes and buildings are being equipped with intelligent technologies, with data processing within each component, and controlled over clouds. Sensors and actuators are heavily distributed inside and outside of buildings. Street elements and objects (lighting, stops, waste bins, etc.), mobile devices or wearables are capable to collect big data [25, 28]. Analyzing and studying these data gathered from many different sources provides city designers, political representation or business enterprises with new knowledge and perspective about processes conducted in neighborhoods, around town and relevant surrounding.

Growing use of digital information modeling methods, a geographic information system (GIS), parametric building information modeling (BIM) allows near to real time data sharing and exchange. An improvement in field of digital technologies and software development helps to design city and its parts, and optimize final design prior final development starts, with potential to simulate activities in model and reactions to conflict situations. 3D visualization tools with active augmented interface information layers are used for communication between all stakeholders to explain changes in existing, or future development in areas of interest.

Smart City virtual modeling used for prediction and simulation is comparable to an idea of twin models in Industry 4.0 Concept.

2 Smart Cities Concept

Concept of Smart cities is the next step in evolution of urbanized city systems development. Retrofitting of existent cities with ITC and computing technologies gives cities new opportunities for dynamic interaction with surrounding and rural area infrastructure. Cities are becoming very complex cyber physical system (CPS), where all physical infrastructure of every subsystem, and growing amount of virtual structure built in virtual world are networked through internet (Internet od Services - IoS, Internet of Things - IoT) and other technologies [16].

2.1 Smart Cities Concept Reasoning

Sustainability of multi-layered city ecosystem and quality of life is a leading reason to recent update activities in city's maintenance and management and to physical renovation of all systems [24, 27]. The force behind application of new technologies is to keep city entropy under control (minimize loss of energy and time, improve inhabitants' satisfaction, etc.). City components with high level of physical – cyber integration are able to connect to each other.

Digital transformation of cities (Smart Cities concept) is shifting its focus to service-domain logic, with higher quality and efficiency of all subsystems, layers and components of city complex Cyber Physical System (CPS) including:

- Commercial activities (employment)
- Public activities (education, security, access to health care)
- Leisure activities (housing, culture, sport)

Smart city approach is to adjust city systems and their existing structure, alongside with organization of processes inside CPS with expectation to minimize use of resources and maximize use of existing infrastructure. The objective is to enhance the whole chain of all processes inside system using deeper knowledge about area using collected and analyzed big data, and further optimized solutions. City is a complex system and minimization of resources and optimization use of existing infrastructure needs to be controlled by new algorithms.

3 Smart City as a Multi-agent CPS

An Artificial Intelligence will be surpassing ability of humans [17] in foreseeable time. This will lead to development of more autonomously operated subjects and systems, including cars, public transportation, freight delivery fleets, manufacturing processes, logistic and control centers, technical infrastructure of intelligent buildings. City with connected infrastructure will gradually start operate as one complex multi–agent system, with less interaction of human as controller of city processes. Self-learning ability will lead toward to higher level of optimization of the most essential city operational subsystems.

New advancement of city structures requires massive sensor, controller and many kinds of data transmitting device placements and distribution around cities to retrofit them to Smart Cities. Collaboration in a secure data sharing process is critical part of next city development and functioning. The failure of this fundamental pre-requisites in Smart City concept could lead to complete city blackout of all key systems.

With advanced connectivity between all city components, aggregated data are collected, moved, and shared through virtual world, and growing amount of asset is circulated in virtual environment and invisibly moved without borders of physical urban system. Higher level of physical – cyber integration, data processing in each physical component, and higher level of connectivity enable create of alliances inside system between multiple agents and delivery faster application or solutions especially in critical or disaster situations. Systems are gaining an ability of dynamical self-reorganization.

Utilizing digital parametric modeling (connected to life data feeds) and ability of visualization of invisible processes in virtual models, augmented with information attached to GPS, allows city managers and system controllers, designers and properties managers improve their services and quality of work. Mirroring physical structure of city (even in simplified forms) using virtual models with opportunity of demonstrating individual process and collaboration of agents, following a prediction of future development of system is starting to be a necessity.

Transition from existing cities to Smart Cities should evolve in sustainable level of balanced environment [23] to be certain, that this future transformation is sufficient and creates a sustainable ecosystem of coexisting human and artificial intelligence society.

This transformation is made in environment of intensive amount of regulations, creating many barriers for smart upgrade of city systems and applying latest techno-logical innovations.

4   Smart City and Adoption of Six Principles Described in Industry 4.0 Concept

From City viewpoint the Industry 4.0 reflects one of city's subsystem. This concept was developed specifically for factories and big enterprises. This concept of multi-agent system designed along whole Manufacturing Value chain (MVC) is predominantly unconnected to other city systems development. Even many of processes of this MVC are supplied from outside of physical borders of production enterprise, by some level of collaborative interaction with surrounding urban development, there is a minimal con-ceptual interaction and interoperability between MVC and entire city CPS. It creates a technologically advanced island in the specific area of city, in relation to the rest of urban development and infrastructure. If surrounding neighborhoods and systems around this island are not ready to accept intelligence of this advanced production enterprise, it may create fatal conflict situations in other city subsystems (for example in transportation system, energy distribution and stability - blackout), and otherwise drops production enterprise's level of productivity or even may stop production. This was a reasoning for searching parallels in I-4.0 Concept and Smart City vision and associated features, and for authors' proposal to apply the same principles, characteristics and functionalities described in Industry 4.0 concept [10] on the rest of city CPS, developed on the similar level of intensively connected and collaborating computationally advanced entities.

4.1   Six Principles of Industry 4.0

The Concept of I-4.0 describes six principles. They are:

1. Interoperability
2. Virtualization
3. Decentralization
4. Real Time Capability
5. Service Orientation
6. Modularity

These principles can be applied through all city systems.

Interoperability

In proposed Smart City near to 4.0 concept, all parts of infrastructure subsystems at each urbanized area should be seamlessly interoperating and maintaining connection points of each subsystem of city Cyber-Physical-Social. They will be networked and communicating to each other each other within secured networks system, including buildings, utilities, integrated transportation system, street elements and structures like smart lighting, smart bins or smart stops, street cameras, hospitals. educational facilities, logistic centers, transportation Hubs, business centers, retail and commercial facilities, energy centers. Networks like Internet of Machines, Internet of Things, Internet of Services, social networks, and other specialized or temporary networks will be interconnected together.

Virtualization

As Industry 4.0 Concept embrace use of digital Twin Models, the similar idea is adopted in Smart Cities Concept. Smart City neat to 4.0 will be mirrored in virtual model Twin City. Models have capability of simulation and prediction, providing visualization of actions in specific area of model, based on analytics coming from linked data sources. Virtual city models could be used for funding a project, development proposals, approval processes, exploration of subsystems' functionality, and much more.

Processes constructed and simulated in digital models may be augmented with GPS related information about any selected component, or areas in screening scenery. Simulation model may be studying traffic flow including pedestrians' behavior [7], public transportation and other factors. Virtualization of processes ongoing activities in city subsystems may be also delivered through specialized devices like glasses, which may be used in educational processes, or flow simulation.

Decentralization

The complexity of Smart City system structure requires decentralized management of all city systems and sub-systems, with an ability to act autonomously, making independent decisions, corrections of their state, creating alliances across systems to solve critical situations or to optimize sharing resources.

It requires an integrated data exchange database crossing silo's virtual communication barriers making silos collaborate in particularly important moments.

Smart City has an ability to collect real time data from physical word (smart street components, intelligent buildings, individual cars or fleets of public transportation, artificial intelligent (AI) elements operating in public space, people with their mobile devices, underground infrastructure, etc.) allows control and operation management of city systems to respond with preferred near to real time solutions. This is, for example, extremely important in city transportation system, or smart energy grid in blackout situation.

Service Orientation

Smart Cities are predominantly focused on service-oriented domain. An interaction of city systems, neighborhoods, intelligent buildings and infrastructure, public transformation and other subsystems with citizens, business entities, visitors of city and others are interconnected through Internet of Services, which leads to delivery of service to much wider audience (Fig. 1).

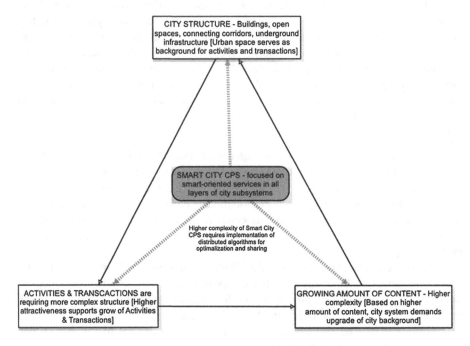

Fig. 1. Smart City shifting focus on smart-oriented service domain

Modularity

Flexibility in service delivery solutions, quick adaptation to change or malfunctioning city subsystems and their components are enabled by interchangeable individual modules of the same function or new modules, carrying better features, or when new type of functionality are added to module. These solutions are expected for example in smart energy grids, transportation, building industry, and others.

5   Adoption of Conceptual Model of Industry 4.0 on Smart City – Smart City 4.0

Analogously to Industry 4.0 [9, 11–15], the same setup of principles, functionality and system characteristics can be applied to Concept of Smart City 4.0, where the whole city is implicitly seen as Production enterprise system to delivery to client's products, predominantly in services-oriented domain.

This paper is proposing a concept of Smart City 4.0, in which the same principles are applied to a Smart City multi-agent cyber physical system with capability dynamically create and change hierarchies, and creating holonic alliances.

All stakeholders of product value chain are vertically and horizontally connected in holonic multi-agent system [29], constantly optimizing entire process.

Horizontal and vertical integration between city stakeholders, subsystems and components will be implemented at each phase of city production chain (CPC) (from vision and design phase, funding, information management od process, production, and follow up of service oriented activities as methods of delivery, Custom Relation Management, asset and property management, or future update of product) to assure optimal and balanced process at each moment of entire Product lifecycle. All subsystems and components within this CPC process has to be able interoperate and collaborate.

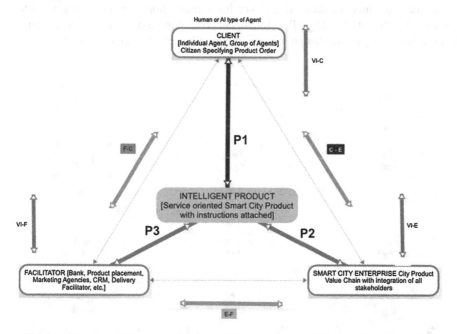

Fig. 2. Triangle rule diagram of industry 4.0 conceptual model adopted on Smart City

Triangle Rule Diagram shown at Fig. 2 was developed as a part of City smartness evaluation (proposed by authors of this paper). It describes a framework of Smart City near to 4.0 and connections within City Value Chain t are shown as well as information integration inside each phase of this OPF process:

- Order (specification)
- Production (within Enterprise – City System)
- Product delivery and CRM (Custom Relationship Management) provided by Facilitator of this part of development.

Industry 4.0 manufacturing production chain is partially carried by Intelligent Product. Concept City 4.0 presumes intelligent product equipped with ability of self-updating instruction set, virtually attached to it, responding to a new information and knowledge about rest of city CPS.

One of characteristic of CPS is ability of independently operated agents to create collaborative alliances with ability of immediate reconfiguration and scalability.

Graphics at Fig. 3 is showing evolution of growing collaboration between agents of City 4.0 concept. Agents in proposed diagrams are:

- Human agent (Ax)
- Intelligent Building as agent (Ax+1)
- Intelligent Transportation System agent (Ax+2)
- Smart Energy Grid agent (Ax+3)

Individual Diagrams describes growing interaction between each subsystem and communication interface (black dots). Web based interaction between human and other agents - Intelligent Building (IB), Intelligent Transportation system (ITS) or Smart Energy Grid (SEG) will change with evolve to alliances of holonic CPS.

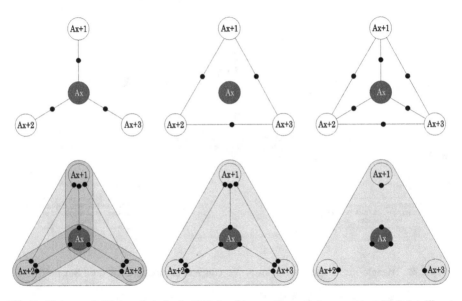

Fig. 3. Entropy of alliances in holonic CPS development between human agent (Ax), intelligent building acting as an agent (Ax + 1), intelligent transportation system (Ax+2), and smart energy grid (Ax+3)

6 Assessment Method of City Smartness

Triangle Rule Diagram Method (TRDM) shown on diagram at Fig. 4, describes framework of assessment method [8] evaluating city smartness, weighting horizontal and vertical integration of all stakeholders along city value production chain. This evaluation is made by cognitive expertise of assessor, electing one of 7 stages of smartness of specific subsystem (by mode and type of subsystem), and layer (management, infrastructure, interconnection, interoperation, open data sharing, services, innovation, etc.).

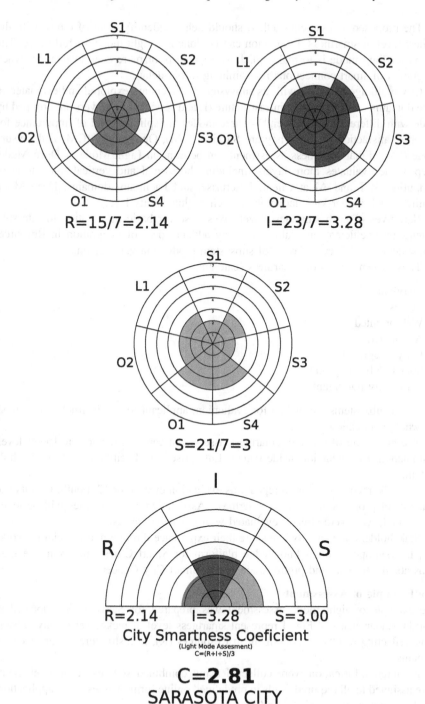

Fig. 4. Radar charts – Sarasota City assessment radar charts for Sarasota City – smartness-meter, sample documenting smartness of resources, infrastructure and service domains in Sarasota City.

The proposed assessment method should help to identify areas of cities, with the highest level of smartness. Evaluation can be done in a light mode, or full mode. The reason for light mode is to make quick assessment prior more deep evaluation, when integration of smart connections is examining in big detail.

City multi agent system with its subsystems – layers are explored and evaluated in three domains – resources (R), infrastructure (I) and services (S). Layers are grouped by mode with different level of weight. Three modes are split by level of importance for citizen's satisfaction of life. They are Survival (SM), Opportunity (OM) and Leisure Mode (LM). Final smartness assessment can be done in Light Mode or Deep Mode. Deep Mode evaluates more layers, including horizontal and vertical integration of computing, ICT and AI at Client, Enterprise, and Facilitator domains. Deep Mode requires much higher knowledge about each evaluated city layer.

Narratives of each smartness level gives observer basic information to rate subsystems by coefficient on scale 1 to 7, by advancement of integration in Resource, Infrastructure and Service layers of subsystem production value chain.

These seven Levels on smartness scale are:

- Marginal
- Modest
- Web-oriented
- Automated
- Fully integrated
- Social-Cyber Physical
- Artificially intelligent

When subsystems are picked for evaluation, applicant follow instructions to finish the whole application.

The procedure of this city smartness assessment can be executed in deeper level, examination also behavior inside Client, Enterprise, and Facilitator sectors of whole system.

It will be recommending to repeat this evaluation every 6 or 12 month. Results and analytics of progression in city's smartness. Association to other cities will be given away to all, who were already evaluated with the same method.

Stakeholders of each city can share their experience through many social networks [22] like synopcity.com - knowledge platform for Smart Cities, and exchange their ideas about solutions and products leading to Smart City Concept.

The Example of Assessment

The example of light mode assessment was prepared for Sarasota city, located in Florida. Radar charts at Fig. 4 represent smartness level of picked set of city subsystems, reflecting results of assessment in Resources (R), Infrastructure (I), and Service domains.

Required information were collected using combined sources. Then coefficients were assigned to all required fields in predefined online form of assessment application, and final scores are calculated and visualized.

7 Conclusion

Existing cities are under process of transition to smart cities by implementing Information and Communication Technologies, with high level of physical – cyber integration and embedded components with data processing ability. Cities are gradually changing from hieratically managed system to multi-agent Cyber Physical System.

Industry 4.0 is concept was created to enhance a manufacturing value chain, integrating all stakeholders, with shifting focus on service-oriented domain. Manufacturing is starting to be more advance then rest of city subsystems and coexistence with the rest of city could generate critical situations in connected infrastructure.

Authors of this paper are proposing an adoption of Industry 4.0 on entire city system, and subsystems, to control balanced upgrade and redevelopment of all subsystems connected in one holonic multi-agent CPS. This concept is based on similar principles, characteristic and functionalities between Industry 4.0 concept and concept of other Smart City individual systems. The highest level of this complex form of CPS could be called Smart City 4.0.

To explore smartness of existing city systems, the framework of assessment method developed by authors is introduced. Compare to other methods used for Smart City evaluation, by means of Key Performance Indicators (KPIs) [19, 21], this method is based on experts' cognitive approach, where no data are needed to be collected as in case of KPIs method. Evaluation can be done in light or deep mode. Simple example of Sarasota city assessment is presented.

Acknowledgment. This work was supported by the Project AI & Reasoning CZ.02.1.01/0.0/0.0/15_003/0000466 and the European Regional Development Fund.

References

1. Svítek, M.: Telematic approach into program of smart cities. In: EATIS 2014, Valparaiso, Chile (2014)
2. Přibyl, O., Svítek, M.: System-oriented approach to smart cities. In: Proceedings of the First IEEE International Smart Cities Conference. IEEE Systems, Man, and Cybernetics Society, New York (2015)
3. Svitek, M.: Applying wave probabilistic functions for dynamic system modelling. IEEE Trans. Syst. Man Cybern. Part C: Appl. Rev. **41**(5), 674–681 (2011)
4. Svitek, M.: Quasi-non-ergodic probabilistic systems and wave probabilistic functions. Neural Netw. World **19**(3), 307–320 (2009)
5. Svitek, M.: Towards complex system theory. Neural Netw. World **25**(1), 5–33 (2015)
6. Svitek, M.: Wave probabilistic information power. Neural Netw. World **21**(3), 269–276 (2011)
7. Bouchner, P., Hajny, M., Novotny, S., et al.: Car simulation and virtual environments for investigation of driver behavior. Neural Netw. World **15**(2), 149–163 (2005)
8. Postranecky, M., Svitek, M.: Assessment method to measure Smartness of Cities. In: Conference Paper, Smart City Conference, Prague 2017 (2017)

9. Roblek, V., Meško, M., Krapež, A.: A complex view of industry 4.0. SAGE Open **6**(2), 1–11 (2016). doi:10.1177/2158244016653987

10. Brettel, M., Friederichsen, N., Keller, M., Rosenberg, M.: How virtualization, decentralization and network building change the manufacturing landscape: an industry 4.0 perspective. Int. Sci. Index Inf. Commun. Eng. **8**(1), 37–44 (2014)

11. Tichý, P., Kadera, P., Staron, R.J., Vrba, P., Tichý, P., Kadera, P., Mařík, V.: Multi-agent system design and integration via agent development environment. Eng. Appl. Artif. Intell. **25**(4), 846–852 (2012)

12. Wang, S., Wan, J., Zhang, D., Li, D., Zhang, C.: Towards smart factory for industry 4.0: a self-organized multi-agent system with big data based feedback and coordination. Comput. Netw. **101**(4), 158–168 (2016)

13. Tao, F., Zuo, Y., Xu, L.D., Zhang, L.: IoT based intelligent perception and access of manufacturing resource towards cloud manufacturing. IEEE Trans. Industr. Inf. **10**(2), 1547–1557 (2014)

14. Frazzon, E.M., Hartmann, J., Makuschewitz, T., Scholz-Reiter, B.: Towards socio-cyber-physical systems in production networks. Procedia CIRP **7**, 49–54 (2013)

15. Recommendations for implementing the strategic initiative INDUSTRIE 4.0, April 2013. http://www.acatech.de/fileadmin/user_upload/Baumstruktur_nach_Website/Acatech/root/de/Material_fuer_Sonderseiten/Industrie_4.0/Final_report__Industrie_4.0_accessible.pdf

16. Behmann, F., Wu, K.: Collaborative Internet of Things (C-IoT): For Future Smart Connected Life and Business. Wiley, Hoboken (2015). [1-118-91374-4; 1-118-91373-6]

17. Veitas, V., Weinbaum, D.: A World of Views: A World of Interacting Post-Human Intelligences (2015). https://arxiv.org/pdf/1410.6915.pdf

18. Anthopoulos, L., Fitsilis, P.: Using classification and roadmapping techniques for smart city viability's realization. Electron. J. e-Gov. **11**(1), 326–336 (2013)

19. Walravens, N.: Qualitative indicators for smart city business models: the case of mobile services and applications. Telecommun. Policy **39**(3–4), 218–240 (2015)

20. Musterd, S., Kovács, Z.: Place-Making and Policies for Competitive Cities, 1st edn. Wiley, Hoboken (2013)

21. Hara, M., Nagao, T., Shinsuke Hannoe, S., Nakamura, J.: New key performance indicators for a smart sustainable city. Sustainability **8**(3), 206 (2016)

22. Anthopoulos, L., Fitsilis, P.: Social networks in smart cities - comparing evaluation models. In: Conference Paper, First IEEE International Smart Cities Conference (ISC2-2015), At Guadalajara, Mexico (2015)

23. Anthopoulos, L., Fitsilis, P., Ziozias, C.: What is the source of smart city value? A business model analysis. Int. J. Electron. Gov. Res. **12**(2), 56–76 (2016)

24. Bibri, S.E., Krogstie, J.: On the social shaping dimensions of smart sustainable cities: a study in science, technology, and society. Sustain. Cities Soc. **29**, 219–246 (2017)

25. Kitchin, R.: The real-time city? Big data and smart urbanism. GeoJournal **79**, 1–14 (2014)

26. Giatsoglou, M., Chatzakou, D., Gkatziaki, V., Vakali, A., Anthopoulos, L.: CityPulse: a platform prototype for smart city social data mining. J. Knowl. Econ. **7**(2), 344–372 (2016)

27. Anthopoulos, L.: Defining smart city architecture for sustainability. In 4th IFIP Electronic Government (EGOV) and 7th Electronic Participation (ePart) Conference (2015)

28. Poncela, J., Poncela, P., Giaffreda, R., De, S., Vecchio, V., Nechifor, S., Barco, R., Aguayo-Torres, M.C., Stavroulaki, V., Moessner, K., Demestichas, P.: Smart cities via data aggregation. Wirel. Pers. Commun. **76**, 149–168 (2014)

29. Mařík, V., Brennan, R., Pěchouček, M. (eds.): HoloMAS 2005. LNCS (LNAI), vol. 3593. Springer, Heidelberg (2005). doi:10.1007/11537847

An Embedded Agent-Based Intelligent Industrial Wireless Sensor Network

Mohammed S. Taboun[✉] and Robert W. Brennan

University of Calgary, Calgary, AB, Canada
mstaboun@ucalgary.ca

Abstract. Advances in cyber-physical systems and the introduction of Industry 4.0 have opened the door for interconnectivity in the industrial automation paradigm. One of the emerging technologies proven to be useful in factory automation is wireless sensor networks. In dynamic situations, wireless sensor networks need to be able to self-reconfigure while maintaining data integrity and efficiency. One solution popular with researchers is the use of multi-agent systems to manage wireless sensor networks. Typically, software agents are located on a server or cloud environment. Recent advances in microcomputers have made it feasible to embed these agents on the devices they control. This requires new reconfiguration and network management protocols. In this paper, an embedded agent architecture for wireless sensor network is proposed and an application specific example is given for an oil and gas refinery. An experiment is also conducted to investigate the effect of cluster sizes and signal frequency on the ratio of lost signals in a wireless sensor network cluster.

Keywords: Embedded multi-agent systems · Wireless sensor networks · Distributed intelligent control

1 Introduction

Recent advances in cyber-physical systems along with the introduction of Industry 4.0, have led to an extensive amount of research in distributed intelligent control along with the development of internet connected devices. Since cyber-physical systems require that devices be aware of their environment, industrial wireless sensor networks (WSNs) have been considered for this application by many researchers. Recent research has shown that multi-agent systems have proven to be a successful technique for managing WSNs in simulations. Typically, this is done through a coupled, or cloud based deployment. Recent advances in technology, such as the introduction of single board micro-computers have led to the feasibility of deploying these intelligent agents directly on the automation hardware, thus creating an intelligent embedded system.

In this paper, a brief background of cyber-physical systems and Industry 4.0 are given. Background on industrial wireless sensor networks and agent based control in wireless sensor networks is examined, and a distinction between embedded and cloud base agents is presented. Related works in agent based WSN, and specifically, their applications in oil and gas refineries are examined, along with the authors' previous sink node embedded, agent based WSN model. A new fully embedded multi-agent

© Springer International Publishing AG 2017
V. Mařík et al. (Eds.): HoloMAS 2017, LNAI 10444, pp. 227–239, 2017.
DOI: 10.1007/978-3-319-64635-0_17

systems managed WSN is presented. For this study, an experiment is conducted to compare the difference in lost signals between the previous sink node embedded model and the current fully embedded model. These results are discussed, conclusions are drawn and future work is discussed.

2 Background

2.1 Industry 4.0 and Cyber-Physical Systems

As previously mentioned, cyber-physical devices and cyber-physical systems are beginning to emerge in industrial applications. A cyber-physical system can be defined as a set of cyber-physical devices that include computing hardware and software that control mechanical activity through embedded processing, networking and connectivity, awareness of the environment and other objects through sensors, and finally a means of interacting with the environment through actuators [1].

Industry 4.0 is a modern area of research which employs these cyber-physical systems. According to reference [2], the term Industry 4.0 describes different changes in manufacturing systems with not only technological but organizational implications. It can be expected that these changes will shift their focus from production to service orientation in industrial systems. This can be extended from manufacturing systems to other types of industrial systems, such as health care systems, logistics, scheduling and oil and gas processing. Evidently, it can be expected that these shifts will lead to new types of enterprises which adopt new specific roles within industry.

2.2 Industrial Wireless Sensor Networks

Cyber-physical systems require awareness of the local environment and other objects can achieve this awareness through sensors. Industrial wireless sensor networks (WSNs) have become a popular area in research due to the advances in processing power for single board micro-computers and reduced battery consumption of embedded battery powered devices. WSNs are composed of wireless sensor nodes, which are small low powered devices with limited processing and computing resources and are inexpensive compared to traditional sensors [3]. More specifically, a WSN sensing and control monitoring system does not require the extensive electrical wiring infrastructure of a conventional sensing and monitoring system. However, the trade-off can be lower speeds, higher latency, and wireless interference.

Two of the primary concerns in a WSN are data routing and aggregation. When a large scale industrial WSN passes a lot of data, this creates a large communication overhead, thus using much of the WSNs available bandwidth. The most widely accepted solution to reduce this overhead clustering the wireless sensor nodes. This clustering process forms a hierarchical structure for the network and allows for more streamlined data aggregation. This hierarchy can then be composed of two types of sensor nodes: sink nodes and "regular" sensor nodes, which can be seen in below Fig. 1 in an environmental monitoring example adapted from the mobile object tracking example presented in [4].

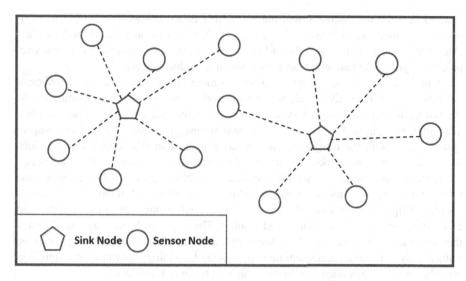

Fig. 1. Sink nodes and regular sensor nodes in a WSN

The nodes which make up the cluster heads are referred to as sink nodes. Sink nodes are responsible for aggregating the data as well as transmitting information from the network to the acquisition system, such as a SCADA system, or base station. Due to the fact that there are many transmissions and data aggregation is required of the sink node, it is often a higher processing, fixed unit. In other words, the sink node is a higher powered, wired unit with a fixed location. As previously mentioned, the sensor nodes which make up the cluster and send sensory data to the sink nodes are often referred to as "regular" sensor nodes or anchor nodes (which is more commonly used in mobile tracking systems).

2.3 Active vs. Passive Sensor Based WSNs

When considering wireless sensor networks, there are two ways of reading sensory data from the sensor nodes WSN. The first is with the use of passively sensing sensor nodes, where the sensor nodes send data without a request from the sink node. For example, a sensor node can send data on a time interval. In other words, the decision and request for sensory data is made on the sensor node level. The second method is using actively sensed sensor nodes, where the sink node sends a request and the sensor node(s) reply with sensory data. In other words, the request for sensory data is made on the sink node level, and the decision to send data is made on the sensor node level. For this study, we consider a passively sensed sensor node.

2.4 Industrial Agents in Wireless Sensor Networks

While several definitions of agents are commonly accepted in the research world, the most commonly accepted definition states that an agent is a computer system that is situated in some environment, and that is capable of autonomous action in this environment to meet its delegated objectives [5]. Agents can also be defined by their characteristics and behaviors. According to [6], agents are autonomous, responsive, proactive, goal-oriented, smart-behaving, social and able to learn.

A multi-agent system is a system of two or more intelligent agents that collaborate to some sort of collective goal, while still working to their own individual goals. According to [6], multi-agent systems have decentralized control and are flexible, adaptable, reconfigurable, scalable, lean and robust. The properties of multi-agent systems align with the design parameters along with other distributed considerations for wireless sensor networks, and are therefore well suited to manage these networks.

A major point of interest with the advances in technology is whether to embed the intelligent agent or to use a coupled or cloud based design. Reference [6] defines a coupled design as a situation where one or more agents collect and process data from an existing structure, in a cloud based fashion. The term "embedded agents" is when the automation platform itself is agent based. While the coupled design can be immediately applicable, and integrate with existing technology, advances in controllers are allowing the embedded intelligent design to become feasible.

3   Related Work

3.1   Agent Based Wireless Sensor Networks

The distributed nature of multi-agent systems aligns with the distributed properties of wireless sensor networks and, for this reason, many researchers have used adaptive, intelligent agents to work on distributed and complex sensor networks. This section briefly addresses some of the following relevant works.

In [7], multi-agent solutions for WSNs are examined. A multi-agent architecture which interconnects a wide range of heterogeneous devices that may possess various levels of resources is proposed in [8]. Similarly, Tynan et al. [9] proposed the development of intelligent sensor networks using multi-agent systems. In this work, the multi-agent system was implemented in the Java Agent Development framework (JADE). Reference [4] compared alternative cluster management approaches using multi-agent systems. This set of simulations also saw the multi-agent system implemented in JADE.

In [10], a multi-agent based application oriented middleware is introduced, in which a multi-agent management system controls a distributed control system using IEC 61499 distributed control function blocks. In this study, the middleware of a WSN referred to a set of tools that reduce the complexity on lower level hardware systems. According to [10], in traditional PLC based systems, this approach is often examined in order to build intelligence into simple programmable controllers. The middleware in [10] is designed specifically for wireless sensor networks that track mobile objects in factory automation.

3.2   WSN for Oil and Gas Refineries

Typically, the primary concern for research in multi-agent systems and wireless sensor networks is manufacturing applications. There are however some research areas that bring this technology to other industries, such as health care or safety. One of these industries of interest is oil and gas refineries.

Reference [11] examined the most promising wireless technologies used in order to cope with the challenges in implementing a WSN in an oil and gas refinery. The authors of reference [12] proposed an outlier detection and accommodation methodology for oil refineries using WSNs. The model was tested on a real monitoring scenario implemented in a major refinery plant.

3.3 Sink Node Embedded, Agent Based WSN for Oil and Gas Refineries

In our previous work [13], an embedded multi-agent system for managing clusters was proposed. This model had 3 intelligent agents embedded in the sink node of a WSN cluster that provide the intelligence required to manage its respective cluster. These agents are the sink node mediator, device manager and task manager. In this model, the device manager is responsible for managing the cluster, the task manager is responsible to task related goals and the sink node mediator mediates between the two other agents.

4 Embedded Agent WSN Model

In this section, a new embedded multi-agent systems managed WSN based on the architecture in reference [13] is presented. Changes in agents in the sink nodes are discussed, as well as the proposal of sensor node agents.

4.1 Sink Node Management

Similar to the model in [13], the sink node has a task manager that is responsible for managing application specific data, a device manager responsible for managing the cluster topology and a sink node mediator agent to mediate the agents on the sink node. Additionally, this model has added a port manager agent in order to manage communication through the wireless transceiver. The architecture is shown in Fig. 2.

In this architecture, the device manager has knowledge of the local environment, the state of each node in the cluster (or nodes situated in the local environment), the power level (i.e. remaining battery life) of each sensor node and finally, the I/O on the node. The device manager is able to communicate only through software APIs. The device manager has skills in conversation, negotiation and decision making.

The task manager has knowledge of each local ask status as well as the critical levels of local tasks. Similar to the device manager, it is only able to communicate through software APIs. The task manager has skill in data aggregation, integration, filtering, conversation, decision making and event handling.

The port manager is essential in managing data moving through the port in which the sink node communicates through. This is necessary due to the elevated number of signals sent and received through the sink node when compared to a sensor node, combined with the port's limited ability in sending or receiving a signal. In other words, the port manager should manage the port since a signal cannot be sent at the

Fig. 2. Agents which are deployed on sink node

same time the device is listening for signals, nor can two signals be sent or received simultaneously. The port manager has knowledge of the local environment, the status of each node, and the status of the WSN port. The port manager agent, like the previous two agents can communicate through software API's, but can also communicate through the WSN port. The port manager has skills in conversation negotiation and decision making.

Finally, the sink node mediator has knowledge of advertisements and calls for bids. It communicates through software API's and other network protocols (for example, internet). It has skills in conversation, collaboration and brokering. The sink node mediator is responsible for mediating messages sent between agents located on a sink node as well as communicating with agents on other sink nodes. The sink node mediator, however, does not mediate messages between sink nodes and regular sensor nodes local to the respective sink nodes.

4.2   Embedded Agents for Dynamic Reconfiguration

Along with the sink node embedded agents, a sensor node agent is embedded in each sensor node. The distinction here is that "sensor node" refers to the hardware platform of the sensor, while term "sensor node agent" refers to the software component, or embedded intelligence.

The sensor node agent has knowledge of the current cluster topology, the neighboring sink nodes, the port status, critical task levels, task status. The sensor node agent is only able to communicate through the WSN port. The sensor node agent has skills in communication, data aggregation and decision making.

4.3   Wireless Sensor Network Architecture

Sensor node agents are deployed on sensor nodes, which allows sensor nodes to communicate with the sink node of their respective clusters through the WSN communication protocols. The sink node embedded agents communicate with the data acquisition system and/or other sink nodes through other network protocols. Since the network architecture follows a clustered topology, scaling the network to more nodes is fairly simple. An industrial WSN can be compose of 1, 2 or Sn sink nodes and 1, 2 or Cn cluster of sensor nodes.

5   Application Specific Example

5.1   Embedded Agent Based WSN for Oil and Gas Refineries

To illustrate an application of the architecture, consider the example of a simple oil refinery, shown in Fig. 3, which has been adapted from reference [14]. In this example, the simple refinery process consists of 4 major types of equipment: separators, compressors, water treatment and storage. For this example, there are two types of separators: stage 1 and stage 2. There are also two types of gas compressors: a low-pressure compressor and a high-pressure compressor.

In this example, which is based on the example presented in [13], unprocessed oil (which consists of a mixture of oil, gas and water) enters the stage 1 separator. The gas that is separated from the stage 1 separator goes to the low-pressure gas compressor. The leftover oil flows to the stage 2 separator. In this stage 2 separator, the remaining gas is separated from the oil. This gas is then sent to the low-pressure gas compressor. After this process, the water that is separated is sent to the water treatment equipment. The refined oil is stored and/or exported after leaving stage 2 separation. After leaving the low-pressure gas compressor, the gas is sent to the high-pressure gas compressor, where it is then exported. The process, along with the responsibility for each cluster is illustrated in Fig. 3.

Some facilities will have more than 1 piece of a certain type of equipment. For example, if it is assumed that a regular sized oil storage tank can be cluster 1.1, and that there are three oil storage tanks in a refinery. It can then be said that cluster 1.1.1 monitors the first storage tank, 1.1.2 monitors the second, and 1.1.3 monitors the third.

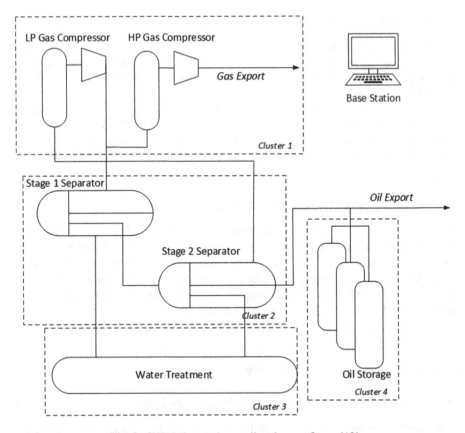

Fig. 3. WSN clusters in an oil and gas refinery [13]

In this case, it would be simple to add one or more storage tanks, or remove an obsolete or damaged storage tank.

One of the key metrics in a refinery is the frequency of data acquired from the processing equipment. Although different types of equipment will have different real-time data acquisition requirements, there will be a minimum threshold of data acquired in order for the equipment to be feasible. In the next section, the effect of increasing the number of sensor nodes as well as increasing the interval of signals sent from the sensor nodes on the quality of service for the WSN.

6 Experiment

In this section, the experiment for this study is discussed. For this study, an experiment was conducted to determine the extent of any effects on cluster size and frequency of sensor node signals for this WSN architecture with passive sensor nodes. This is essential to the development of agent based hardware. Much of the research on agent based WSNs is done through simulations, without considering actual hardware implementation. This experiment is designed to see how communication of agents through a hardware implemented WSN protocol performs in terms of quality of service. In this experiment, we implement we test the performance of the before mentioned WSN architecture on hardware.

As previously mentioned, this architecture was implemented on a hardware testbed. The testbed was developed using Raspberry Pi 3, Raspberry Pi Zero and XBee ZigBee modules. For this experiment, the testbed was configured to have between 5 to 10 sensor nodes and 1 sink node.

The multi-agent system was built using JADE and deployed on this testbed. Tests were run according to the statistical design presented in Sect. 6.2, and results were analyzed. The experimental design is discussed in the next section starting with the metric in Sect. 6.1.

6.1   Lost Signal Ratio

In large scale factory wireless sensor networks, one of the most critical metrics is the number of signals making it through to the data acquisition system. The lost signal ratio (Ls) is defined as:

$$L_s = \frac{n_{sent} - n_{received}}{n_{sent}} \tag{1}$$

where n_{sent} is the number signals sent in a cluster and $n_{received}$ is the number of signals received by the sink node.

While an acceptable lost signal ratio is application specific, typically a goal is to minimize the lost signal ratio. A lower lost signal ratio is the product of more of the signals sent by the sensor node read by the sink node. A higher lost signal ratio, on the other hand is a product of the sink node not receiving the signals sent by the sensor nodes in its' cluster. Lost signals result in lost information, which in turn degrades the quality of any monitoring and/or control processing. Therefore, a lower lost signal ratio contributes to a higher quality of service.

6.2   Statistical Design

In this experiment, we investigate the effect of two factors on the lost signal ratio of a wireless sensor network cluster. The first factor is the number of sensor nodes in a cluster. When increasing the number of sensor nodes, the sink node requires more bandwidth, so we expect to see increased signal congestion and a corresponding increase in lost signal ratio. In this experiment, this factor has six levels – the cluster size ranging from 6 to 10 sensor nodes.

The second factor is the time between sent signals. In a WSN with passive sensor nodes, the sensor nodes send signals based on a factor internal to the sensor node. In this experiment, the sensor nodes are inspected based on a time frequency. This factor has two levels: 5 s and 10 s.

Given the factors previously introduced factors, a statistical scheme for experimentation can be devised. There are 2 factors, 1 of which is 6 levels and 1 of which is 2 levels. With a full factorial design outlined according to [15], we will have the following design:

$$r_{base} = 6^1 2^1 \tag{2}$$

where r_{base} is the number of base runs. With 12 base runs and 5 replications per run, there are 60 runs total.

To reduce the effects of external factors, according to [15] it is widely suggested to randomize the running order of the runs for the experiment. In this study, the running order of the experiment was randomized using python and UNIX bash scripting.

6.3   Significance of Experiments with Respect to Embedded Agents

In this section, the significance of the experiment to embedded agents in WSN are discussed. As previously mentioned, it is widely accepted that multi agent systems are an ideal solution for managing wireless sensor networks. Much of the research to date focuses on battery conservation and data routing, and only considers simulated experiments. In the application specific example presented in Sect. 5, one of the primary concerns for oil and gas refineries is quality of service in terms of WSN data. This equates to a lower number of lost signals. The experiment in this study tests hardware embedded agents' ability to deliver a feasible quality of service that would be required in industrial applications.

6.4   Experimental Results

In this section, the results of the experiment are discussed. For this experiment, we tested the effect of two factors on the lost signal ratio. In this experiment, we expected the increase in cluster size to increase the lost signal ratio. We also expected the increase in the time between sensor node signals sent to decrease the lost signal ratio. First the effects of cluster size are discussed following with the transmission interval time differences.

Effect of Cluster Size
In this experiment, different cluster sizes were examined, ranging from 5 to 10 sensor nodes. There were to transmission times: 5 and 10 s. The effect of the cluster size for both 5 and 10 s intervals are analyzed using 1-way ANOVA (for each) and a Tukey post-hoc test.

For a transmission interval of 5 s, there was a statistically significant difference between groups as determined by one-way ANOVA ($F(5,24) = 718.7$, $p = .000$). A Tukey post hoc test revealed that the lost estimation ratio became statistically significantly higher whenever an extra sensor node was added, as summarized in Fig. 4.

For a transmission interval of 10 s, there was a statistically significant difference between groups as determined by one-way ANOVA ($F(5,24) = 887.5$, $p = 0.000$). A Tukey post hoc test revealed that the lost estimation ratio became statistically significantly higher whenever an extra sensor node was added, as summarized in Fig. 5.

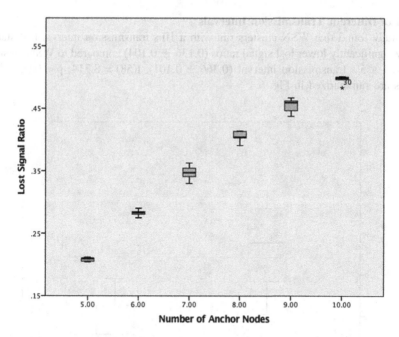

Fig. 4. Effect of cluster size on lost estimation ratio for 5 s transmission intervals (F(5,24) = 718.7, p = .000)

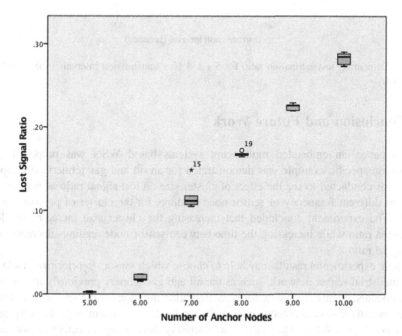

Fig. 5. Effect of cluster size on lost estimation ratio for 10 s transmission intervals (F(5,24) = 887.5, p = .000

Effect of Different Transmission Intervals

This study found that WSN clusters run with a 10 s transmission interval had statistically significantly lower lost signal ratios (0.136 ± 0.104) compared to WSN clusters run with a 5 s transmission interval (0.366 ± 0.101), $t(58) = 8.714$, $p = 0.000$. The results are summarized in Fig. 6.

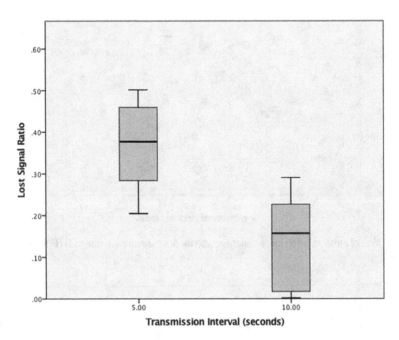

Fig. 6. Comparing lost estimation ratio for 5 s and 10 s transmission intervals ($t(58) = 8.714$, $p = 0.000$)

7   Conclusion and Future Work

In this paper, an embedded multi-agent systems based WSN was proposed. An application specific example was demonstrated for an oil and gas refinery. An experiment was conducted to see the effect of cluster size on lost signal ratio as well as the effect of different frequency of sensor node readings for the cluster of passive sensor nodes. The experiment concluded that increasing the cluster size increases the lost estimation ratio while increasing the time between sensor node readings decreases the lost signal ratio.

These experimental results may help to choose which sensors to prioritize in a large scale industrial sensor network, such as the oil and gas refinery previously mentioned. The embedded agents also allow for reconfiguration decisions at the sensor node level. These reconfiguration protocols may arguably be more efficient with actively read sensor nodes in a WSN. The authors are currently developing an active sensor node architecture for a reconfigurable WSN to compare to this architecture.

References

1. Broy, M., Schmidt, A.: Challenges in engineering cyber-physical systems. Computers **47**(2), 70–72 (2014)
2. Lasi, H., Fettke, P., Kemper, H., Feld, T.: Industry 4.0. Bus. Inf. Syst. Eng. **6**(5), 239–242 (2014)
3. Callaway, E.: Wireless Sensor Networks: Architectures and Protocols. CRC Press, Boca Raton (2003)
4. Gholami, M., Taboun, M.S., Brennan, R.W.: Comparing alternative cluster management approaches for mobile node tracking in a factory wireless sensor network. In: 2014 IEEE Conference on Systems, Man and Cybernetics (SMC), San Diego (2014)
5. Woolridge, M.: An Introduction to Multiagent Systems. Wiley, Hoboken (2009)
6. Leitao, P., Karnouskos, S.: Industrial Agents: Emerging Applications of Software Agents in Industry. Morgan Kaufmann, Burlington (2015)
7. Hla, K.H.S., Choi, Y., Park, J.S.: The multi agent system solutions for wireless sensor network applications. In: Nguyen, N.T., Jo, G.S., Howlett, R.J., Jain, L.C. (eds.) KES-AMSTA 2008. LNCS, vol. 4953, pp. 454–463. Springer, Heidelberg (2008). doi:10.1007/978-3-540-78582-8_46
8. Karlsson, B., Bäckström, O., Kulesza, W.: Intelligent sensor networks - an agent oriented approch. In: Workshop on Real-World Wireless Sensor Networks (2005)
9. Tynan, R., Ruzzelli, A.G., O'Hare, G.M.: A methodology for the development of multi-agent systems on wireless sensor networks. In: 17th International Conference on Software Engineering and Knowledge Engineering (SEKE 2005), Taipei, Taiwan (2005)
10. Cai, N., Gholami, M., Yang, L., Brennan, R.W.: Application oriented middleware for distributed sensing and control. IEEE Trans. Syst. Man Cybern. Part C Appl. Rev. **42**(6), 947–956 (2012)
11. Sevazzi, S., Guardiano, S., Spaganoli, U.: Wireless sensor network modelling and deployment challenges in oil and gas refinery plants. Int. J. Distrib. Sens. Netw. **9**(3), 383168 (2013)
12. Gil, P., Santos, A., Cardoso, A.: Dealing with outliers in wireless sensor networks: an oil refinery application. IEEE Trans. Control Syst. Technol. **22**(4), 1589–1596 (2014)
13. Taboun, M.S., Brennan, R.W.: Sink node embedded, multi-agent systems based cluster management in industrial wireless sensor networks. In: Borangiu, T., Trentesaux, D., Thomas, A., McFarlane, D. (eds.) Service Orientation in Holonic and Multi-Agent Manufacturing. SCI, vol. 640, pp. 329–338. Springer, Cham (2016). doi:10.1007/978-3-319-30337-6_30
14. Devold, H.: Oil and Gas Production Handboook (2013). http://www.lulu.com
15. Montgomery, D.C.: Design and Analysis of Experiments. Wiley, Hoboken (2005)

Multi-robotic Area Exploration for Environmental Protection

Tomas Lazna[1,2]([⊠]), Tomas Jilek[1,2], Petr Gabrlik[1,2], and Ludek Zalud[1]

[1] CEITEC - Central European Institute of Technology,
Brno University of Technology, Purkynova 656/123, 612 00 Brno, Czech Republic
{tomas.lazna,tomas.jilek,petr.gabrlik,ludek.zalud}@ceitec.vutbr.cz
[2] Department of Control and Instrumentation, FEEC, BUT,
Technicka 3082/12, 616 00 Brno, Czech Republic

1 Introduction

Area guarding, exploration, and environmental measurement constitute both major necessities and open challenges for current robotics. As Industry 4.0 has quickly found its place in various domains of manufacturing, applications that use autonomous robots to considerably increase safety and security with no need of additional operators have become effectively and widely marketable.

The article analyzes only a small portion of related problems but considers their potential to be extended to other sub-problems. More concretely, two robots from our newly developed Autonomous Telepresence Robotic System (ATEROS) are used to fulfill one mission. An image of the robots included in ATEROS is shown in Fig. 1. Further, an unmanned aerial vehicle (UAV) equipped with an appropriate sensor subsystem acts as a 3D mapping device, and an unmanned ground vehicle (UGV), an Orpheus robot, exploits gamma radiation sensors to monitor the radiation area, make a 'radiation layer', or search for radiation sources. The risks involving such sources are described in, for example, [1].

Since the data come from different sources, proper referencing is a vital task and a central precondition of success. Although, potentially, the radiation measurement data may be padded to any referenced 3D map, the advantage of

Fig. 1. The robots included in ATEROS.

© Springer International Publishing AG 2017
V. Mařík et al. (Eds.): HoloMAS 2017, LNAI 10444, pp. 240–254, 2017.
DOI: 10.1007/978-3-319-64635-0_18

structuring such a map at the time of the radiation measurement embodies a major asset: maps provided by other sources are often unreliable, obsolete, intentionally distorted, or even completely useless in the case of an unexpected event (a technological accident, war, or natural disaster).

The capabilities presented herein form only one part of the ATEROS system, in which significantly more challenges are to be solved. For instance, a set of robots patrolling a predefined industrial area can definitely possess mutliple functions, including area guarding against unauthorized entries, monitoring sudden or longer-term spatial changes to diagnose a wide range of issues ranging from criminal/terrorist acts to technological accidents, and even observing natural processes or vegetation development.

The text comprises several chapters describing relatively independent procedures and aspects. In Sect. 2, high-precision photogrammetry with no need of ground control points (GCP) for light UAVs is characterized. Section 3 discusses precise self-localization, including the necessary equipment. The given process is indispensable for navigation, as described in Sect. 4. Section 5 then outlines the basics of radiation mapping, inclusive of directional measurement and the algorithms to speed up a point radiation source.

2   Aerial Mapping

An aerial map embodies an essential element within the planning of a mission in an unknown environment. Common aerial imagery is obtained using manned aircraft, from the altitude of hundreds or thousands of meters, or utilizing satellites deployed in space. In most cases, the resolution and accuracy of the orthophotos produced via this kind of imagery is not sufficient for the precise navigation of small mobile robots. Another restraining factor rests in that the landscape can change quickly due to changing seasons, construction activities, or natural disasters; consequently, the corresponding maps are rendered out-of-date. Such preconditions then establish an opportunity for the use of UAVs.

2.1   UAV Photogrammetry

UAVs can be a very effective tool for aerial mapping due to their low overall cost and safe and fast operation. Micro and light[1] UAVs are able to operate in low altitudes, producing the aerial imagery of local areas with very high ground resolution and almost as often as needed. Basically, two ways to georeference the imagery are available: using GCPs, whose positions are man-measured, and via onboard positioning equipment to measure the position (and orientation) of every single image. The indirect and direct approaches to georeferencing both have their advantages and disadvantages; in this paper, however, the direct mode is used because it satisfies the basic requirement of being usable in environments that pose risks to the human health.

---

[1] UAV classification according to [2]. Micro: less than 5 kgs; light: 5 to 50 kgs.

For the purposes of aerial mapping, a multirotor UAV DJI S800 was equipped with a multisensor system (Fig. 2) developed for the precise georeferencing of aerial imagery. This system comprises a digital camera Sony Alpha A7, a global navigation satellite system (GNSS) receiver Trimble BD982, an inertial navigation system (INS) SBG Ellipse-E, and a single board computer Banana Pi R1. The GNSS receiver is able to measure position with centimeter-level accuracy when real time kinematic (RTK) correction data are transmitted, and as it is equipped with two antennas for vector measurement, the device also measures orientation around two axes. The position and orientation data are used as an auxiliary input for the INS, which provides data output at a frequency of up to 200 Hz. Since all the sensors are precisely synchronized, once an image is captured, the position and orientation data are saved into the onboard SSD data storage. The multisensor system is described in more detail within [3].

Fig. 2. The applied UAV equipped with a multisensor system.

2.2   Image Acquisition and Processing

A UAV equipped with a multisensor system was used for the aerial mapping of a region where a potential radiation source is located. During an 8-min automatic flight, 137 photographs were taken across the area of approximately 3 ha. The flight trajectory and image capture period were set to meet the requirement of 80% side overlap and 80% forward overlap. As the full-frame camera was fitted with a 15 mm lens and the flight altitude corresponded to 50 m above the ground level (AGL), the ground resolution of the images is about 2 cm/px. Figure 3 shows the detail of one of the aerial images captured by the UAV (right), comparing it with an orthophoto from the CUZK[2] (left).

---

[2] The State Administration of Land Surveying and Cadastre of the Czech Republic, a body to provide web map service (WMS) containing orthophotographic, topographic, cadastral, and other map layers.

Fig. 3. A detail of the orthophoto from the CUZK [5] (left) and the orthophoto produced by the UAV photogrammetry (right).

Both the image data and the position data logs were imported into the Agisoft Photoscan Professional photogrammetric software. This tool is capable of processing image data and reconstructing terrain geometry, finding use in the creation of a digital elevation model (DEM) and orthophoto generation. The digital terrain model is georeferenced directly in the course of image processing because every image has been assigned a position measured using onboard sensors. The accuracy of the digital model was determined via 30 ground test points, exhibiting 1.6 cm RMS and 2.6 cm RMS for the longitude and latitude, respectively, and 1.5 cm RMS for the vertical axis. These results almost achieve the accuracy of indirect georeferencing, which is presented in, for example, [4].

Once the georeferenced orthophoto and the DEM have been formed, they can be used in the planning of a trajectory for terrestrial robots. The data were imported into the QGIS geographic software, which is able to work with a georeferenced raster, vector layers, and WMS layers. Using the orthophoto and DEM layer, a target polygon with the area of $438\,m^2$, where the terrestrial mapping should be executed, was determined. The situation is illustrated in Fig. 4. The polygon coordinates are used to generate the trajectory for the terrestrial robot, described in greater detail within the following sections.

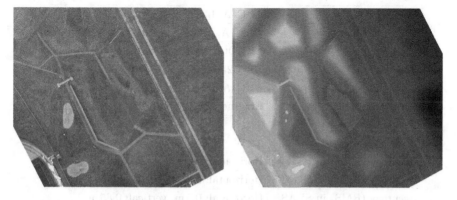

Fig. 4. The georeferenced orthophoto (left) and DEM (right) created using UAV photogrammetry. The green polygon represents the target area for the actual terrestrial mapping. (Color figure online)

3   Robot Self-localization

The modular concept is applied to design the self-localization of a mobile robot, allowing for the quick and easy integration of localization data from different sources. A GNSS is used as the main source of localization data due to the outdoor use of the mobile robot. Currently, the self-localization module comprises integrated submodules for odometry and AHRS/INS. Environments with a good open sky view facilitate using a solution based on the GNSS only. A Trimble BD982 GNSS receiver is employed for the GNSS localization solution.

The Trimble BD982 is an OEM receiver of GNSS signals. It enables the reception of GPS, GLONASS, Galileo, BeiDou, and QZSS signals. The receiver can work as a single stationary or moving base station or as a rover. In all its modes, the device can provide for different localization solutions. In situations with no external correction data available, the receiver works in the autonomous mode; if correction data distributed from satellites are accessible, it operates in the satellite-based augmentation system (SBAS) mode; and on the condition that the receiver uses data from ground correction stations or networks, it functions in the ground-based augmentation system (GBAS) mode. In the last mentioned cycle, the device can ensure differential GNSS (DGNSS) or RTK solutions. The DGNSS solution is a code-based one, and the RTK solution uses the measurement of the phase of the carrier signals. The RTK mode is the most accurate type of solution from those mentioned above; it is the primary solution employed in our applications. The main parameters of the BD982 receiver are summarized in Table 1.

Table 1. The main parameters of the Trimble BD982 GNSS receiver [7]

Parameter	Value
Update rate	Max. 50 Hz
Latency	Max. 20 ms
GPS signals	L1 C/A, L2E, L2C, L5
GLONASS signals	G1 C/A, G2 C/A, L2 P, L3 CDMA
Galileo signals	L1 BOC, E5A, E5B, E5AltBOC
BeiDou	B1, B2
QZSS	L1 C/A, L1 SAIF, L2C, L5
Connectivity	Ethernet, USB 2.0, CAN, RS-232, UART
Weight	92 g
Power consumption	2.3 W
Accuracy (RMS) in RTK	Horizontal: 0.008 m, vertical: 0.015 m
Accuracy (RMS) in DGNSS	Horizontal: 0.25 m, vertical: 0.5 m
Accuracy (RMS) in SBAS	Horizontal: 0.5 m, vertical: 0.85 m

Due to the high position accuracy in the RTK mode, position measurement in two points on the short base lines can be used for very accurate heading measurement. We utilize two GNSS antennas connected to the rover module. The signals from the first antenna are employed in two RTK engines: the first one ensures the position measurement of the mobile robot (using corrections from an external base or network), and the second one is used for the heading/tilt measurement of the mobile robot (via corrections based on the signals from the second antenna of the rover). A typical configuration is shown in Fig. 5.

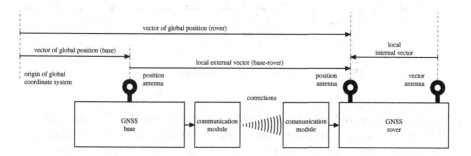

Fig. 5. Using the dual antenna GNSS receiver for 5DOF self-localization.

4   Robot Navigation

The mobile robot exploits an embedded control algorithm to track the required trajectory of motion. The algorithm, designed by our laboratory, is implemented as a separate module of the robot control system; it uses the data of the current position and orientation from the self-localization module, computing the control efforts for the motor drivers to track the requested trajectory. A simplified block scheme of the navigation algorithm is presented in Fig. 6.

The block that computes the navigation solution to track the current waypoint with coordinates φ_N and λ_N from the current position with coordinates φ_R and λ_R is shown in Fig. 7. Out of these coordinates, we then compute the

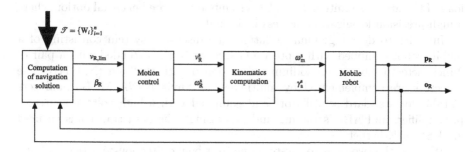

Fig. 6. A simplified block scheme of the navigation algorithm.

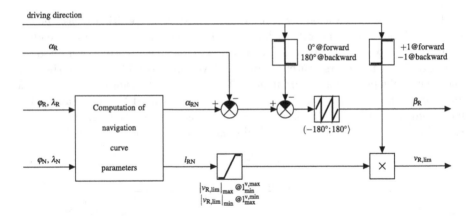

Fig. 7. The principle of the navigation solution.

start azimuth α_{RN} and length l_{RN} of the navigation curve [8]. The azimuth error is obtained from α_{RN} (setpoint) and from the current azimuth α_R (feedback) of the mobile robot. All the computations are performed natively in the WGS-84 coordinate system. A more detailed description of the algorithm is available in [6].

The navigation module also integrates an application interface for external control. In the context of autonomous area exploration, the external module with a path planning algorithm generates a sequence of waypoints that describes the requested robot motion trajectory.

5   Radiological Source Localization

According to papers [9,10], UAVs are applicable in obtaining radiation distribution maps. The disadvantage of this solution consists in the low precision of the source localization: Even when the UAV is equipped with a precise self-localization module, such as that described earlier, a problem arises with increasing distance from the sources due to the UAV's high flight altitude AGL. The drawback can be compensated for by using higher volume detectors; the useful load of the drone is limited. Thus, UGVs embody a more beneficial option where a high-precision localization process is desired.

In order to detect gamma radiation, the discussed system consisting of a mobile robot equipped with a precise GNSS receiver is extended with a pair of 2-inch detectors based on sodium iodide doped with thallium (NaI(Tl)). The detectors are complemented by multi-channel Nuvia NuNA MCB3 analyzers suitable for standard scintillators and equipped with a high voltage source, a preamplifier, and ADC sampling and processing. The data transfer is ensured via USB or Ethernet.

We used the two-detector system due to it being direction-sensitive and utilizable in advanced localization algorithms. In order to intensify the directional sensitivity, the detectors are separated by a 4 mm thick layer of lead. The idea is inspired by the system comprising three NaI(Tl) detectors introduced in [11] and the semiconductor detector setup with shielded layers discussed in [12]. An image of the whole robotic system is proposed in Fig. 8.

Fig. 8. Robot carrying equipment for gamma radiation measurement.

A scheme of the system components related to the actual radiation measurement is shown in Fig. 9. All the connections are realized through either the TCP or the UDP protocols. The main component consists in the control module which is a PC program performing data collection and the generation of commands for the navigation module.

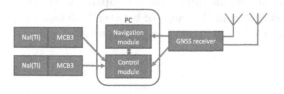

Fig. 9. A scheme of measurement system components.

The radiation measurement period is set to 1 s. The data are sent on request, which is synchronized by GNSS timing. The radiation intensity is represented by the number of pulses in each channel. The total count can be obtained by summing the partial counts. When the detector has been energetically calibrated or the response matrix operator is known, the dose rate can be obtained too [13].

5.1   Basic Mapping Algorithm

There are many different strategies to locate a radiation source in a pre-specified area. One of these lies in riding through the whole area along parallel lines with defined spacing. This method is well-known and has been characterized in multiple reports, e.g., [14]. To facilitate such an operation, two input parameters are needed: a list of vertices defining the polygon to be mapped, and the spacing of the measurement lines, whose relevant optimal value can be calculated for the weakest source to be found.

At the initial stage, the control program needs to compute the waypoints for the navigation module, calculating the equations of the lines parallel to one of the polygon's edges; the corresponding distance is given by the spacing. For each line, intersections with the polygon are identified. The waypoints are equally distributed along the line segments delimited by the intersections. Generally, this algorithm works well for convex polygons; however, when each parallel line has just two intersections with the polygon, it need not be convex. Apparently, the situation depends also on the choice of the edge to which the lines are in parallel. The resulting list of waypoints is arranged such that the points follow each other appropriately, and it is then sent to the navigation module accompanied by the command to start the passage. A schematic example of such a trajectory is shown in Fig. 11 (left).

The result of the mapping procedure is a set of scattered points, and these are not very suitable for visualization and further map processing, including, for example, the conversion to a 3D point cloud. Thus, radiation intensity calculation in the points of a regular grid is needed; this step is performable, for example, through a Delaunay triangulation [15]. At this stage, the data can be visualized, and the position of the sources can be marked manually.

The automatic computation of the position comprises three phases. First, the local maxima have to be found. To eliminate false positive detections, we used a custom 2D peak detector and tuned it with data acquired from real experiments. Basically, each point in the data set is compared to its neighbor as shown in Fig. 10, and its absolute value is compared to the threshold. The value of parameter k is chosen in the range of between 0.95 and 1.00, with parameter Th set to the double of the lowest measured intensity.

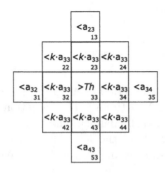

Fig. 10. A scheme of the kernel for peak detection.

Afterwards, the measured data points within the radius defined around each maximum are selected for further processing. These points are then fitted with a suitable function. In general terms, it is possible to use a paraboloid to carry out rough approximation because the fitting can performed analytically, using the least-squares method. With the set of points (x, y, z) where z is the intensity, the vector of the paraboloid parameters can be calculated by solving matrix equation [16]

$$\mathbf{p} = \begin{bmatrix} p_1 \\ p_2 \\ p_3 \\ p_4 \\ p_5 \\ p_6 \end{bmatrix} = \begin{bmatrix} \mathbf{1} \ \mathbf{x} \ \mathbf{y} \ \mathbf{x^2} \ \mathbf{xy} \ \mathbf{y^2} \end{bmatrix}^{-1} \mathbf{z}. \tag{1}$$

The components of the matrix on the right-hand side are column vectors composed of point coordinates. The following formulas then enable us to find the coordinates of the maximum of the paraboloid described by the parameter vector from Eq. 1. They fit to coordinates of the searched source [16].

$$x_{max} = \frac{p_3 p_5 - 2 p_2 p_6}{4 p_4 p_6 - p_5^2} \tag{2}$$

$$y_{max} = \frac{p_2 p_5 - 2 p_3 p_4}{4 p_4 p_6 - p_5^2} \tag{3}$$

5.2   Strong Source Search Algorithm

When timing is important and the presence of only one strong source can be assumed in the area of interest, the algorithm discussed in this chapter is applicable; it exploits the dynamic change of the measurement trajectory in accordance with the data already measured.

First, the same trajectory as in the case of mapping is planned. After the robot has reached the end of a line, the data are searched for peaks in the radiation intensity. If such peaks are found in two neighboring lines and the distance of their projections to the current line is smaller than some threshold, the trajectory is altered, and new waypoints are planned in the direction perpendicular to the current line, with intersection in the center between the peak projections. The robot follows this new line denoted as *normal line* until another radiation intensity peak occurs. Another line is planned in the direction perpendicular to the normal line (and, therefore, is parallel to the original lines), with intersection in the newly measured peak. The line may be shorter than the original ones. A schematic example of such a trajectory is shown in Fig. 11 (right).

After the new waypoints have been passed, the control program is expected to have collected enough data to interpolate the position of the source, using the same method as in the case of basic mapping. The only difference rests in that no local maxima are searched, and the global maximum is used instead. Three

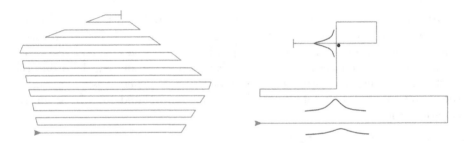

Fig. 11. The radiation mapping trajectory (left) and the strong source localization trajectory (right).

parameters influence the behavior of the algorithm: the first one affects the peak detection; the second one defines the allowed threshold for the neighboring peak projection distance; and the third one determines the length of the last planned line.

5.3   Experiment Results

Both of the presented algorithms were tested in experiments with real radiation sources. For basic mapping, three gamma radiation sources were used, namely, Cobalt-60 (^{60}Co) with the activity of 8.0 MBq; ^{60}Co with the activity of 220 kBq; and Caesium-137 (^{137}Cs) with the activity of 350 kBq. The polygon defined in Sect. 2 served as the measurement area. The spacing of the parallel lines was set to 1 m. The passage through the area took approximately 15 min. The interpolated radiation map can be seen in Fig. 12 (left), and the estimated positions of the sources are marked with crosses. The difference between the estimated position of the strong ^{60}Co source and the measured position (with the GNSS receiver) corresponds to approximately 7 cm; the value is comparable to the reference measurement error.

The second experiment tested the strong source search algorithm in the same measurement area, using ^{137}Cs with the activity of 65.6 MBq. The control module detected the corresponding peaks already in the first two lines, directing the robot to the source. After the detection of the next peak, the final waypoints are planned within 2 m radius. The resulting trajectory with the measured points is visualized in Fig. 12 (right), and the estimated position of the source is marked with a cross. The entire passage lasted 3 min. As in the previous experiment, the difference between the estimation and the reference measurement is approximately 7 cm.

The time of the experiment apparently depends on the source position. In the discussed case, the source was approximately in the middle of the measured area, and the period needed to locate the source was reduced 5 times. If a real radiation-related incident happened, a wider area would be roughly explored first, using means such as a helicopter [17]. The polygon for precise ground

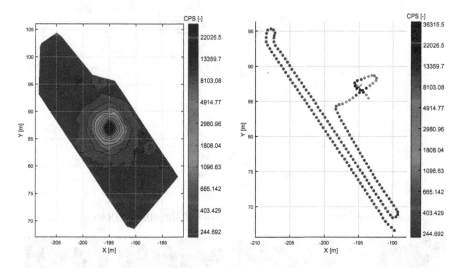

Fig. 12. The results of the radiation mapping (left) and strong source localization (right).

measurement would be defined in accordance with the rough data, leading to the assumption that the strongest source is in the center.

Proposed methods provide higher precision than more common airborne systems. In paper [14], the accuracy of a localization is several meters while our robotic system has the position error lower by two orders. There are several other methods described in a scientific literature but usually they are not tested in real conditions or they deal with slightly different problems. In terms of source localization, the second proposed algorithm is rather unique.

The evaluated directional characteristics of the applied radiation detection system are shown in the polar plot within Fig. 13. The robot's forward direction is denoted as 0°, and the number of the mean measured counts relative to the forward direction is on the radial axis in percent. Thanks to the system geometry and the lead shielding layer, both the detectors exhibit different sensitivity to the radiation arriving in various incident angles. The radiation coming from angles around 180° (through the robot) is notably attenuated. New algorithms that employ the direction-sensitive system are currently being developed; they are based on Bayesian techniques and the Monte Carlo method [18,19] and should be able to quickly locate more than one strong source.

The designed system is suitable for localizing the static point sources of gamma radiation. The approach, however, appears to be inconvenient for dynamic processes such as monitoring the progression of a radiation cloud. Due to the low speed of the robot, it is also incapable of tracking fast fluctuation of a radiation field; an airborne system would be markedly more beneficial in this type of mission.

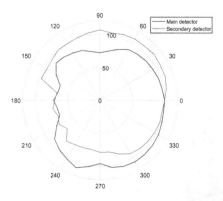

Fig. 13. The directional characteristics of the applied detectors.

Fig. 14. The final map containing both the orthophoto and the radiation map.

6 Conclusion

A multi-robotic system capable of fully autonomous 3D map building, inclusive of the environmental parameters, was presented. In our case, the primary 3D map was structured using a light UAV, and the gamma radiation measurement exploited an Orpheus UGV. The key component to facilitate such precise mapping and navigation of the robots is exact self-localization. This step is, as is presently common, performed through fusing data from multiple sources. As regards the UAV, we use the combination of a MEMS-based INS and an RTK GNSS, and in the UGV the combination of a vector RTK GNSS and odometry is employed. The obvious drawback of the RTK GNSS-based self-localization and navigation rests in the necessity of correcting the data to render them available for the solution. In our case, a custom base-station, which is a solution suitable for most stationery missions, is exploited; the other option would be to purchase of the correction data from providers, depending on the country of operation. The final georeferenced map is shown in Fig. 14.

As is demonstrated, the proposed solution is currently feasible using even relatively small robotic platforms. The presented UAV exhibits the maximum payload capacity of 3 kg, but it is capable of precise photogrammetry with georeferenced output thanks to the incorporated miniature RTK GNSS and INS combined with a hi-resolution full-frame camera. The UGV used also embodies a smaller outdoor machine, with the approximate weight of 60 kg and the operation time of 60 min per charging cycle at the minimum.

As it was already mentioned, the presented mission forms only one part of the intended usage. Once the system has been built, the addition of other functions, such as victim search or autonomous map-difference identification, appears to be relatively simple. The robots can be easily equipped with supplementary sensors to measure additional environmental parameters and/or related risks, including CBRN ones. The proposed self-localization methods can be perceived as an auxiliary tool to help effectively handle such risks, but the measurement and searching algorithms still require changes according to the character of the sensors and measured quantities.

Acknowledgements. The completion of this paper was made possible by the grant No. FEKT-S-17-4234 – 'Industry 4.0 in automation and cybernetics' financially supported by the Internal science fund of Brno University of Technology. This work was also supported by the Technology Agency of the Czech Republic under the projects TE01020197 – 'Centre for Applied Cybernetics 3' and TH01020862 – 'System for automatic/automated detection/monitoring radiation situation and localisation of hot spots based on a smart multifunctional detection head usable for stationary and mobile platforms incl. unmanned.'

References

1. Ferguson, C.D., Kazi, T., Perera, J.: Commercial radioactive sources: surveying the security risks. Monterey Institute of International Studies, Center for Nonproliferation Studies, Monterey, California (2003). https://www.nonproliferation.org/wp-content/uploads/2016/09/op11.pdf. Cited 15 Mar 2017
2. Arjomandi, M., Agostino, S., Mammone, M., Nelson, M., Zhou, T.: Classification of unmanned aerial vehicles. University of Adelaide, Adelaide, Australia (2006). http://afrsweb.usda.gov/SP2UserFiles/Place/62351500/Unmanned.pdf. Cited 17 Apr 2014
3. Gabrlik, P., Jelinek, A., Janata, P.: Precise multi-sensor georeferencing system for micro UAVs. IFAC-PapersOnLine **49**(25), 170–175 (2016)
4. Barry, P., Coakley, R.: Field accuracy test of RPAS photogrammetry. ISPRS - Int. Arch. Photogramm. Remote Sens. Spat. Inf. Sci. **XL–1/W2**, 27–31 (2013)
5. WMS View Service - Orthophoto. In: CUZK: Geoportal (2010). http://geoportal.cuzk.cz/. Cited 15 Mar 2017

6. Jilek, T.: Autonomous field measurement in outdoor areas using a mobile robot with RTK GNSS. IFAC-PapersOnLine **48**, 480–485 (2015)
7. Trimble: BD982 Datasheet. Trimble, pp. 1–2 (2014)
8. Rapp, R.H.: Geometric Geodesy Part I. The Ohio State University, pp. 71–85
9. Hartman, J., Barzilov, A., Novikov, I.: Remote sensing of neutron and gamma radiation using aerial unmanned autonomous system. In: 2015 IEEE Nuclear Science Symposium and Medical Imaging Conference (NSS/MIC). IEEE (2015)
10. Aleotti, J., Micconi, G., Caselli, S., et al.: Unmanned aerial vehicle equipped with spectroscopic CdZnTe detector for detection and identification of radiological and nuclear material. In: 2015 IEEE Nuclear Science Symposium and Medical Imaging Conference (NSS/MIC). IEEE (2015)
11. Schrage, C., Schemm, N., Balkir, S., Hoffman, M.W., Bauer, M.: A low-power directional gamma-ray sensor system for long-term radiation monitoring. IEEE Sens. J. **13**, 2610–2618 (2013)
12. Uher, J., Frojdh, C., Jakubek, J., Pospisil, S., Thungstrom, G., Vykydal, Z.: Directional radiation detector. In: IEEE Nuclear Science Symposium Conference Record, vol. 2, pp. 1162–1165 (2007)
13. Stacho, M., Hinca, R., Sojak, S., Slugen, V.: Spectral dose rate calculation using whole spectrum processing approach within energy range up to 10 MeV. In: 22nd International Conference Nuclear Energy for New Europe, Bled, Slovenia (2013). http://www.djs.si/proc/nene2013/pdf/NENE2013_805.pdf. Cited 15 Mar 2017
14. Joshi, T., Quiter, B., Maltz, J.: Measurement of the energy-dependent angular response of the ARES detector system and application to aerial imaging. IEEE Trans. Nucl. Sci. (2015). IEEE
15. Amidror, I.: Scattered data interpolation methods for electronic imaging systems: a survey. J. Electron. Imaging **11**(2), 157–176 (2002). http://molly.magic.rit.edu/~mac/test/paper_pdf.pdf. Cited 15 Mar 2017
16. Lazna, T.: Autonomous robotic gamma radiation measurement. Faculty of Electrical Engineering and Communication, Department of Control and Instrumentation, Brno University of Technology, Brno (2017)
17. Guillot, L., Bourgeois, C.: The use of the airborne system Helinuc for orphan sources search. In: Proceedings of International Conference on the Safety and Security of Radioactive Sources, IAEA-CN-134, Bordeaux (2005)
18. Morelande, M.R., Ristic, B.: Radiological source detection and localisation using Bayesian techniques. IEEE Trans. Signal Process. **57**, 4220–4231 (2009)
19. Cortez, R.A., Papageorgiou, X., Tanner, H.G., Klimenko, A.V., Borozdin, K.N., Lumia, R., Priedhorsky, W.C.: Smart radiation sensor management. IEEE Robot. Autom. Mag. **15**, 85–93 (2008)

Human-in-the-Loop Control Processes in Gas Turbine Maintenance

Michael Barz[1]([⊠]), Peter Poller[1], Martin Schneider[2], Sonja Zillner[2], and Daniel Sonntag[1]

[1] German Research Center for Artificial Intelligence (DFKI), Campus D3.2, 66123 Saarbrücken, Germany
{michael.barz,peter.poller,daniel.sonntag}@dfki.de
[2] Corporate Technology Siemens AG, Otto-Hahn-Ring 6, 81739 München, Germany
{martin.schneider,sonja.zillner}@siemens.com

Abstract. In this applied research paper, we describe an architecture for seamlessly integrating factory workers in industrial cyber-physical production environments. Our human-in-the-loop control process uses novel input techniques and relies on state-of-the-art industry standards. Our architecture allows for real-time processing of semantically annotated data from multiple sources (e.g., machine sensors, user input devices) and real-time analysis of data for anomaly detection and recovery. We use a semantic knowledge base for storing and querying data (http://www.metaphacts.com) and the Business Process Model and Notation (BPMN) for modelling and controlling the process. We exemplify our industrial solution in the use case of the maintenance of a Siemens gas turbine. We report on this case study and show the advantages of our approach for smart factories. An informal evaluation in the gas turbine maintenance use case shows the utility of automated anomaly detection and handling: workers can fill in paper-based incident reports by using a digital pen; the digitised version is stored in metaphacts and linked to semantic knowledge sources such as process models, structure models, business process models, and user models. Subsequently, automatic maintenance and recovery processes that involve human experts are triggered.

Keywords: Cyber Physical System (CPS) · Human-in-the-loop · Industry 4.0 · Smart factory · Case study · Handwriting recognition · Gesture recognition · Anomaly handling · Business Process Model and Notation (BPMN) · Anomaly detection · Semantic Knowledge Base

1 Introduction

Human-computer interaction for control processes is one of the key development issues in cyber-physical systems (CPS) [6]. Especially in industrial settings, incorporating workers in the manufacturing process as *humans-in-the-loop* is promising for decision-making [5,27]. Further, efficient and secure manufacturing requires the standardisation of business processes [13].

© Springer International Publishing AG 2017
V. Mařík et al. (Eds.): HoloMAS 2017, LNAI 10444, pp. 255–268, 2017.
DOI: 10.1007/978-3-319-64635-0_19

In this paper, we propose a cyber-physical system (CPS) architecture for smart factories enabling a real-time semantic data analysis from multiple sources, which is controlled by a standardised BPMN model (see also [16]). We evaluate our method in the use case of gas turbine maintenance. Maintaining industrial facilities is of high relevance—it helps to significantly reduce operating costs and to improve productivity of the plant operations and the quality of the product [1]. However, as of today, the integration of production and maintenance processes is only realised and implemented in a very limited way. With the increase in automation, electrification, and digitalisation of plants, more and more monitoring and maintenance devices and applications in cyber-physical environments are emerging. In this way, single parts or components of plants are serviced by dedicated predictive maintenance applications. In general, those techniques should complement preventive maintenance strategies (i.e., strategies including predetermined periodic basis components of the plant that are taken off-line for inspection). In addition, due to the complexity of the underlying processes and operations, employees that are most experienced with handling the machines and plant components are no longer actively involved in the maintenance process. In summary, the following shortcomings in maintenance applications on plants at various levels can be observed[1]:

- The **knowledge and expertise of production employees** is no longer integrated in an effective manner in the maintenance process.
- Many separate **monitoring applications** provide important insights about plant components. However, often they do not include a comprehensive view on the plant performance.
- The **semantic knowledge** about the plant structure and its basic principles are not incorporated into the maintenance processes.

With our CPS architecture, we provide an approach to overcome these limitations. It supports a seamless alignment of human-generated expert know-how with machine-generated maintenance know-how in a semantically consistent manner for improving the analytic-based maintenance application. In particular our system enables: (1) a seamless integration and processing of expert knowledge by smart pen technology (directly transferred from [21–23]); (2) modelling and executing of workflow knowledge in form of BPMN [15] models; (3) incorporating structural knowledge about the plant and its operations by means of a semantic model (semantic modelling/storage of components, products, and reports in metaphacts); and (4) usage of this integrated data source as input for analytical applications aiming to produce new valuable insights and to trigger automatically recommended actions.

2 Related Work

A general overview for the current status and the latest advancement of CPS in manufacturing is given in Wang et al. [26] and Sonntag et al. [24]. Herman et al. [7] analysed literature on Industry 4.0 scenarios, which include CPS,

---

[1] We extracted these shortcomings from interviews with domain experts.

and extracted essential design principles for such systems. Our system complies with *Interoperability* by incorporating humans-in-the-loop, *Virtualisation* by modelling processes with BPMN and with *Decentralisation, Real-time capabilities, Service orientation* and *Modularity* given by our flexible smart factories server infrastructure. Wang [25] introduce an Intelligent Predictive Maintenance (IPdM) system targeting zero-defect manufacturing in smart factories. They include preventive and predictive maintenance approaches [1], but lack from incorporating the workers that can provide valuable inputs. Zamfirescu et al. [27] introduce a reference model for anthropocentric cyber-physical systems (ACPS). They consider the worker as a composite factor of a general hybrid manufacturing system ("human-in-the-loop"). We adhere to the "human-in-the-loop" principle and build the platform for a holistic IPdM system in our maintenance scenario.

Petersen et al. [17] present a semantic model for representing smart factories as ontology instances. However, their system is limited to monitoring applications. In contrast, our system allows us to trigger relevant actions upon monitoring events. Mayer et al. [14] propose the Open Semantic Framework and show its utility for increasing worker safety in industrial settings. Both publications rely on standards concerning the semantic knowledge representation, but lack a standardisation for the business processes in which they are integrated. A very good and comprehensive overview for industrial standards mapped to the ISA95 model[2] is given in Lu et al. [13]. Furthermore, Lee et al. [12] propose a guideline for implementing Industry 4.0-based manufacturing systems similar to the ISA95 model and defined a sequential workflow order of implementation for two major functional components of a CPS. Our case study is an ISA95 model level 3, similar to Panfilenko et al. [16].

3   Technical Architecture

Our goal is to implement a system architecture that allows us to integrate, align, analyse, and manage machine and human generated data to produce faster response times for anomaly recovery. The most important aspect of our architecture is its flexibility with respect to the attached software components and hardware devices facilitating fast adoption to different industrial use cases. We developed a decentralised service-oriented architecture with the *Smart Factories Server* at its core (see Fig. 1). It serves as request proxy (services can sign up; client requests are processed accordingly) and event broadcasting node (data publisher and subscriber can register). The communication is based on XML-RPC [11]. This approach enables an easy integration of a BPMN engine managing the business processes and a semantic knowledge base providing the necessary concepts of the domain. We use the Camunda[3] BPMN workflow server and the metaphactory platform of metaphacts[4]. Further, it allows for a seamless

---

[2] www.isa.org/.

[3] Camunda, https://camunda.org/.

[4] Metaphacts, http://www.metaphacts.com.

integration of any user input device and machine sensor streams as data publisher. In particular, we integrated smart pens with networking capabilities and machine sensors. The following section provides further details about a concrete use case implementation.

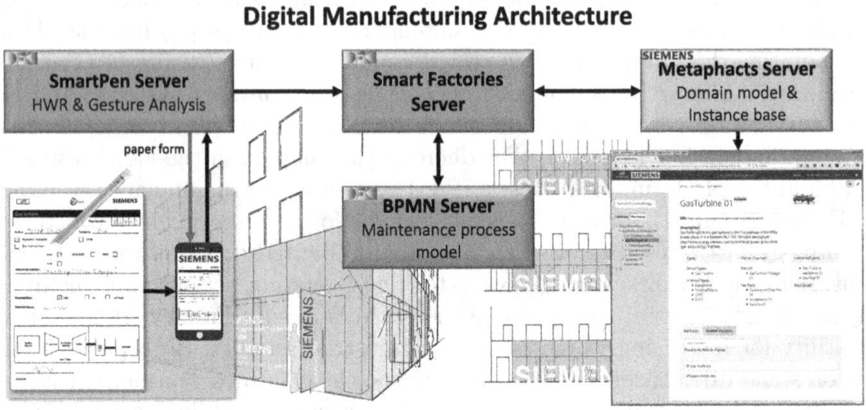

Fig. 1. Smart factories server architecture, see the use case video on the *GALLERY* tab: http://dfki.de/smartfactories

4   Use Case

Anomaly detection and recovery is of high relevance in manufacturing as failures lead to high cost. In industrial environments, anomalies are usually detected by workers or technicians that are familiar with the production facility; this includes visitors from other organisational units with technical knowledge. Another approach is the automated detection of anomalies through automatic analysis of data from sensors monitoring the production processes. However, such systems are often constrained to a single component whereas a failure would propagate to interconnected components, for example in a production line. Due to the high flexibility end extensibility of our CPS architecture, it can be applied for improving these and multiple other scenarios. In this section, we describe the use case of *gas turbine maintenance* and emphasise the potential of our architecture with a focus on human-in-the-loop error recovery.

4.1   Gas Turbine Maintenance

This business scenario focuses on the operation and maintenance of gas turbines, in particular, we considered the Siemens gas turbine (SGT-750) as reference object. We focussed on seamlessly incorporating workers in the maintenance process (human-in-the-loop) without the need for workers to change their daily practice. The maintenance processes, which were elaborated in extensive expert interviews, are modelled with BPMN (see Fig. 2). This standardisation is central to our approach. To this end, a BPMN engine manages all incidents based on this model as indicated in Fig. 1. The model further includes the integration of humans into the workflow. The human-in-the-loop functionality allows a worker to fill in paper-based incident reports with a smart pen, or to call a technician in the case of high risk incidents. A detailed description of all components is provided next.

4.2 Implementation

In this section we describe the core aspects, major components and functionalities of our implementations for the gas turbine maintenance use case. These include the standardised BPMN workflow models, the pen-based incident reporting for integrating humans-in-the-loop and the underlying semantic modelling and knowledge representation (see Fig. 1). The target is to automatically process incident reports and, depending on how critical the case is, to intervene in real-time by alerting experts. The individual software components were designed and implemented in close cooperation with domain experts, especially concerning the BPMN-based workflow and the semantic models. We illustrate one possible implementation of our general CPS architecture.

Gas Turbine Maintenance BPMN 2.0 Model. The maintenance processes including the handling of incident reports are realised as BPMN process models, which were elaborated in expert interviews. We use the Camunda BPM server for automatically mapping reported incidents to maintenance steps of the gas turbine in real-time (see Fig. 2). The process can be explained as follows: first, an incident is observed in a facility, which yields a filled report modelled as a BPMN event. It is evaluated by our classification components, and a report page is inserted into the metaphacts knowledge base. Further, "proceed to further processing" keeps record and passes the incident on to the next decision point. Eventually, "compute risk" calls a risk level assessment (in the current model *high* and *low*). Depending on the risk level, user tasks (human-in-the-loop) and automated activities are initiated. If the risk is low, the Remote Diagnostic Center (RDC) shall be notified via email and the production technician, who can manually adjust the configuration, is informed. In case of a high risk, a service expert is called and the RDC department receives an alert. A use case video helps to understand this process of anomaly detection within a distributed digital manufacturing architecture.[5]

Smart Pen Technology. In the industrial context, the interaction with pen and paper forms is well known to the users and fits into established business processes, e.g., documentation, maintenance, repair, or reporting processes.

---

[5] Smart Factories, http://dfki.de/smartfactories/?page_id=82.

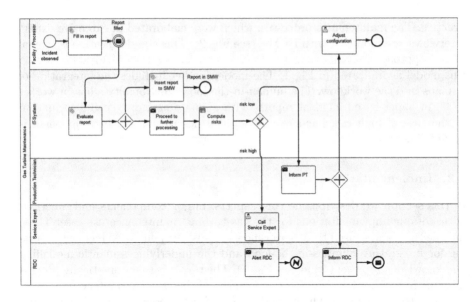

Fig. 2. Gas turbine workflow model in BPMN 2.0

Thus, introducing the digital pen technology for these tasks requires only low training effort and cost. The major advantage of smart pens is that the acquired data can be processed and integrated in real-time into corresponding software systems which enables continuous knowledge acquisition with worst-case execution time (WCET) capabilities. We use the highly innovative and networked *Neo Smartpen N2* facilitating digital user interaction on specially prepared papers [20]. These special paper forms contain an almost invisible grid structure for identification of the form and localisation of the pen strokes. A filled paper form is immediately synchronised via Bluetooth or Wifi with the screen of an iPhone or tablet computer (DFKI provides additional streaming technology). On confirmation by the user, the raw data is sent to the *SmartPen Server* which is responsible for detecting the form and for managing the handwriting and stroke gesture analysis. The handwriting recognition and gesture/shape analysis is performed by using a commercial software library integrated into our system architecture (myscript.com).

Preparation of Domain Specific Paper Sheets. The individual data fields have been derived by intensive discussion with our technology partner Siemens and can be described as follows: author and company name are important data for further incident tracing and recommendation for task assignments; the identity of the author influences the reliability of provided risk estimates, e.g., technicians know the production line from daily work while service experts possess a much deeper knowledge of the technology; incident type and description provides a simple classification; potential risk gives subjective user risk assessment. The graphical sketch representation is used to enable the workers to easily locate the

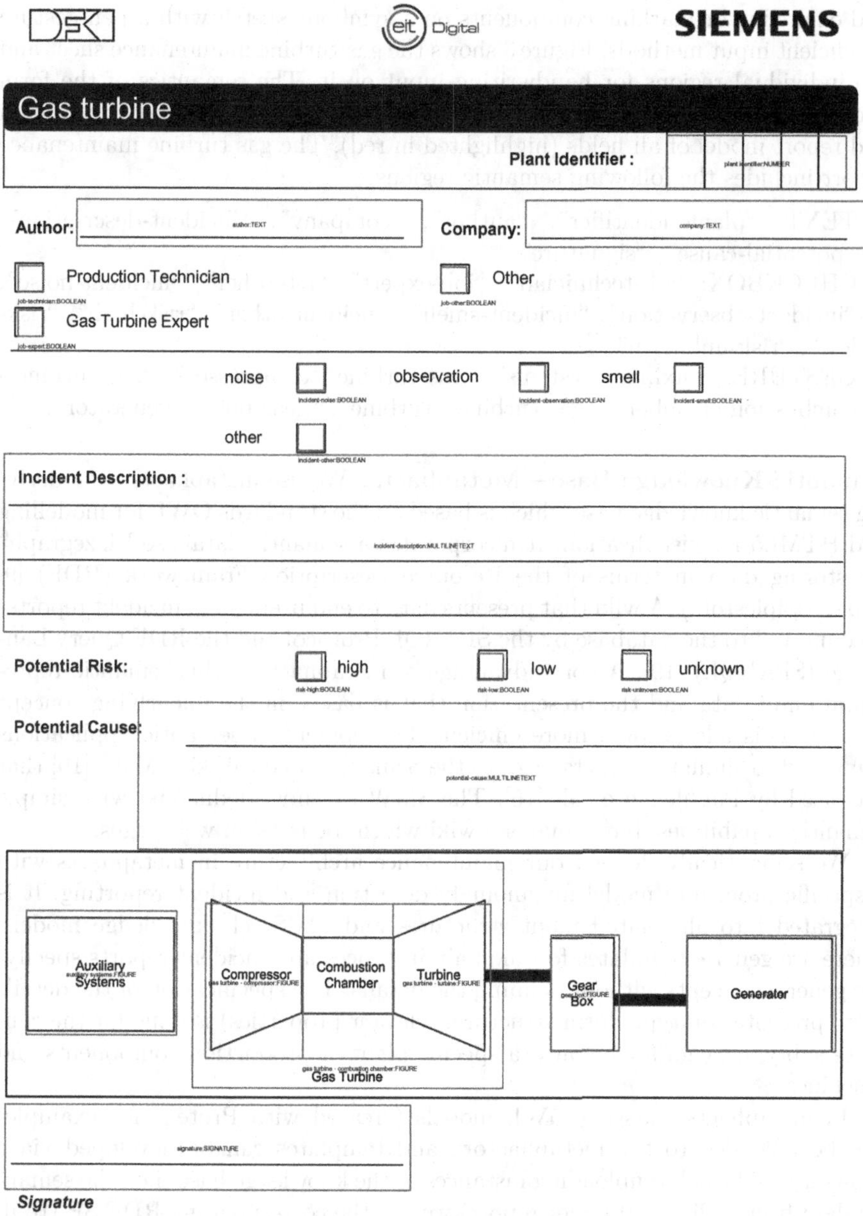

Fig. 3. Specification of the semantics of the gas turbine maintenance report (Color figure online)

incident by marking it on the printed illustration of the machine. The layout of the sheet has been determined in close cooperation with layout designers and experts of the application domain. We identified checkboxes, handwritten text, and encircling or marking components on a symbolic sketch with a pen gesture as efficient input methods. Figure 3 shows the gas turbine maintenance sheet and the individual regions for handwriting input on it. The semantics of the form is defined by the geometric location, the input type and the underlying domain and report model of all fields (highlighted in red). The gas turbine maintenance report includes the following semantic regions:

- TEXT: "plant identifier", "author", "company", "incident-description", "potential-cause", "signature"
- CHECKBOX: "job-technician", "job-expert", "job-other", "incident-noise", "incident-observation", "incident-smell", "incident-other", "risk-high", "risk-low", "risk-unknown",
- GESTURE: "auxiliary systems", "gas turbine - compressor", "gas turbine - combustion chamber", "gas turbine - turbine", "gear box", "generator".

Semantic Knowledge Base—Metaphacts. We use metaphacts as underlying semantic knowledge base which is based on the standards OWL for modelling and HTML5 for visualisation. It incorporates a semantic database Blazegraph[6] for storing data in terms of the Resource Description Framework (RDF) [9] triples (triplestore). A wiki that presents data to end users (e.g., incident reports) is connected to the database by the SPARQL Protocol and the RDF Query Language (SPARQL) [19]. A core advantage of metaphacts is this semantic representation of data and the presentation that is based on the underlying concept models. This allows for a more efficient development of semantic applications compared to similar products, e.g., to the Semantic MediaWiki (SMW) [10] that was used by Panfilenko et al. [16]. The SMW extends MediaWiki with simple semantic capabilities, but remains a wiki which focusses on web pages.

We semantically defined our maintenance architecture in metaphacts with a specific procedure model for anomaly detection and incident reporting. It is integrated into all related plant structures and I2MSteel[7] knowledge models. There are generic templates for anomaly instances and incident reports specifying generic concepts without defining the details. The specification of the details (e.g., presentation type, form structure, relevant properties) is done for the concrete subtypes, e.g., a company, a specific plant or production components and machines.

In metaphacts, existing OWL models (created with Protégé for example) can be uploaded to the metaphactory and templates can be developed via a browser interface. For uploading instances to the knowledge base (i.e., the semantic data from a digitised paper report) we use the corresponding RDF SPARQL commands transmitted via metaphacts' REST interface and the standard turtle/TTL syntax (see the example below). The ttl description includes a header defining the namespace prefixes and the semantic data triples that were extracted from the incident report. The corresponding PDF document is uploaded to the knowledge base as reference and integrated into the resulting incident report page (see Fig. 4). Here's an Turtle/TTL example:

---

[6] Blazegraph, https://www.blazegraph.com/.

[7] I2MSteel, https://www.cetic.be/I2MSTEEL.

```
@prefix: <http://siemens.com/energy/vocab/gasTurbineExample#>.
@prefix gtd: <http://siemens.com/energy/schemas/gasturbineDomain#>.
@prefix owl: <http://www.w3.org/2002/07/owl#>.
@prefix rdf: <http://www.w3.org/1999/02/22-rdf-syntax-ns#>.
@prefix xml: <http://www.w3.org/XML/1998/namespace#>.
@prefix xsd: <http://www.w3.org/2001/XMLSchema#>.
@prefix ppex: <http://siemens.com/energy/vocab/gasTurbineExample#>.
@prefix rdfs: <http://www.w3.org/2000/01/rdf-schema#>.
@prefix report: <http://siemens.com/reporting/schemas/generic#>.
@base <http://siemens.com/energy/vocab/gasTurbineExample>.
### http://siemens.com/energy/vocab/gasTurbineExample#TestReport_02:TestReport_02
rdf:type report:IncidentReport, owl:NamedIndividual;
rdfs:label "Gas Turbine Report Incident 170314_100508";
report:incidentType "Noise";
report:hasDate "2017-03-14 10:05:08";
report:authorsCompany "Siemens AG";
report:potentialRisk "unknown";
report:authorType "Other";
report:potentialCause "bearings worn out?";
report:author "Schneider";
rdfs:comment "rumbles very much";
report:locatedAtComponent:Generator01;
report:pdflink "/assets/reports/gasturbine/form-44f106ed-f262-4122-941c-b0173160ca8b.pdf".
```

5 Maintenance Case Study

One case study with domain experts is presented to illustrate the usefulness of our service-oriented CPS architecture for industrial applications. In this case study we explore the impact of our approach on the efficiency of maintenance processes in the gas turbine use case. Through interviews and case studies with domain experts, we iteratively designed and realised a seamless integration of workers in the model-driven and standardised workflow using smart pen technology. Incident reports are automatically analysed in real-time based on semantic domain knowledge which initiated proper prevention or recovery activities. We investigate the strengths and limitations of our architecture.

Maintaining industrial facilities is of great importance for reducing cost and for improving product quality. In contrast, state-of-the-art processes in many factories include simple pen and paper forms for incident reporting inducing long processing and thus reaction times. In addition, these reports cannot be used for analysing failures and for extracting their causes. This case study is based on a qualitative assessment of our system extracted from interviews with expert users that tested it in the gas turbine maintenance use case. Key advantages that were reported are:

- Incident reports are immediately digitised, aligned and integrated into the semantic knowledge base (digitalisation) within a few seconds which enables:
  - Immediate data analysis (WCET) and over time, e.g., augmented with sensor data
  - Very fast response times

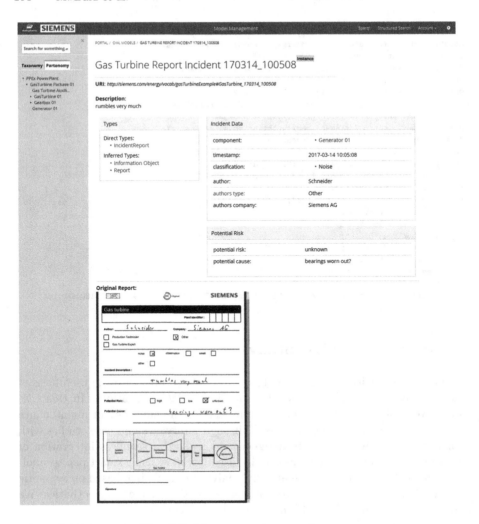

Fig. 4. Incident report in metaphacts

- Intuitive and clear visualisation by filtering/searching for incidents with certain criteria (e.g., component, time interval, incident type or keywords within comments)
- Easy alignment to other business processes due to standardisation with BPMN (well established in the industrial domain)
- Low overhead concerning change management as workers are already familiar with pen and paper.

Interestingly, in comparison to tablet-based applications, the pen based application was preferred as it was easier to handle and use in the working environment. The experts also mentioned the potential for other industries, such as automotive, that are still relying on analog paper-based reporting. In general, we can state that the future potential of these applications has been recognised by our expert partners in a very positive manner and in nearly all discussions, they mentioned further scenarios and processes that could benefit from this technology.

6   Conclusion and Outlook

We proposed a service-oriented architecture for seamlessly integrating workers in industrial cyber-physical production environments. This enables automatic data processing based on standardised models (BPMN and semantic concepts). A case study with domain experts (maintenance processes for a gas turbine) has shown the usefulness of our approach. It also demonstrated the flexibility of our architecture and thus its potential for improving efficiency in many other Industry 4.0 use cases (such as the hot rolling mill). The tools (Camunda BPM server and metaphacts) and hand writing input modes used for implementing this use case turned out to be suitable candidates for further developments in similar domains.

The second use case is about the hot rolling mill plant in Eisenhüttenstadt [8]. The I2MSteel[8] project (intelligent and integrated manufacturing in steel production) has set up a comprehensive knowledge base for this kind of facility. It contains a broad model library for steel manufacturing processes including product models, process models, structure models, measurement models, order models, and storage models. This practical application scenario for the hot rolling mill in Eisenhüttenstadt combines two anomaly treatment approaches: (1) the manual (human-in-the-loop) incident reporting by using a smart pen, and (2) the automatic processing of a Semantic Sensor Network (SSN) compliant to W3C SSN Ontology [4]. The approach for pen-based incident reporting will be similar to the gas turbine use case. The automated anomaly detection relies on a collection of smart sensors that are placed in the production environment, e.g., attached to machines, products, or the production environment. All sensors are represented in a semantically modelled sensor network (SSN), which describes the sensor capabilities, their measurement processes, and typical observations. Based on a corresponding reasoning mechanism, inconsistent sensor values, broken sensors, or sensor values exceeding predefined limits are immediately detected as anomalies. These can then be integrated into the database and immediately processed at detection time. Depending on the underlying anomaly model, recovery actions can be triggered automatically.

Our extensible CPS platform suggests the integration of further input channels. Prange and Sonntag proposed pen-based form filling using tablet computers in the medical domain [18]. It would be interesting to transfer their approach and evaluate the utility and usability in the industrial context. Further, we would like to investigate speech dialogues with gaze-based deictic reference resolution similar to [3] and combine speech with gaze-guided object classification [2] to map gaze to semantic concepts. Another promising direction is the integration

---

[8] I2MSteel, https://www.cetic.be/I2MSTEEL.

of smart environmental sensors (SSN) for predictive maintenance. Multimodal multisensor input channels and corresponding recovery actions could be used to train deep networks for holistic and automatic business process modelling as suggested in [24].

Acknowledgment. This research was funded in part by the European Institute of Innovation and Technology (EIT) in the CPS for Smart Factories project, see http://dfki.de/smartfactories/. The responsibility for this publication lies with the authors.

References

1. Alsyouf, I.: The role of maintenance in improving companies' productivity and profitability. Int. J. Prod. Econ. **105**(1), 70–78 (2007). http://www.sciencedirect.com/science/article/pii/S092552730600065X
2. Barz, M., Poller, P., Sonntag, D.: Evaluating remote and head-worn eye trackers in multi-modal speech-based HRI. In: Mutlu, B., Tscheligi, M., Weiss, A., Young, J.E. (eds.) Companion of the 2017 ACM/IEEE International Conference on Human-Robot Interaction, HRI 2017, Vienna, Austria, 6–9 March 2017, pp. 79–80. ACM (2017). doi:10.1145/3029798.3038367
3. Barz, M., Sonntag, D.: Gaze-guided object classification using deep neural networks for attention-based computing. In: Lukowicz, P., Krüger, A., Bulling, A., Lim, Y., Patel, S.N. (eds.) Proceedings of 2016 ACM International Joint Conference on Pervasive and Ubiquitous Computing, UbiComp Adjunct 2016, Heidelberg, Germany, 12–16 September 2016, pp. 253–256. ACM (2016). doi:10.1145/2968219.2971389
4. Compton, M., Barnaghi, P., Bermudez, L., García-Castro, R., Corcho, O., Cox, S., Graybeal, J., Hauswirth, M., Henson, C., Herzog, A., Huang, V., Janowicz, K., Kelsey, W.D., Phuoc, D.L., Lefort, L., Leggieri, M., Neuhaus, H., Nikolov, A., Page, K., Passant, A., Sheth, A., Taylor, K.: The SSN ontology of the W3C semantic sensor network incubator group. Web Semant.: Sci. Serv. Agents World Wide Web **17**, 25–32 (2012). http://www.sciencedirect.com/science/article/pii/S1570826812000571
5. Fantini, P., Tavola, G., Taisch, M., Barbosa, J., Leitao, P., Liu, Y., Sayed, M.S., Lohse, N.: Exploring the integration of the human as a flexibility factor in CPS enabled manufacturing environments: Methodology and results. In: IECON 2016–42nd Annual Conference of the IEEE Industrial Electronics Society, pp. 5711–5716, October 2016
6. Gaham, M., Bouzouia, B., Achour, N.: Human-in-the-loop cyber-physical production systems control (HiLCP2sC): a multi-objective interactive framework proposal. In: Borangiu, T., Thomas, A., Trentesaux, D. (eds.) Service Orientation in Holonic and Multi-agent Manufacturing, pp. 315–325. Springer International Publishing, Cham (2015). doi:10.1007/978-3-319-15159-5_29
7. Hermann, M., Pentek, T., Otto, B.: Design principles for industrie 4.0 scenarios: a literature review. Technische Universität Dortmund, Dortmund (2015)
8. Kahle, P.: Hot-rolled strip production. EKO Stahl. http://www.arcelormittal-ehst.com/ameh/uploads/file/Warmbanderzeugung.pdf
9. Klyne, G., Carroll, J.J.: Resource description framework (RDF): concepts and abstract syntax, February 2006. https://www.w3.org/TR/2004/REC-rdf-concepts-20040210/

10. Krötzsch, M., Vrandečić, D., Völkel, M.: Semantic mediaWiki. In: Cruz, I., Decker, S., Allemang, D., Preist, C., Schwabe, D., Mika, P., Uschold, M., Aroyo, L.M. (eds.) ISWC 2006. LNCS, vol. 4273, pp. 935–942. Springer, Heidelberg (2006). doi:10. 1007/11926078_68

11. Laurent, S.S., Dumbill, E., Johnston, J.: Programming Web Services with XML-RPC. O'Reilly & Associates Inc, Sebastopol (2001)

12. Lee, J., Bagheri, B., Kao, H.A.: A cyber-physical systems architecture for industry 4.0-based manufacturing systems. Manuf. Lett. **3**, 18–23 (2015)

13. Lu, Y., Morris, K.C., Frechette, S.: Standards landscape and directions for smart manufacturing systems. In: 2015 IEEE International Conference on Automation Science and Engineering (CASE), pp. 998–1005. IEEE (2015)

14. Mayer, S., Hodges, J., Yu, D., Kritzler, M., Michahelles, F.: An open semantic framework for the industrial internet of things. IEEE Intell. Syst. **32**(1), 96–101 (2017)

15. Object Management Group: Business Process Model and Notation (BPMN) Version 2.0. Techical report, Open Management Group (2011). http://www.omg.org/spec/BPMN/2.0

16. Panfilenko, D., Poller, P., Sonntag, D., Zillner, S., Schneider, M.: BPMN for knowledge acquisition and anomaly handling in CPS for smart factories. In: 2016 IEEE 21st International Conference on Emerging Technologies and Factory Automation (ETFA), pp. 1–4. IEEE, September 2016. http://ieeexplore.ieee.org/document/7733686/

17. Petersen, N., Galkin, M., Lange, C., Lohmann, S., Auer, S.: Monitoring and Automating Factories Using Semantic Models. Springer International Publishing, Cham (2016)

18. Prange, A., Sonntag, D.: Digital PI-RADS: smartphone sketches for instant knowledge acquisition in prostate cancer detection. In: 29th IEEE International Symposium on Computer-Based Medical Systems, CBMS 2016, Belfast, UK and Dublin, Ireland, 20–24 June 2016, pp. 13–18. IEEE Computer Society (2016). doi:10.1109/CBMS.2016.23

19. Prud'Hommeaux, E., Seaborne, A.: SPARQL query language for RDF, January 2008. https://www.w3.org/TR/rdf-sparql-query/

20. Sonntag, D., Liwicki, M., Weber, M.: Digital pen in mammography patient forms. In: Proceedings of the 13th International Conference on Multimodal Interfaces, ICMI 2011, NY, USA, pp. 303–306 (2011). doi:10.1145/2070481.2070537

21. Sonntag, D., Romanelli, M.: A multimodal result ontology for integrated semantic web dialogue applications. In: Proceedings of 5th Conference on Language Resources and Evaluation, LREC 2006 (2006). http://www.lrec-conf.org/proceedings/lrec2006/pdf/288_pdf.pdf

22. Sonntag, D., Sonnenberg, G., Nesselrath, R., Herzog, G.: Supporting a rapid dialogue system engineering process. In: Proceedings of 1st International Workshop on Spoken Dialogue Systems Technology, IWSDS (2009)

23. Sonntag, D., Weber, M., Cavallaro, A., Hammon, M.: Integrating digital pens in breast imaging for instant knowledge acquisition. AI Mag. **35**(1), 26–37 (2014). http://www.aaai.org/ojs/index.php/aimagazine/article/view/2501

24. Sonntag, D., Zillner, S., van der Smagt, P., Lörincz, A.: Overview of the CPS for smart factories project: deep learning, knowledge acquisition, anomaly detection and intelligent user interfaces. In: Jeschke, S., Brecher, C., Song, H., Rawat, D.B.R. (eds.) Industrial Internet of Things, pp. 487–504. Springer International Publishing, Cham (2017). doi:10.1007/978-3-319-42559-7_19

25. Wang, K.: Intelligent predictive maintenance (IPdM) system-industry 4.0 scenario. WIT Trans. Eng. Sci. **113**, 259–268 (2016)
26. Wang, L., Törngren, M., Onori, M.: Current status and advancement of cyber-physical systems in manufacturing. J. Manuf. Syst. **37**(Part 2), 517–527 (2015)
27. Zamfirescu, C.B., Pirvu, B.C., Gorecky, D., Chakravarthy, H.: Human-centred assembly: a case study for an anthropocentric cyber-physical system. Procedia Technol. **15**, 90–98 (2014)

Author Index

Printed in the United States
By Bookmasters